Hanif Kureishi

MANCHESTER
UNIVERSITY PRESS

CONTEMPORARY WORLD WRITERS

SERIES EDITOR   JOHN THIEME

ALREADY PUBLISHED IN THE SERIES

Peter Carey   BRUCE WOODCOCK
Kazuo Ishiguro   BARRY LEWIS
Timothy Mo   ELAINE YEE LIN HO
Toni Morrison   JILL MATUS
Alice Munro   CORAL ANN HOWELLS
Ngugi Wa Thiong'o   PATRICK WILLIAMS
Salman Rushdie   CATHERINE CUNDY
Derek Walcott   JOHN THIEME

Hanif Kureishi

BART MOORE-GILBERT

Manchester University Press
Manchester and New York

distributed exclusively in the USA by Palgrave

Published by Manchester University Press
Oxford Road, Manchester M13 9NR, UK
and Room 400, 175 Fifth Avenue, New York, NY 10010, USA
http://www.manchesteruniversitypress.co.uk

Distributed exclusively in the USA by
Palgrave, 175 Fifth Avenue, New York, NY 10010, USA

Distributed exclusively in Canada by
UBC Press, University of British Columbia, 2029 West Mall,
Vancouver, BC, Canada V6T 1Z2

British Library Cataloguing-in-Publication Data
A catalogue record for this book is available from the British Library

Library of Congress Cataloging-in-Publication Data applied for

ISBN 0 7190 5534 2 *hardback*
     0 7190 5535 0 *paperback*

First published 2001
10 09 08 07 06 05 04 03 02 01   10 9 8 7 6 5 4 3 2 1

Typeset in Aldus
by Koinonia, Manchester
Printed in Great Britain
by Bell and Bain Ltd, Glasgow

For Deborah Lanyon

Contents

Acknowledgements

Many friends and colleagues have helped in the production of this book, through conversations and debate, help with references and other expressions of interest; these include Émilienne Baneth, Chris Baldick, Philippe Birgy, Josh Cohen, Geoff Davis, Jean-Pierre Durix, Nigel Gearing, Olivia Jennings, Yu-Cheng Lee, Susheila Nasta, Alix Sierz, Mark Stein, Andrew Teverson and my series editor John Thieme, who read and responded to draft material in a supportive fashion. I owe a particular debt to Conor Carville for tracking down sources and in checking references. Thanks also to Parv Bancil, Bidisha, Vincent Ebrahim, Shyama Perera, Atima Srivastava, Max Stafford-Clark, Meera Syal and Jatinder Verma for answering questions about aspects of Kureishi's work, and to Zephyr Films for supplying a pre-release video of *My Son the Fanatic*. I am also indebted to Hanif Kureishi for checking the 'Chronology', for finding time for several interviews, for lending me unpublished material and answering questions on the phone – all without ever trying to influence my interpretation of his work. I would also like to record my gratitiude to both Goldsmiths College and the Arts and Humanities Research Board for sabbaticals which have enabled me to complete this text sooner than I would otherwise have done. Thanks also to Matthew Frost at MUP for his patience.

Finally, thank you, Deborah, for your love, encouragement, sense of humour and sense of perspective.

Series editor's foreword

Contemporary World Writers is an innovative series of authoritative introductions to a range of culturally diverse contemporary writers from outside Britain and the United States, or from 'minority' backgrounds within Britain or the United States. In addition to providing comprehensive general introductions, books in the series also argue stimulating original theses, often but not always related to contemporary debates in post-colonial studies.

The series locates individual writers within their specific cultural contexts, while recognising that such contexts are themselves invariably a complex mixture of hybridised influences. It aims to counter tendencies to appropriate the writers discussed into the canon of English or American literature or to regard them as 'other'.

Each volume includes a chronology of the writer's life, an introductory section on formative contexts and intertexts, discussion of all the writer's major works, a bibliography of primary and secondary works and an index. Issues of racial, national and cultural identity are explored, as are gender and sexuality. Books in the series also examine writers' use of genre, particularly ways in which Western genres are adapted or subverted and 'traditional' local forms are reworked in a contemporary context.

Contemporary World Writers aims to bring together the theoretical impulse which currently dominates post-colonial studies and closely argued readings of particular authors' works, and by so doing to avoid the danger of appropriating the specifics of particular texts into the hegemony of totalising theories.

List of abbreviations

B	*Borderline* (1981 edition)
BA	*The Black Album*
BS	*The Buddha of Suburbia*
FBP	*The Faber Book of Pop*
HK	*Interviews with Hanif Kureishi by Bart Moore-Gilbert*
I	*Intimacy*
LBT	*Love in a Blue Time*
LKM	*London Kills Me*
MAD	*Midnight All Day*
MBL	*My Beautiful Laundrette and Other Writings*
MSF	*My Son the Fanatic*
OOP	*Outskirts and Other Plays*
SR	*Sammy and Rosie Get Laid: The Script and the Diary*
SWM	*Sleep With Me*
TT	*Tomorrow-Today!*

Chronology

1954 Hanif Kureishi born 5 December in Bromley, Kent.

1965–70 Attends Bromley Technical High School, Kent (which becomes Ravenswood Comprehensive). In 1969, at the age of fourteen, determines to become a writer.

1971–73 Attends Ravensbourne College of Art, for 'A' levels.

1973–74 Reads philosophy at Lancaster University. Expelled at the end of the year.

1974–77 Reads philosophy at King's College, London.

1976 *Soaking the Heat* given a Sunday night reading at the Royal Court Theatre Upstairs.

1977–79 Works as assistant stage manager for Steven Berkoff.

1980 *The King and Me* opens at Soho Poly.

The Mother Country, his first full-length play, opens at Riverside Studios.

You Can't Go Home (play) broadcast on BBC Radio.

1981 *Outskirts* opens at the Royal Shakespeare Company's (RSC) Warehouse Theatre.

Wins the Royal Court's George Devine Award and is appointed Writer-in-Residence.

Tomorrow-Today! opens at Soho Poly.

Borderline opens at the Royal Court after a short tour with Joint Stock Theatre Company.

Voted 'Most Promising New Playwright' by *Drama* magazine.

Co-adapts Janusz Glowacki's *Cinders* for the Royal Court Theatre Upstairs.

1982   *Borderline* is judged best play in Thames Television's Bursary scheme.

Co-adapts Ostrovsky's *Artists and Admirers* for Riverside Studios.

Adapts Kafka's *The Trial* for BBC Radio.

1983   *Birds of Passage* opens at the Hampstead Theatre, London. The play is published by Amber Lane Press.

John Calder publishes *Outskirts, The King and Me, Tomorrow-Today!* in a single volume.

First Visit to Pakistan.

1984   Adapts Brecht's *Mother Courage and Her Children* for RSC at the Barbican.

Second visit to Pakistan.

1985   *My Beautiful Laundrette* is premiered at the Edinburgh Film Festival. It goes on general release in November.

1986   *My Beautiful Laundrette* wins the *Evening Standard* Award for Best Film of 1985 and is nominated for BAFTA's Award for Best Screenplay. Wins New York Critics' Award and Oscar nomination for Best Screenplay.

My Beautiful Laundrette and *The Rainbow Sign* published by Faber.

1988   *Sammy and Rosie Get Laid* opens in London in January.

Sammy and Rosie Get Laid: The Script and the Diary published by Faber.

1990   *The Buddha of Suburbia* published by Faber. It wins the Whitbread Prize for Best First Novel in 1990.

1991   Makes his debut as a director with *London Kills Me*, opening at the London Film Festival.

The script is published by Faber.

Death of father.

1992   *Outskirts and Other Plays* published by Faber.

1993   Co-writes *The Buddha of Suburbia* as a four-part BBC series.

Birth of twins, Carlo and Sachin.

Adaptation of Brecht's *Mother Courage and Her Children* revived at the National Theatre (Cottesloe) after a short tour.

1995   *The Black Album* published by Faber.

Co-edits *The Faber Book of Pop,* published by Faber.

1996   *My Beautiful Laundrette and Other Writings* published by Faber.

1997   *Love in a Blue Time* published by Faber.

Premiere of *My Son the Fanatic* at the Cannes Film Festival. The film opens in Britain at the London Film Festival, before going on general release.

The script of *My Son the Fanatic* published by Faber.

1998   *Intimacy* published by Faber.

Birth of third son, Kier.

1999   *Sleep With Me* opens at the National Theatre (Cottesloe).

Sleep With Me and *Midnight All Day* published by Faber.

2001   *Gabriel's Gift* published by Faber.

Intimacy, a film directed by Patrice Chéreau, based on Kureishi's *Intimacy* and material from *Love in a Blue Time* is released.

Contexts and intertexts

Introduction: Kureishi and the thematics of 'world writing'

Since this text appears in a series called 'Contemporary World Writers', it is worth beginning with a consideration of the implications of the label for an understanding of Kureishi's work. To some extent, its appropriateness depends on where the reader of his work is located.[1] From Princeton, Sydney or Nairobi, the world which Kureishi describes might well appear cosmopolitan, even exotic. To British readers – and more particularly to London-based ones – however, Kureishi might seem a local, even parochial, kind of writer[2] – at least in comparison with authors like Toni Morrison, Peter Carey or Ngugi wa Thiong'o, to whose work companion volumes in this series are dedicated. For such readers, these latter artists might be deemed to address more obviously 'global' issues like slavery and its legacies, the histories and effects of settler colonialism and the sometimes brutal realities of today's 'Third World'; and in doing so they may seem to construct much more expansive imaginative histories and geographies than Kureishi's.

The temporal reach of Kureishi's writing rarely extends further back than the 1970s and his settings are confined largely to London and the South-east. Despite a year spent at Lancaster University, the rest of England, indeed the rest of the United Kingdom, barely registers until recent work like the play *Sleep With Me* (1998). The essay 'Bradford' (1986, MBL) has an anthropological feel which vividly expresses how alien Kureishi felt on his excursion to this provincial city - later used as the setting for the film *My Son the Fanatic* (1997) – barely two hundred miles from London. Nor is the wider world outside Britain registered in any substantial way in his *oeuvre*. A short section of the novel *The Buddha of Suburbia* (1990) is set in New York, and Paris is the backdrop for 'Midnight All Day' (MAD). 'With Your Tongue Down My Mouth' (LBT) partly takes place in Pakistan, which is also described in the essay 'The Rainbow Sign' (MBL). Otherwise, the decolonised or postcolonial world is notable by its absence in Kureishi's work. Characteristically, the outer limits of his imaginative milieu are leafy suburbs to the south of the capital like Bromley and, at its core, are the squats, housing estates, cafes and clubs of inner- city London.

Paradoxically, however, these circumscribed settings provide clues to some of the ways in which Kureishi can legitimately be described as a 'world writer', even for a local readership. For example, in the apparently quintessentially English[3] culture of the South London suburbs, Kureishi traces the imprint of world- historical events in the post-war world from which, his work recurrently suggests, even such materially privileged and tradition-bound milieux cannot in the end insulate themselves. In the play *Birds of Passage* (1983), David concludes a paean to Sydenham with the claim that 'the suburbs are a feature of English life that has succeeded and deserves to endure for at least a thousand years' (OOP, 188). However, what the drama itself reveals is that David's speech is better seen as a eulogy to a way of life, set of values and sense of identity which are already crumbling. Thus, when his sister-in-law Eva suggests that 'if you want to see what England's really like, come out to Chislehurst sometime' (OOP, 181), the reader/viewer – as well as the new Pakistani lodger Asif, to whom the comment is addressed – are in reality being invited to witness how received conceptions of 'Englishness' are being challenged in their very heartland by a variety of developments. Indeed, Kureishi's *oeuvre* can, on one level, be understood as a record of the decline of what his novel *The Black Album* (1995) calls 'the whole Orwellian idea of England' (BA, 89).

In this respect, Kureishi belongs to a tradition of inquiry into the 'state of the nation' and the meanings of 'Englishness' which reaches back well into the nineteenth century. For example, his novels engage with 'condition of England' writers as varied as Dickens and H. G. Wells. More immediate forebears whom his writing cites in this respect include J. B.Priestley, T. S. Eliot and Orwell himself. In contrast to their various fears about the threats posed by fascism, mass unemployment or mass culture, for Kureishi the key issue is the unanticipated rapidity and scale of the unravelling of Britain's long history as an imperial power. As recently as 1947, the country still controlled more than a quarter of the world's population and territory; within two decades, this empire had, ostensibly, all but disappeared.

The short story collection *Love in a Blue Time* (1997) typifies Kureishi's consistent perception that even the most trivial details of everyday British life indicate how imbricated in this imperial past the nation nonetheless remains. Thus, whenever Nina leaves her home, she must pass 'South Africa Road and the General Smuts pub' (LBT: 72). At times, indeed, Kureishi suggests that despite formal decolonisation, the former empire has simply been reconstituted in a different form - not outside Britain this time, but within.[4] In the film *Sammy and Rosie Get Laid* (1988), for example, Danny anatomises what he describes as the system of 'domestic colonialism' (SR, 21) which is endured by large numbers of so-called 'New Commonwealth' immigrants[5] from the former empire. Time and again, Kureishi anatomises the quasi-colonial attitudes, institutional structures and social hierarchies which subordinate such minorities within contemporary British society. The most immediate and dramatic echo of the histories of colonialism occurs in the violence which so often accompanies the racism of the 'host' society. More subtle mechanisms of discrimination are embedded in the job market, educational institutions and housing. Equally evocative of imperialism is the geographical concentration of immigrants in certain areas of the inner city, which recalls the ethnic zoning in colonial cities like Chandrapore in E. M. Forster's *A Passage to India* (1924), a recurrent intertext of Kureishi's writing.

Amongst Kureishi's major preoccupations, then, are the consequences of formal decolonization – in psychological, political, cultural and material terms – for the 'native' British population. For much of his career, Kureishi identifies a serious malaise in national life and self-image, which is reflected primarily in the difficulties that Britain has experienced in adapting to a diminished status in the modern world and in throwing over anachronistic attitudes towards nation, race, ethnicity[6] and cultural difference. Susan's comments on her work as an investigative journalist in the (investigative, journalistic) play *Borderline* (1981) describe equally well the focus and stance of much of Kureishi's own writing: 'I want to show how things are changing under the skin of England. I want to chart the pricking of a certain kind of imperial inflation' (OOP, 122). At the same time, his work testifies to the very real problems which are involved in any attempt to reformulate and extend something so all-encompassing yet nebulous, so deeply if often unselfconsciously felt, as national identity. One of the key questions posed in his work is: 'So what does it mean to be British?' (MBL, 100). Most of his writing up to 1995, at least, constitutes an evolving set of analyses of – and attempted answers to – this problematic.

Kureishi recognises that Britain's demise as a world power is not, of course, simply a consequence of decolonisation but of political re-alignments and economic restructuring on a global scale in the period since 1945. In *My Son the Fanatic* it is a resurgent Europe, represented by the aggressive businessman Schitz (identified in the original script simply as 'the German'), which provides one context in which Britain's decline must be understood. By contrast, most of his earlier work reflects Kureishi's conviction that the 'US [now] has the central role in the world which England had in the nineteenth century' (SR, 108), a position which has been consolidated since the collapse of the Soviet-dominated 'Second World' (a theme of *The Black Album*). This collapse has hastened the integration of the global economy and the emergence of a single international division of labour, which requires the increasing mobility of both capital and labour power. To the extent that Kureishi's writing registers such developments, the treatment of globalisation – though it is never named as such in his work – provides another way in which Kureishi can be understood as a 'world writer'.

The implications of globalisation are hotly debated. For Marxists, it signals a new era of more ruthlessly efficient, US-led western domination of the rest of the world; 'liberals',[7] especially in the United States, often see in it the beginnings of 'a new world order', characterised by the potential for greater peace, prosperity and social justice for humanity. Equally, debate rages over whether globalisation involves the increasing homogenisation of the world in the image of the West and/or encourages its greater cultural diversification.[8] On the latter issue, Kureishi is divided. In *Love in a Blue Time*, Nina is astonished when she first meets her cousin Nadia from Pakistan, remarking that 'you look as if you live in Enfield' (LBT, 67). Conversely, *The Black Album* and *My Son the Fanatic* see the rise of 'fundamentalism' in the contemporary era as a reaction against the threat to 'local' cultural tradition which the homogenising tendencies of globalisation represent.[9] If, as the example of Schitz suggests, it cannot be fully equated with Americanisation in Kureishi's work, the United States is nonetheless represented as the principal motor of globalisation. Consequently, while little of his writing is set in the United States, much of it is informed by a keen interest in the implications of America's influence on, even hegemony over, the rest of the world.

At times, Kureishi expresses dismay at the seemingly inexorable consolidation of US political power, describing 'American interference' as the bane of the 'Third World' (MBL, 90). But while at times he represents the United States as taking on Britain's formerly dominant role in the non-western world, one of his most important insights is that this process has had profound consequences for the identity and autonomy of long-established western states, including Britain itself. He recalls of a visit to Pakistan how 'the Karachi wits liked to ask me when I thought the Americans would decide the British were ready for self-government' (MBL, 92). Kureishi has also deprecated 'Thatcher's attempt to convert Britain to an American-style business-based society' (MBL, 116). He has further criticised the effects of US 'cultural imperialism' on Britain. As *The Black Album* suggests, to the extent that American culture has succeeded in displacing the indigenous one, Britain sometimes appears to be in danger of becoming just one more of the United States's 'cultural colonies'. In the film *London Kills Me* (1991), the cult of Elvis has taken hold in the remotest reaches of the English countryside and one of the central characters re-invents himself in the image of Clint Eastwood. 'Sometime With Stephen' (SR), by comparison, describes the attitude of 'cultural cringe' prevalent amongst British film-makers of the 1980s towards Hollywood. Against such trends, Kureishi comments approvingly that, until the 1980s at least, 'Britain's cornucopia of music prevented the country from becoming … the complete victim of US cultural power' (OOP, xii).

Elsewhere Kureishi is much more positive about the influence of the United States. The lure of America is a theme which is established early in his career. Plays such as *The King and Me* (1980), which explores the obsession of a young working-class couple with visiting the home of Elvis, and *Birds of Passage*, in which Stella sees New York as the best place to start a new life, set up the grounds for a comparison between America and Britain – to the latter's disadvantage – which is elaborated upon in many later texts. Both Farouk in *Borderline* and Chili in *The Black Album* view the United States as a country which offers greater material opportunities to immigrants; in *The Buddha*, Charlie Hero and Karim each see New York as more varied and libertarian than London, which seems distinctly backward by comparison. Equally, Kureishi often criticises the anti-Americanism which has traditionally informed British Left thinking. In *The Buddha*, for example, Karim reproves his radical friends by pointing out the crucial role played by the United States in the emergence of the 'new social movements' such as feminism, the gay rights movement and contemporary mobilisations around race and civil rights. Thus, for Imran in the early unpublished play *The Mother Country* (performed in 1980), Eldridge Cleaver and Stokely Carmichael are inspirational icons.

In many parts of his work Kureishi also expresses admiration for American culture. Karim's girlfriend Jamila favours the African-American writers who came to prominence in the 1950s and 1960s over 'the old, dull, [British] white stuff' which she is taught at school (BS, 95). Kureishi himself has been strongly influenced by this tradition to the extent that one could argue that he initially found more relevance in the African-American model for understanding contemporary British minority experience, including that of Asian Britain, than any other. The exploration of Shahid's 'invisibility' in *The Black Album* owes much to Ralph Ellison's *The Invisible Man* (1952). Perhaps the greatest inspiration, however, was James Baldwin. (MBL, 77) What is possibly Kureishi's most important single essay, 'The Rainbow Sign' (MBL), derives its title from the same spiritual which supplies the title of his mentor's *The Fire Next Time* (1963) and Kureishi's characteristic mingling of issues of ethnicity, politics and 'deviant' sexuality draws on Baldwin's precedent. Kureishi has debts to other kinds of American writer, too. As an adolescent, the novelists whom he most admired were Kerouac and Salinger. Later, he was deeply impressed by the Jewish-American Philip Roth (whose wife, Claire Bloom, acted in *Sammy and Rosie*).[10] He learned much from Roth's negotiation of what Kobena Mercer has described as 'the burden of representation'[11] (see below) endured by minority writers, as well as Roth's frank and explicit treatment of sexuality. Recently, Kureishi has confessed to being influenced as a short-story writer by Singer, Cheever and Carver. Compared with all these figures, their British contemporaries often seemed to him disappointingly timid and inward-looking. (HK)

Kureishi has expressed equal admiration for the part played by the United States in extending received definitions of 'culture' in the twentieth century, particularly through its role in the development of the visual media. He is almost unique amongst British writers of his generation in having worked extensively in film and television and he has often commented approvingly on the vibrancy of American film culture, especially in the 1970s, when he first began to take a serious interest in cinema. One important intertext for *My Beautiful Laundrette* (1985) is Francis Ford Coppola's *The Godfather* (1972, 1974); in *Sammy and Rosie*, Woody Allen's *Annie Hall* (1977) is a crucial influence and in *My Son the Fanatic*, Martin Scorsese's *Taxi Driver* (1976) is equally determining. Thus, while Kureishi was keen to assist in the revival of British cinema in the 1980s, the most important model on which he drew was Hollywood. (His first three films all contain an American, whose vision of Britain provides a comparative perspective on the 'state of the nation'.)

Moreover, as texts from *The King and Me* to *The Black Album* recognise, America has been the source of some of the most admired popular music of the contemporary era. Much of Kureishi's work – notably *The Buddha* – maps itself in relation to the pop music of the time and the films often use pop to great emotional effect. At moments, Kureishi suggests that it is the first truly 'global' cultural form – even more so than film, which is more limited by its language of transmission. He has argued that from the 1960s onwards, '[p]op music and youth culture were enfolded with a world-wide common vocabulary and code' (OOP, xii) and has claimed that the Beatles 'spoke directly to the whole world' (MBL, 113). He also recalls, of a visit to Pakistan, how his contemporaries there listened 'to the Stones, Van Morrison and Bowie' (MBL, 88). While never underestimating the extent to which pop music is a global *commodity*, (thus in *The Buddha*, Charlie finds himself in New York concocting and selling a certain kind of 'Englishness' through his records), Kureishi also sees it as a template for the progressive processes of hybridisation and cross-fertilisation in which he is most interested. He consistently corroborates Dick Hebdige's argument that pop music has led the way in cross-racial cultural syntheses and transfers more specifically.[12] Thus in *London Kills Me*, the white Tom-Tom has internalised reggae culture to the point of presenting himself in the style of a rasta and adopting Black-British patois. Similarly, Strapper in *The Black Album* has

absorbed 'some Jamaican attitude' through exposure to club-
bing. 'Hippy' culture in The Buddha is notably eclectic; as with
George Harrison (BS, 31), Haroon, Karim and and Eva alike
demonstrate how East and West can be drawn together through
music and clothes. Kureishi's interest in pop culture, then, provides a more specific way in which Kureishi can be understood as
engaging with 'global' themes.[13]

Elsewhere, pop is represented as symbolic of a 'cultural
revolution' which has helped to radically democratise and expand
the horizons of post-war British society and, in doing so, has
adumbrated liberating new kinds of (cultural) politics. Kureishi
has claimed that without the Beatles, the nation's recent history
would have been genuinely different (MBL, 113). As 'Eight
Arms to Hold You' (MBL) suggests, the Liverpool band epitomises for Kureishi the promise of greater social mobility and a
more meritocratically-organised society. More specifically, pop
is valued by Kureishi because it articulates both the political
protest and the 'sexual revolution' associated with the 1960s
which, in theory at least, pointed the way towards more tolerant
and flexible conceptions of sexuality and gender roles as well as
of class identities. (Kureishi has recently commented that
'dressing up and being girlish was [always] part of English
pop'.)[14] Indeed, pop is sometimes ascribed a cultural/political
significance beyond that of any other genre in Kureishi's work.
His conviction of its potency is apparent from the earliest work,
like The Mother Country, where Imran chooses music rather
than conventional political activism as the most effective
medium through which to educate mainstream society away
from its racist attitudes. (Rock Against Racism had been
established in 1976 and was instrumental in the emergence of
the Anti-Nazi League the following year.)[15]

In fact, while concerned to promote what he sees as the
long-overdue democratisation of British society, Kureishi is
generally sceptical about traditional kinds of oppositional politics.
Like a range of minority cultural critics, including Stuart Hall,
Homi Bhabha and Paul Gilroy, Kureishi sees Labour politics in
particular as compromised by a history of institutional racism.

His unease with class politics must also be related to his perception that, as *Laundrette* graphically suggests, the most immediate and violent expressions of racism have tended to emerge from working-class formations. He is equally sceptical about the politics of cultural nationalism, which he objects to on the grounds that it is often organised around essentialist notions of minority identity. His work consistently reflects the belief that gender, sexuality and ethnicity are categories of (self-)identification which, while relational, are just as important as those centred in absolutist conceptions of race, class and nation.[16] Kureishi's vision of identity is thus anti-foundational: the self is always seen as mobile, fissile and plural. As Chapter 4 will demonstrate, pop culture is valued so highly by Kureishi precisely because it adumbrated such models of identity long before the advent of post-structuralism.

Kureishi's popularity amongst younger British audiences relates not just to the fact that the predicament of youth is one of his primary subjects, or to his abundant, earthily irreverent humour, but because he has been one of the first 'serious' writers to take its sub-cultures seriously and to have emulated some of their vivid expressiveness. His belief that pop needs to be recognised as comparable in merit to more established 'high' cultural forms is evident in a number of contexts. In essays, Kureishi has claimed that pop is 'the richest cultural form of post-war Britain' (MBL, 117). In 1995 he co-edited *The Faber Book of Pop*, and in the 'Introduction' to *Outskirts and Other Plays* (1992) he records why, at the outset of his career, he had been unimpressed by concerns over the supposedly imminent 'death of the novel'. Its demise 'didn't appear regrettable, only inevitable, and anyhow, because the music was so abundant and so good, little was being lost and much gained' (OOP, xiii).

However, Kureishi's attitude to pop culture is more complex than this account might suggest. Even in *The Mother Country*, some scepticism about its progressive political ambitions is apparent. Imran's friend Joe is unimpressed by the claim that Imran's band can help achieve social justice: 'Selling records to shop-girls. To relieve them. Pap.'[17] Joe's Adornian cynicism about the narcotic effect of pop as a mass cultural commodity seems to be partly endorsed by *The King and Me*. Here the music of Elvis provides a focus for the exploration of new and liberating forms of self-identification for Marie and Bill, as is implied by the negative response which their enthusiasm provokes from their conservative neighbours. At the same time, however, it clearly also functions as a kind of psychological opium which prevents them (especially Marie) from confronting the difficult circumstances in which they live.

The doubts evident in these early treatments of pop culture are amplified considerably in later texts like *The Black Album* which, as Chapter 4 will argue, expresses deep concern about the future of the traditional 'high' cultural canon in the face of the unrelenting expansion of popular and 'mass' forms of cultural expression.[18] Kureishi's changing perspectives express an ever-increasing disenchantment with the claims made on behalf of the 'cultural revolution' inaugurated in the 1960s. While he himself was a bitter opponent of her policies throughout the 1980s, many of Kureishi's more recent characters endorse the Thatcherite counter-revolution, especially in the novella *Intimacy* (1998) and some of the short stories, many of whose protagonists view their youthful radicalism as jejune and have consequently defected to the bracing world of enterprise.

As the presence in the suburbs of the Pakistani lodger Asif in *Birds of Passage* demonstrates, however, it is not American culture alone which is now being exported round the world. In the wake of both decolonisation and the increasingly globalised world order of which it was an early symptom, Kureishi continually reminds us, has come an astonishing degree and variety of human migration and cultural flows around the world, not least from former imperial territories to the West.[19] In the 'Author's Note' to the first edition of *Borderline*, he argues that 'the immigrant is a kind of modern Everyman, a representative of the movements and aspirations of millions of people' (B, 4).[20] In the case of Britain, much – though by no means all – of this migration has come from the Indian subcontinent and the Caribbean. A major consequence of these trans-global flows has been a rich, confusing and sometimes conflictual juxtaposition and mixing of peoples and cultural traditions. This has had radical implications for established conceptions of national, cultural and personal identity alike, not just for 'host' societies, but for these diasporic formations, too.

The principal sites of this new pattern of inter-cultural mixing are, of course, the great metropolitan cities of the West, like London. From one perspective, texts like *The Black Album*, which so clearly express what Kureishi has called his 'love and fascination for inner London' (SR, 101), belong squarely in the tradition of great 'London novels' like Dickens's *Bleak House* (1852–53) or Woolf's *Mrs Dalloway* (1925) and his first three films attempt, to some degree, to provide a cinematic equivalent. Kureishi's work can thus also be understood as an effort to record the way in which the already cosmopolitan national and imperial capital is being transformed into a 'world city' in the contemporary era.[21] From another perspective, Kureishi's treatment of London attests to the emergence of a new, 'fourth England', to be added to the three which J. B. Priestley identified in *English Journey* (1934), a text which particularly interested Kureishi (MBL, 129). As Chapter 3 will show, like many contemporary cultural commentators Kureishi is concerned to demonstrate how the modern inner city is an easier 'England' to identify with for diasporic populations than the rural, industrial and suburban 'Englands' which Priestley anatomised.

This points to the most obvious, if most general, way in which Kureishi can be compared with writers like Morrison, Carey and Ngugi. All are in important ways the product of 'global' processes of migration and 'translation',[22] though the dynamics of these need to be carefully distinguished in each case. Morrison writes out of, and about, the Black diaspora, which saw millions of Africans transported to the plantations of the Americas, mainly in the seventeenth and eighteenth centuries. Carey is the product of, and engaged by the consequences of, a quite different but no less dramatic population transfer which led to the settling of large areas of the world by European populations, notably in the nineteenth century. By contrast, as an exile from Kenya since the early 1980s, Ngugi represents the fate of millions in the period since 1945 who have been involuntarily displaced by political or economic problems in their homelands.

Biographical contexts

However, while he is also partly a product of the diasporic flows of the post-war world, Kureishi belongs to a quite different category of migrant from that of a figure like Ngugi. His father Rafiushan was from a relatively affluent Muslim family from Madras and came to Britain in 1947 (MBL, 73) to read law (most of the family moved to Pakistan after Partition). Discontinuing his studies, Kureishi's father took up a clerical job in the embassy of Pakistan, the newly created state he had never set foot in. Having met and married his English wife Audrey, Rafiushan remained in Britain, where he lived until his death in 1991. (The father–son relationship is a central theme of Kureishi's work, partly reflecting his own complex relationship to Rafiushan, himself a frustrated writer of fiction.)[23]

Kureishi, who was born in Bromley in 1954, represents what the opening paragraph of *The Buddha* famously describes as a 'new breed' of Englishman in a number of different senses. He can be categorised initially as one of the first generation of children of 'New Commonwealth' origins to be born in Britain, but this description is complicated by Kureishi's Anglo-Pakistani/Indian parentage, which makes him a minority within a minority. Indeed, the respective nationalities of his parents made his family unusual even amongst the mixed-race households which emerged in the wake of the migration to Britain of former colonial subjects (then, as now, Anglo-Caribbean children were much more common.) Kureishi was certainly made to feel his difference from mainstream society as he grew up. Indeed, he was sometimes bullied to the point that, as he confesses: 'I couldn't tolerate being myself' (MBL, 76). In work as diverse as 'The Rainbow sign' (MBL), *The Buddha, The Black*

Album and 'We're Not Jews' (LBT), Kureishi provides harrow-
ing accounts of the torment and self-hatred to which racism can
lead young people from such minorities.[24]

In an interview in 1997, Kureishi discussed how his complex
personal background impinges upon his work:

> I came from two worlds ... There was my Pakistani family,
> my uncles, aunts and so on. Then there was my English
> family, who were lower-middle or working class. My grand-
> father had pigeons and grey-hounds and all that. And
> having an Indian father ... So, finding my way through all
> that ... I wrote all those books to make sense of it.[25]

Such comments might encourage one to read Kureishi's work as
a species of autobiography, a temptation which is encouraged –
wittingly or not – in a number of other ways. Much of it describes experiences similar to the author's.[26] *The Buddha* provides
insights into the kind of secondary education which Kureishi
received (he attended the same Bromley school as pop icons like
David Bowie and Billy Idol). *The Black Album*, another 'portrait
of the artist as a young man', draws on memories of Kureishi's
student life in the 1970s. *The Buddha*, again, reflects at length
on Kureishi's near decade-long involvement in 'fringe' theatre.
Both novels' protagonists are first-generation British-Asians
(Karim is mixed-race) from outside London 'proper', and their
trajectory towards a new life in the inner city reflects Kureishi's
own similar journey. Of *Laundrette*, Kureishi has observed:
'The two boys are really the two sides of me: a Pakistani boy and
an English boy, because I'm half Pakistani and half English. I got
the two parts of myself together ... kissing'.[27] Many of the
recent short stories involve writers – of drama, screenplays and
fiction – and reflect self-consciously on the methods, purposes
and challenges of these various crafts in which Kureishi has been
involved. As Chapter 5 will demonstrate, much of Kureishi's
most recent work overtly muddies the borders between fiction
and autobiography.

More specific encouragement to biographical readings of
Kureishi's work is provided by his curious habit of naming

characters after members of his own family in a teasing, even
pointed way. Fractious mothers who share his mother's name
include the Audreys in *Birds of Passage* and *The Buddha* – and,
in the play *Tomorrow-Today!* (1980), Ben's aunt, who is not
seen on-stage. In *Borderline*, the young militant Yasmin shares
Kureishi's sister's name and in both *Borderline* and *Sammy and
Rosie*, principal characters are called Ravi/Rafi, the shortened
form of Kureishi's father's name. In the same film, the lesbian
Rani is named after an aunt of Kureishi's, in revenge for the
outrage which she expressed over *Laundrette*'s exploration/
celebration of the 'deviant' sexuality of British-Pakistanis (SR,
64). Tracey Scoffield, the mother of his twins and Kureishi's
former editor at Faber, is alluded to in the family of Scoffields
who live in Karim's street in *The Buddha* and in the forename
given to the unpleasant, politically correct, black actress whom
Karim encounters. Kureishi has also admitted to basing some of
his characters on other people he has been close to. In
Laundrette, Johnny is modelled on an adolescent friend (MBL,
74) and the lead female character in *Sammy and Rosie* was
drawn from a lover of several years, Sarah (Sally) Whittall,
whom Kureishi had met as an undergraduate.

Kureishi's handling of biographical material has sometimes
been vigorously condemned. For example, the depictions in both
his fiction and non-fiction of his maternal family have been
challenged by his sister. In a letter to *The Guardian* in 1998 she
claimed that Kureishi gave 'a false impression of our family life';
she insisted that her grandfather 'was not a "cloth cap working
class person"', but owned three shops, and that her parents were
well-off enough to send her to ballet school.[28] Kureishi's mother
corroborated Yasmin's acount in an interview in *The Observer*
shortly afterwards: 'I suppose it's trendy nowadays for an
author to pretend they had a working-class background, but
Hanif had everything he wanted as a child.'[29] *Intimacy* drew a
particularly hostile reaction from Tracey Scoffield, who argued
that Kureishi's intention towards the family he had recently left
was 'malicious' and claimed that 'nobody believes it's just pure
fiction. You might as well call it a fish'.[30] Reactions to Kureishi's

use of his acquaintances have also, at times, been vituperative. Once Glynn Roberts, the model for Clint, saw *London Kills Me*, he 'denounced ... [Kureishi] as a middle-class exploiter'.[31] And the resemblance of Rosie to Kureishi's university girlfriend led her to retitle the film sarcastically 'Hanif Gets Paid, Sarah Gets Exploited' (SR, 122).

Kureishi has reacted to such criticisms in various ways. At a reading of *Intimacy* at the Purcell Room in June 1998, he responded to his mother and sister by remarking that it was perhaps inevitable that different members of the same family would interpret 'facts', or remember events, differently.[32] Elsewhere, by contrast, he has expressed some regret for the way that he has used real-life sources in his work. He acknowledges that, in basing the lead female role in *Sammy and Rosie* on his former lover, he had failed to maintain a sufficient distance from his source: 'I know that in certain passages I've been spiteful' (SR, 66), an expression of contrition augmented by the disarming admission that 'there's some autobiography' in the 'jerk' Sammy (SR, 87). Kureishi has elsewhere insisted that his work is not faithful in detail to his experience: 'Like *Laundrette*, *Sammy and Rosie* is quite a personal story, autobiographical, not in its facts, but emotionally' (SR, 65). At the reading of *Intimacy*, moreover, Kureishi argued that, while writers cannot help but draw on their own experience, they adapt, edit or add to it in conformity with the demands of the story and other elements of aesthetic form. Thus, while writers 'constantly investigate the lives of the people they are involved with [and] keep private records of these private relationships' (SR, 68), *Intimacy* cannot be taken as a diary of the break-up of his own relationship; rather it was only the basis for an essentially imaginative 'falling-out-of-love book'.[33]

Such issues are a recurrent theme within Kureishi's work. As early as *Borderline*, the artist's right to appropriate the life experiences of those with whom he is closely connected is debated. The would-be novelist Haroon admits that the work he is writing will include a representation of his former girlfriend's forthcoming wedding – a decision which is to some degree inspired by pique at her decision not to return to him. The theme recurs in 'With Your Tongue Down My Throat' (LBT), and in *The Buddha*, similarly, Karim's determination to base his role in Pyke's play on personal acquaintances provokes a strong reaction from family and friends. In detailing the hurt which Changez, in particular, initially feels at the way that Karim has (mis)appropriated aspects of his experience, Kureishi perhaps implicitly acknowledges the pain he may have caused in the past to some of those closely connected to him – without, however, conceding that it is illegitimate for the artist to use whatever material comes to hand for aesthetic ends. This, at least, is the defence offered by the writer-narrator in 'That Was Then' (MAD), when a former lover confronts him over the way she has been (mis)represented in his work.

Kureishi's audiences

What is finally important (for those who are not closely involved with Kureishi, at least) in considering the biographical contexts of his work is whether or not he shapes his own experience so that it resonates beyond the confines of his real family and acquaintances. In managing to attract an international as well as a domestic British audience, Kureishi has clearly succeeded in generalising his own experience of the cultural 'in-betweenness' faced by millions of migrants and their descendants the world over – and, more specifically, by those who have gravitated from the non-western world to the great cities of the West. A major theme of Kureishi's work is the need to give voice to such minorities by the 'telling of new stories' (OOP, xvi) about their lives. Kureishi's reputation rests to a considerable degree on the fact that he is the first locally-born writer of real quality to articulate British-Asian experience to a substantial degree.[34] In *Birds of Passage*, Eva comments to Asif: 'You're the first Pakistani I've met. We hear a lot about them' (OOP, 176). Despite the recent rapid increase in the visibility of British-Asian cultural production (see Chapter 6), for a domestic white audience/readership, certainly, Kureishi's work is still likely to provide the first encounter with Asian Britain in the aesthetic domain.

However, Kureishi's desire to make this community a subject to write about should not be confused with a wish to be seen only as a spokesman for Asian Britain. As will be seen in subsequent chapters, the question of the responsibility of the artist with an 'ethnic' background to his/her community of origin is a recurrent theme of Kureishi's work, from *Borderline* to *The Black Album*, and the issue clearly causes considerable anxiety, both to the author and to those of his protagonists who are artists. Haroon and Shahid (and the actor Karim in *The Buddha*) are subjected to strong pressure to put their work at the service of the social group to which they are supposed to belong, a responsibility which they all at most only partially accept. In more recent work Kureishi has been even more resistant to accepting 'the burden of representation' so often placed on minority writing. At the launch of *Love in a Blue Time* in 1997 Kureishi insisted that he wanted to be regarded simply as a writer and rejected labels like 'ethnic', 'minoritarian', 'Asian' or 'British-Asian' as adequate categorisations of his work. At the Purcell Room reading of *Intimacy*, moreover, Kureishi argued that some of the work of the African-American film director Spike Lee had been 'ruined' by his mistaken assumption of the duty to provide 'politically correct' representations of his community.

One reason for his disavowal of any mandate, even duty, to speak (only) on behalf of Asian Britain is precisely Kureishi's awareness that he is untypical of the community - and not just in the ways described earlier. For example, he was raised not in the inner cities in which immigrants from the subcontinent have generally gathered, but in the relatively affluent suburbs to the south of London. Moreover, he was educated in the privileged surroundings of King's College, London (where he read philosophy)[35] and now earns his living as a highly successful writer. In describing one uncle's library as having been 'bought in the 1940s in Cambridge, where he was taught by [Bertrand] Russell'

(MBL, 98), Kureishi reminds one that his father's family, at least, was upper-middle-class. Furthermore, like most of his protagonists, Kureishi is monoglot – something which has on occasion caused him embarrassment, as on his visit to the Muslims of Bradford (MBL, 136). Also, while much of his paternal family is based in Pakistan, Kureishi feels no strong links to that country; he has only visited it twice, for short periods, the last time way back in 1984 (HK). Consequently, Kureishi sees himself as something of an outsider *vis-à-vis* 'mainstream' Asian Britain. The research for *Borderline* took him into what he describes as the quite alien territory, culturally, geographically and in class terms, of the predominantly British-Asian area of Southall in west London and he has expressed strongly equivocal feelings about writing 'a play based on people I hardly knew, whose experiences I have never had, most of whom are from countries I've never visited' (B, 4). Scepticism about Kureishi's 'right' to represent Asian Britain has been echoed by others, sometimes violently, as his account of his visit to Bradford testifies (MBL, 130). In New York Pakistani activists picketed the cinema where *Laundrette* was released and both his own family and several minorititarian cultural critics have questioned Kureishi's integrity as an artist on this score.[36]

As Kureishi's comments on *Borderline* imply, moreover, labels like 'British-Asian' are conveniences which, while sometimes necessary and useful, can also unhelpfully obscure the diversity of the social formation(s) which they aspire to describe just as surely as majoritarian terms of blanket abuse like 'Paki'. Even well-meaning liberals betray this tendency to homogenise. As Minoo complains of the Fingerhuts in *My Son the Fanatic*: 'They couldn't tell the difference between a Pakistani and a Bengali' (MSF, 6). Kureishi's work continually reminds one that Asian Britain is internally differentiated to the extent that there is no single community for him to be spokesman for, even if he so wished.[37] There are strong differences between new migrants, like Ravi in *Borderline* or Changez in *The Buddha*, and those who have been born in Britain, such as Karim. There are also important class distinctions within the community. In *Laundrette*, Nasser patronises Omar as 'one of those under-privileged types' and laughs at Hussein's 'black-hole flat' (MBL, 16). Meanwhile in *My Son the Fanatic*, Fizzy's increasing prosperity complicates his relationship with Parvez. Figures like Asif in *Birds of Passage* or Anwar in *The Buddha* belong to the elite in their countries of origin and their passage to Britain is smoothed by education, money and connections, advantages which are not available to the persecuted Bangladeshi family on the 'sink' estate in *The Black Album*. In *Birds of Passage*, Asif is damning about such people:

> Most English don't realise that the immigrants who come here are the scum of Pakistan ... They've given us all a bad reputation because they don't know how to behave. I couldn't talk to them there, except to give them orders. And I won't be solid with them here. (OOP, 200)

Indeed, Kureishi's work suggests that at times materially successful immigrants like Asif participate in the exploitation of their disadvantaged fellow-countrymen in a way which aligns them with dominant fractions of the 'host' society. Thus, in *Laundrette* Salim's eviction of the squatters, who include an elderly fellow-countryman, spurs one onlooker to describe him as a collaborator with the white man (MBL, 19).

The differentiated nature of Asian Britain is further apparent in the range of linguistic, religious and ethnic groups registered in Kureishi's work (though caste, interestingly, is never addressed). In *Borderline*, for example, Ravi works in a restaurant with fellow-migrants from a wide variety of locations in the subcontinent, with whom relations are often prickly. One of the most important divisions within these communities occurs across generational lines. Much of Kureishi's work is concerned with the conflict between the claims of inherited cultural tradition, to which older British-Asians in his work tend to be loyal, at least in the context of family life, and the aspirations of their children to participate more fully in mainstream British society. (At times, of course, notably in *My Son the Fanatic*, the attitudes of the respective generations is reversed.)[38] To the extent that it is so often the sexuality of British-Asian women around which such debates rage, Kureishi's work reminds one that gender is another important fissure within Asian Britain.

Describing Kureishi as an 'ethnic' or 'minoritarian' writer runs other dangers against which he wishes to guard. Above all, perhaps, such labels might give the impression that Kureishi is primarily addressing, or only interested in, Asian Britain – which, despite his mixed-race origins, is often erroneously supposed to be his only community of origin. This has never been the case at any point in his career. At its outset, Kureishi recalls, the 'questions that a *multi-cultural* society had to ask had hardly been put' (OOP, xvi) (my emphasis). Kureishi's work characteristically attempts to register the points of tension or incompatibility between the dominant and minority cultures, and to imagine new kinds of synthesis, complementarity or linkage which might lead to greater mutual understanding and harmony than has often been the case in British race relations, particularly since the 1970s. While Kureishi has certainly participated in the project of trying to give Asian Britain a stronger cultural voice and a more confident sense of its identity, a consistent premise of his writing has been that for inter-cultural relations to be improved, the ignorance of the dominant culture about the new minorities must be addressed and dispelled. As Kureishi recalls of his collaboration with the Joint Stock Theatre Company, under the directorship of Max Stafford-Clark, which resulted in *Borderline*: 'Max was continually reminding me how little English people know about Asians living amongst them and that the theatre can, in whatever minimal sense, educate [English] people' (B, 4). But the reverse is also true. Kureishi detects in Asian Britain a propensity to ignorance and inwardness which is no less marked and potentially damaging. To this end, Kureishi has argued, what is needed are 'stories about the new British communities, by cultural translators, as it were, to interpret one side to the other' (OOP, xvi).

Aside from not confining himself to minoritarian cultural institutions and outlets for his work, the principal way in which

Kureishi attempts to construct this dual audience and to engage in fostering a better understanding between different social formations is through a comparative, cross-cultural focus on moral and social issues within his work. One of the most important effects of this is to show what is common to different communities in contemporary British society without suggest-ing, however, that such groups and their predicaments, values or life choices are simply equivalent or interchangeable, still less that different groups are equal in terms of their social status and opportunities. For example, many of the life choices confronting Del in the play *Outskirts* (1981) or Stella in *Birds of Passage* are faced by Haroon in *Birds of Passage* and Shahid in *The Black Album* as well, for whom South London and the community of their birth are also nets which they must fly by if they are to fulfil their personal and professional ambitions. However, the intimidation which Johnny faces from former cronies in *Laun-drette* has less force than the pressure on Haroon in *Borderline* to remain loyal to his roots. Anwar's appeal – 'Don't lose touch with your own people' (OOP, 112) – echoes Genghiz's warning to Johnny, but to be set adrift in the mainstream 'white' world clearly poses a quite different order of problem for each protagonist.

This comparative perspective is also evident in Kureishi's treatment of the family, another recurrent theme of his work and characteristically represented as a highly dysfunctional institution. In *Birds of Passage* Stella comments: 'Families - I hate you' (OOP, 194); to which her brother Paul later adds: 'Families are divisive anyway. Why care for someone more because they came out of the same hole as you?' (OOP, 217). It is hard to think of a family which functions with more than moderate success in Kureishi's work, and recent writing like *Intimacy* and the short story collection *Midnight All Day* (1999) reflects a deepening cynicism about its effects. However, con-trary to one common 'positive' stereotype (and one much beloved by Kureishi's favourite *bête noire*, Thatcher), the British-Asian (or mixed-race) family is not represented in any better light than its British equivalent.[39] This is evident from early work like

Borderline, in which Amjad consistently bullies both his wife and daughter, reducing Banoo to a state of vegetative depression and provoking Amina to rebellion, to *The Buddha,* where Haroon proves himself no more faithful or attentive to the emotional needs of Audrey than Eva's husband has been to his wife. In this context, too, however, Kureishi does not suggest complete equivalence between the experience of the dominant and minority formations. Most obviously, while daughters such as Stella in *Birds of Passage* are subject to parental pressure, this is never to the degree experienced by figures like Banoo in *Borderline* or Jamila in *The Buddha,* whose fathers can insist that they marry spouses chosen for them. Yasmin sees Amjad as typical of the British-Asian paterfamilas in this respect, commenting: 'I had a father like you.' To which Haroon replies: 'We've all had 'em' (OOP, 115).

Kureishi's culturally comparative treatment of such social issues is often subtle and effective. In the context of the family, for example, it prevents readers/viewers from the ethnic majority from feeling any comfortable sense of superiority about the supposedly emancipated status of women in mainstream metropolitan society, without giving comfort to minoritarian cultural nationalists who believe that traditional family roles are necessarily better for British-Asian women than the alternatives offered in the 'host' society. Audrey in *Birds of Passage* and Banoo in *Borderline* are both oppressed to a comparable degree by the near-impossible demands of reconciling child-rearing with badly paid and unfulfilling jobs, which finally grind each of them down to the point of passive acceptance of their subordinate position.

As its consistent attention to issues of youth and gender suggests, moreover, pinning labels such as 'minoritarian' or 'British-Asian' on Kureishi's writing might give the erroneous impression that issues relating to race and ethnicity are his only concern. In the novels, the cross-race relationships are in part approached through the prism of a self-conscious awareness of the feminist work of figures like Simone de Beauvoir, Germaine Greer and Kate Millett. Moreover, Kureishi has commented that: 'Just as one of the excitements of British culture in the Sixties was the discovery of the lower middle class and working class as a subject, one plus of the repressive eighties has been cultural interest in marginalized and excluded groups' (SR, 63). Such constituencies are the subject of much of Kureishi's work. In *Sammy and Rosie*, for instance, Rosie announces the invitation list for her party thus: 'We'll just have to round up the usual social deviants, communists, lesbians … with a sprinkling of the mentally sub-normal' (SR, 31). In *The Buddha*, Kureishi references a gay tradition of writing from Wilde and Gide to Genet and Paul Bowles as self-consciously as he does the African-American tradition. Indeed, no ethnic minority characters appear in early work like *Tomorrow-Today!* or *Outskirts*, and in *London Kills Me* neither the black tramp nor the British-Asian Bike has a speaking role. In most of Kureishi's recent stories, as well as *Sleep with Me*, ethnicity is simply not, ostensibly, an issue. Thus, if his primary attraction for the student of 'world writing' remains his analysis of diasporic experience, it is crucial to recognise the ways in which - and the extent to which – these are articulated with other other modes of (self-)identification, such as age, class, nationality, sexuality and gender.

Intertexts and issues of style

While Shahid in *The Black Album* studies the Indian empire between 1857 and 1947 at college, Kureishi's own work pays little attention to colonial histories *per se*. Thus, the mention in 'We're Not Jews' (LBT) of Lord Macaulay, author of the Indian 'Minute on Education' (1835), is quite exceptional. Alice in *Sammy and Rosie* is the only English character with a colonial background in his *oeuvre*. Equally, while colonial literature forms part of Shahid's college syllabus, it is rarely invoked in Kureishi's writing. In *The Mother Country*, Imran's 'A' Level syllabus includes Forster's *A Passage to India*, for the progressive vision of inter-racial relations in which Kureishi has expressed admiration.[40] To some degree, the relationship between

Imran and Joe (and, indeed, between Omar and Johnnie in *Laundrette*) recalls the one between Aziz and Fielding in Forster's text, with a similar – though less bitter – separation at the end – and there is a shared interest in the problems and possibilities of cross-cultural understanding. The most extensive dialogue of this sort is with Kipling. In *The Buddha*, prominent intertexts include *The Jungle Books* and – less obviously – *Kim*. In 'The Rainbow Sign' Kureishi imagines his Pakistani cousins will be like 'little Mowglis' (MBL, 73), and the predicament of Alice in *Sammy and Rosie* has intriguing parallels with one of Kipling's earliest short stories, 'Lispeth'. However, while Kureishi may be reworking Kipling's story of an Indian girl who waits for the English lover who has abandoned her, a more obvious source for Alice is Miss Havisham in Dickens's *Great Expectations*. Otherwise, the engagement of Kureishi's work with 'colonial discourse' takes place at a fairly generalised level. Thus, in 'With Your Tongue Down My Throat' (LBT), the narrator ironically compares his/her account of the sometimes grim realities of modern Pakistan to 'stories of tigers and elephants and rickshaw wallahs' (LBT, 64) which one might take to be a dig at the more vapid forms of literary 'Orientalism'.

All this is in strong contrast to more obviously post-colonial writers like Chinua Achebe and Ngugi, much of whose work is thoroughly engaged with, and haunted by the ghost of, colonial literature. Both have intimated that it was a disgust with colonial representations of Africa, and a desire to offer alternatives to these, which motivated them to begin their own writing careers. For example, Achebe has stated: 'At the university I read some appalling novels about Africa (including Joyce Cary's much-praised *Mister Johnson*) and decided that the story we had to tell could not be told for us by anyone else no matter how gifted or well-intentioned'.[41] By contrast, as someone born in Britain, Kureishi writes from, as much as to back to, the West and its cultural traditions; he is more an insider, or more accurately an insider/outsider, than simply an outsider.

While *The Black Album* mercilessly satirises cultural nationalist writing of the kind produced by Riaz (BA, 56, 59, 194)

– largely on the grounds that unmediated political polemic and the production of 'positive stereotypes' is incompatible with literature proper,[42] this is not to suggest that Kureishi is any less concerned than such writers to contest or hybridise the discursive legacies of colonial representation, particularly as these determine the construction of peoples of non-western origin in the contemporary world. *My Son the Fanatic* discusses western misrepresentations of Islam in a manner which strongly suggests the influence of Edward Said's *Orientalism* (MSF, x). Kureishi consistently both directly challenges and parodically reworks stereotypes, tropes and motifs which have their roots in colonial discourse. In *Birds of Passage*, for instance, David and Eva enter carrying Asif's trunk, which is described as 'the brown man's burden' (OOP, 175), an ironic appropriation of the image of 'the white man's burden' which Kipling famously used to describe the 'responsibility' of the West to the non-West in his poem of that name. In *Borderline*, by comparison, Haroon's advocacy of a strategy of infiltration of the dominant order subverts the colonial trope of disguise, which figures the penetration of the culture of the colonised for purposes of control.[43] Whereas colonial literature emphasises the savagery and immorality of the subject peoples, Kureishi's immigrant characters associate these qualities with the British. Minoo complains in *My Son the Fanatic* that the English are forever 'stealing and drugging' (MSF, 40). Salim's animadversions in *Sammy and Rosie* against the 'lazy English' performs a similar function *vis-à-vis* the colonialist trope of the 'lazy native',[44] as well as challenging the common perception that immigrants 'steal' their hosts' jobs. At moments, moreover, Kureishi's immigrants represent their pioneering spirit in the same quasi-religious register as the nineteenth-century British overseas. Most obviously, perhaps, throughout Kureishi's work the concept of an immigrant 'invasion' parodically inverts the spatial dynamics of western imperialism. In *The Mother Country*, for example, Hussein describes his growing business as 'the Indian empire. You, me, your uncles, we'll practically take over South London.'[45]

However, just as Kureishi eschews any detailed or sustained engagement with the decolonised world *per se* in his writing, so there is little dialogue with non-western cultural traditions, whether Pakistani literature (despite the fact that his aunt Maki is one of the most distinguished English language poets there), postcolonial writing more generally or, indeed, other kinds of 'world writing'. The only historical example of non-western writing that Kureishi refers to is *One Thousand and One Nights*, which he describes as 'perhaps the greatest book of all' (MSF, xii). He has alluded to an early play, soon abandoned, which was influenced by V. S. Naipaul (SR, 81) and there are some intriguing markers of orality in *The Buddha* (see Chapter 4). There are parallels between Ralph Singh in Naipaul's *Mimic Men* (1966) and Rafi in *Sammy and Rosie* and perhaps fortuitous echoes in *The Black Album* of *Gora* (1924) by the Bengali Nobel prize-winner, Rabindranath Tagore (who is also mentioned in *The Buddha*); each has a character called Brownlow whose apparent liberalism and interest in other cultures masks an authoritarian attitude towards the 'subaltern'. However, the source of Brownlow's name is more likely to be the seemingly benevolent figure in Dickens's *Oliver Twist* (1837–38). The story of the fraudulent guru in *The Buddha* is anticipated in *As Time Goes By* (1971), a play by Mustapha Matura, a leading light at the Royal Court when Kureishi began work there in the 1970s. Despite occasional references to writers like Márquez (BA, 85, 102, 111) and Keri Hulme (MAD, 7), and expressions of admiration for writers like Soyinka, whose work Kureishi has described as being sedimented in his imagination,[46] there is little evidence of the direct influence of non-western cultural traditions or 'world writing' in other parts of his writing.

It is a similar story as regards Kureishi's work in the visual media on which, as was suggested earlier, Hollywood is the predominant influence. He has acknowledged the influence of *Tokyo Story* (1953), by the Japanese director Yasujiro Ozu, on his conception of *Sammy and Rosie*, but, despite his confession that 'I started off thinking of [the latter] as a contemporary remake of this desperately moving and truthful film' (SR, 81), the links in fact are strictly limited. Satyajit Ray, the great Bengali film maker, is alluded to in *The Buddha* but there is no evidence of his influence, or that of any other non-western *cineaste*, on Kureishi's screenplays – though they vigorously contest the discursive legacies of colonialism represented by the 'Raj Revival' in 1980s British cinema (see Chapter 3). Also, despite the explosion of 'world music' in the period since Kureishi's career began, very little of this is referred to in his writing, one notable exception being Nusrat Fateh Ali Khan, the great Pakistani *qawwali* singer. (Although some 'world music' features in the soundtracks for Kureishi's films, most of it is western in provenance.)

The most important exception to this general pattern is Salman Rushdie. Kureishi has described Rushdie as a friend (MBL, 6) and has acknowledged that: 'The idea for *My Son the Fanatic*, as for *The Black Album*, was provided by my thinking about the fatwa' (MSF, vii).[47] There are general analogies between *Midnight's Children* (1981) and *The Buddha* insofar as each is centred on a young man of mixed-race origins who represents the potential emergence of a new model of national identity in their respective homelands. Like Saleem Sinai's, Karim's grandfather is a Bombay doctor; and noses are a motif common to both texts. Like Saleem (who at one point acquires the nickname 'Buddha'), Karim flirts with the Left and Jamila listens willingly to his stories in the way Padma does to Saleem. Another echo of *Midnight's Children* occurs in *Sammy and Rosie*, where the expulsion of the carnivalesque caravan of travellers recalls the dispersal of the magicians' ghetto in Rushdie's text. Similarly, there are some common thematic interests in *Satanic Verses* and *The Black Album* insofar as both texts explore the conflict of cultural loyalties and identities amongst migrants and the effects of such migration on London. Equally, the relationship between Anwar and Haroon in *The Buddha* has clear parallels with that of Saladin and Gibreel in *Satanic Verses* and involves a comparable debate between the respective claims of assimilationism and fidelity to 'roots'.[48]

However, Rushdie's style has clearly not been an influence

on Kureishi's, which is generally resolutely realist in mode. There is some sophisticated and self-conscious narrative trickery in 'With Your Tongue Down My Mouth' (LBT), and – as already suggested – the borders between fiction and documentary are self-consciously blurred in some recent writing. Kureishi has also drawn attention to the 'the mixture of realism and sur-realism' in *Sammy and Rosie* (SR, 64) but, as this implies, even at the rare moments when his work is stylistically avant-garde, realism does not completely disappear. Little of it exemplifies the 'magic realism' which is so characteristic of 'world' and post-colonial literature. (Homi Bhabha, for example, claims that the mode is 'the literary language of the emergent post-colonial world'.)[49]

Kureishi has explained his stylistic orientation partly in terms of the fact that, whereas certain parts of the world may seem, or indeed be, magical or bizarre, there is precious little magic in South London (HK). However, the attachment to realism also derives from Kureishi's desire to engage with pressing social issues and to bring these to a wide audience, a task in which it has traditionally proved extremely effective. From his early days in the theatre Kureishi has tried to construct a popular readership/audience which he feels might be intimi-dated or confused by experimentalism. Thus he has commented: 'You have to ensure your work is accessible. You can't indulge yourself' (SR, 95). Realism is also a strong personal preference, as Kureishi's comments on some recent European writing indicate: 'I'd hated the Robbe-Grillet, Duras and Sarraute method, which I found arid and dull, a dead-end' (OOP, xviii). Finally, Kureishi's penchant for realism can be related to what he has described as his limited capacity for fully imagining things with which he is unfamiliar. He attributes the uncon-vincing representation of the travellers' commune in *Sammy and Rosie*, for example, to the fact that it 'wasn't based on anything I'd known' (SR, 70).

Kureishi's use of language also bears little resemblance to the practices of many 'world' and postcolonial writers. One consequence of both the histories of British imperialism and current American domination of the world's media has been the entrenchment of English as a, or even the, 'world language'. Writers such as Achebe have responded by insisting that as such, it must submit to a variety of inflections which reflect the myriad cultural contexts and geographical locations in which English is now used. The contemporary African writer, for example, must develop 'a new English, still in full communion with its ancestral home but altered to suit its new African surroundings'.[50] Similarly, Rushdie has commented that 'we can't simply use the language the way the British did … it needs remaking for our own purposes.'[51]

By contrast, Kureishi's grammar, syntax and vocabulary conform overwhelmingly to the norms of Standard Received English. Kureishi recalls that his father had great respect for people 'who could speak or write "good English" … "He writes beautiful English," he'd say of someone, as if this facility were yoked to humane values, and the mellifluous manipulation of sentences would produce people who were good, magnanimous and polite' (OOP, ix). While there is some obvious irony in this reflection, and Kureishi has shown himself adept at capturing the nuances of many non-standard varieties of spoken English, whether these are inflected by class, sub-cultural, regional or ethnic identities, it is striking that when a third-person narrative voice is deployed in his work, it is generally mediated in terms which largely correspond to his father's paradigm. In contrast to a writer like Rushdie, there is little attempt to 'chutnify' English by the intermingling of non-western words. In 'We're Not Jews' (LBT), Azhar's father writes 'Bombay variety, mish and mash' (LBT, 47), but Kureishi himself never does so. Because Kureishi is monoglot, there are few traces of subcontinental languages in his work beyond an occasional Urdu expletive, usually from a first-generation migrant character. (One notable exception is the scene in *Sammy and Rosie*, where the feminists attack Rafi.)

As all this might lead one to infer, the intertexts and orientations of Kureishi's writing are overwhelmingly western - as will be detailed more fully in subsequent chapters. In his plays, the principal influences range from the classical European theatre of Ibsen, Strindberg and Chekhov (who is probably the most important single intertext in Kureishi's work as a whole) to contemporaries like Joe Orton and Steven Berkoff. As already suggested, the films look to Hollywood, while also engaging with two strands of contemporary British film-making, 'Raj Revival' and 'Heritage' cinema. While also engaged with the African-American novel, Kureishi's fiction draws primarily on British and European traditions of social realism, comic as well as serious, and the genres of *Bildungsroman* and *Künstler-roman*. The short stories gesture not only towards Cheever, Carver and Singer, but towards Joyce, Maupassant and Calvino.

The cultural/political meanings of Kureishi's reliance on western intertexts are not easy to resolve. On the one hand, it might feed the suspicion that Kureishi's work is too parochially Eurocentric to qualify as 'world writing'. Equally, the post-modern elements of Kureishi's work[52] (the moral relativism,[53] the distrust of traditional kinds of oppositional politics, the anti-foundational conception of identity, the mixing of high and popular cultural forms, the predeliction for straightforward pastiche as much as for more politically-oriented kinds of hybridisation) might give comfort to those who assert that Kureishi – following so many of his British-Asian businessman protagonists – has fully assimilated himself to the cultural norms, values and hierarchies of the dominant formations in British society. However, there is evidence to support the oppo-site interpretation, that Kureishi's strategy has been to subvert those dominant values and perspectives, nowhere more obviously than in his attempt to redefine and expand traditional conceptions of 'Englishness' – and to show how it has come under pressure from global developments. Equally, one might argue that his work reconfigures the postmodern in the name of the diasporic (and postcolonial) by adapting some of its modes, conventions and epistemological perspectives to migrant experi-ence, an encounter which cannot but expose the putative Euro-centrism of postmodernism. Finally, one might argue that Kureishi's *oeuvre* is too differentiated to support either inter-pretation wholesale, or that he occupies a troubling 'in-between' position or 'third space' in respect of these conflicting positions.[54] Such controversies are the very stuff of Kureishi's writing and we can now trace them in greater detail in the chapters which follow.

The plays

Introduction

At the launch of *Love in a Blue Time* in April 1997, Kureishi commented that he had no plans to return to writing drama.[1] Furthermore, he asserted, he had little regard for the plays he had produced at the outset of his career, except for *Outskirts*, which he considered the only one to have stood the test of time.[2] Given the extent of his investment in writing for the theatre, which included not only several original plays (for radio as well as stage), but versions of the work of Kafka, Brecht and Ostrovsky, as well as the critical acclaim he received, Kureishi's self-deprecatory attitude to his early work is, on the face of it, somewhat surprising. From 1976, when his short play *Soaking the Heat* was given a Sunday night reading at the Royal Court Theatre Upstairs, until 1984, when he started to think about the script of *My Beautiful Laundrette*, drama occupied Kureishi full time and seemed destined to be the medium in which he would realise his artistic ambitions.

As an aspiring young writer in the early 1970s, Kureishi's decision to focus on drama was not adventitious. As he later recalled, at that time 'the film industry seemed impossible to break into' (OOP, xiii) for a lower-middle-class youth of mixed racial origins from the unfashionable North Kent suburbs. Despite his eager experiments in fiction as a teenager, Kureishi was discouraged by his intial contacts with the industry,[3] which seemed no more welcoming to someone with his background than film: 'The novel was posh, written by gentlemen like

Graham Greene, and published by upper-crust Bloomsbury types' (OOP, xiv). Besides, as the last chapter indicated, Kureishi had doubts about the continuing viability of fiction in the face of the increasing authority of a variety of modes of popular cultural expression.

By the 1970s, in contrast, what William Gaskill – a leading director until 1972 at the Royal Court Theatre, and still a powerful presence when Kureishi began his apprenticeship there – described as having been twenty years earlier 'the most reactionary branch of the arts',[4] had transformed itself into probably the most dynamic and innovative 'high' cultural form in Britain.[5] New impetus had been given to British theatre from the late 1950s by a combination of factors. The 1955 premiere of Beckett's *Waiting for Godot* had introduced the dramaturgy and philosophical vision of European 'absurd' drama; the opening of Osborne's *Look Back In Anger* (1956) announced the vigorous renaissance of social realism in the form of 'kitchen-sink' drama; and the visit of Brecht's Berliner Ensemble in the same year introduced British theatre to a radically new set of production techniques, harnessed to an uncompromising socialist politics. Such developments helped to precipitate the emergence of 'fringe' theatre in the subsequent decade, especially after the abolition of stage censorship in 1968. Catherine Itzin has calculated that whereas at the beginning of 1968 there were only half-a-dozen such groups, a decade later there were in excess of a hundred.[6]

For Kureishi, the appeal of 'fringe' lay essentially in its democratic thrust, which manifested itself in a number of ways. In the first place, it offered relatively easy access to the hitherto culturally disenfranchised as producers of art. In theory, anyone so minded could put on a 'fringe' drama, partly because it required far less than conventional theatre in terms of material resources like casts, sets, lighting and props. David Hare has recalled the minimalism embraced by his company, Portable Theatre, which operated by 'tumbling a group of actors out of a van ... with only the crudest and most makeshift scenery'.[7] Such flexibility enabled 'fringe' to bypass traditional venues and operate in all manner of *ad hoc* spaces. As Kureishi recalls, from the early 1970s drama began to be performed 'all over London, in basements, above pubs, in tents, in the street and even in theatres' (OOP, xiv). As a student, he regularly visited new spaces like the Soho Poly, the King's Head, the Open Space and The Almost Free Theatre (HK). The rapid expansion of 'fringe', which generally favoured limited runs of short new plays, meant unprecedented opportunities for aspiring authors like Kureishi. Throughout the 1970s, the Soho Poly alone commissioned roughly twenty new plays a year. Itzin estimates that at its height, 'fringe' created a pool of roughly 250 new playwrights.

'Fringe' also sought to revolutionise theatre as a social and cultural institution at the point of consumption by extending the cultural franchise to constituencies which conventional theatre did not customarily address or appeal to. The proliferation of 'fringe' beyond disused warehouses and pubs into the streets and thence into factories and 'sink' housing estates was one symptom of this ambition, as was the attempt to create a broader theatrical constituency through community-based theatre groups, in which amateurs drawn from the community in question would often take part as actors or in script development. Such communities were also to be enticed into theatre by making them the subject of dramatic representation to a far greater extent than had traditionally been the case.

The democratic thrust of 'fringe' was evident in two other ways which enthused Kureishi. First of all, it was concerned to challenge the established hierarchies and working practices of theatre, thus addressing John Arden's complaint that the 'so-called *revolution* at the Royal Court and Theatre Workshop in the late fifties had been largely a revolution of *content* ... the structure of theatre management had scarcely altered a jot'.[8] More important, perhaps, much 'fringe' was strongly orientated towards exploration of questions of social justice and morality. In the Introduction to *London Kills Me*, Kureishi describes how he was 'stimulated by the idea of drama having a use or purpose, to facilitate society's examination of itself and its values' (LKM, ix). The often fugitive and occasional nature of 'fringe' gave it a licence in these respects which, even in the more liberal atmosphere created by the abolition of stage censorship, mainstream theatre was more reluctant to exploit. Indeed, Kureishi felt that 'fringe' was able to engage with issues of social justice and morality in a less inhibited way than any other cultural form of the time, making it the most 'independent political forum, [for] dealing with [topics like] sexuality, the security services, Northern Ireland and the corruption of politicians and the state' (OOP, xiv–xv).

Kureishi's jaundiced judgement of his early plays at the launch of *Love in a Blue Time* contrasts starkly with the excitement which theatre inspired in him at the outset of his writing career – though his comments are perhaps less surprising in the light of the fame and critical prestige he has subsequently enjoyed as a novelist and writer of screenplays. Nonetheless, they are still worth close examination, not least because they adumbrate many of the characteristic features of his later work. Kureishi's career develops incrementally; even though he has moved apparently quite abruptly from genre to genre (from drama to films to novels to short stories) there is a considerable degree of thematic and stylistic unity in his work, at least between 1979 and 1995. This is partly reflected in a constant tendency to revisit, adapt and expand aspects of his earlier texts.

For example, Kureishi has himself drawn attention to the recurrence of certain character types from his plays in subsequent work: 'A character from *The King and Me* ... turned up in *London Kills Me*. The lives of the suburban couple Ted and Jean [*sic*, her name is actually Eva] from *Birds of Passage* were extended in *The Buddha of Suburbia*, and the boys from *Outskirts* were the genesis of the boys in *Laundrette*' (OOP, xix–xx). Similarly Asif in *Birds of Passage* is reworked into both Salim in *Laundrette* and Chili in *The Black Album*. *Borderline* proved a particularly rich source in this respect. Ravi is developed into a more complex version of the baffled and naive new immigrant Changez in *The Buddha*. Banoo, the oppressed wife who yearns to return to Pakistan, reappears as Minoo in *My Son the Fanatic*. Meanwhile Haroon prepares the ground for the embattled would-be artist Shahid in *The Black Album*, who faces many of the same problems and dilemmas as his predecessor. Even between plays this pattern is clearly evident. Bill and Ben from *Tomorrow-Today!* are immediately rejigged into Del and Bob in *Outskirts* and there are strong parallels between each of these pairs and Joe and Imran in *The Mother Country*.

The state of the nation

There are equally clear continuities of subject matter between Kureishi's drama and his later writing. As he has commented, 'all these plays were a setting-out of themes that would absorb me for a long time, as if I were beginning to discover what my subject would be' (OOP, xix). At the most general level Kureishi's plays can be understood as a preliminary instance of his recurrent engagement with 'the condition of England' between the late 1960s and the millennium. The time scheme of *Outskirts* demarcates the temporal boundaries of the plays, extending from 1969 to 1981. This was a time of particular turbulence and difficulty in contemporary British history which, from a Left-liberal perspective at least, began with quasi-revolutionary optimism and ended in deep reaction. In *Borderline*, Kureishi makes his first use of a trope which will recur in his later work, employing the perspective of the outsider, in this case the recently arrived Ravi, to comment on the depressed state of the nation in this period (compare Nadia in 'With Your Tongue Down My Throat' and Changez in *The Buddha*.) Ravi's expectations of the former imperial power are repeatedly disappointed from the moment he gets the airport bus to London. Asif in *Birds of Passage*, who has had longer to acclimatise, nonetheless confirms Ravi's disobliging vision of his new home and, in doing so, reminds the audience of the extent of the nation's decline in the perceptions of the rest of the world: 'The English haven't done anything good since 1945 … We say you are a Third World country. You know, under-developed' (OOP, 201, 211).[9]

In common with much other 'fringe' theatre of the time, Kureishi's plays focus their debate about the 'condition of England' on the increasingly apparent failures of the Welfare State. There is a constant emphasis on material impoverishment. Indeed, some of the settings of *Tomorrow-Today!* and *Outskirts*, with their bomb sites and patches of derelict wasteland, evoke an England which has still not fully recovered from the ravages of World War Two. Such damage has been compounded by insensitive programmes of reconstruction like the 'sink' housing estates invoked in *The King and Me*, *Borderline* and *Birds of Passage*, or the motorways which the youths frequent in *Outskirts* and *Tomorrow-Today!* in the absence of other amenities. There are abundant references to more immediate symptoms of economic decline in the wake of steep rises in the price of oil in 1973 and 1979. (By the early Thatcher years, unemployment had reached an historic high of 3 million, as Britain was subjected to an aggressive policy of de-industrialisation which shifted the country towards a new, service-based economy.) Haroon observes lugubriously of his neighbourhood in *Borderline*: 'The factories are closing down and everything' (OOP, 112). Dole queues are one of the first things Ravi sees and the blight of unemployment is central to *Outskirts*, where Bob and his friends are long-term unemployed, and to *Birds of Passage*, where Paul is jobless, Audrey gets laid off and Ted and Eva's business collapses.

This trajectory of economic decline and the increasingly threadbare nature of social provision which it entails is accompanied by a loss of hope in the future which is reflected in the large number of Kureishi's characters who suffer from frustration, helplessness and lethargy, or – by contrast – resentment and anger. Such feelings express a disenchantment with established social institutions and arrangements which is seemingly irreversible, particularly among those at the margins of society, on whose life experience – like so much other 'fringe' – Kureishi's drama is primarily focused. As Bill complains in *The King and Me*, after the failure of his attempt to win the Elvis lookalike competition: 'We're still in this muck – no money, them kids, no nothing' (OOP, 24). Fantasies of escape and nostalgia for the past provide one way of mitigating current difficulties for many of Kureishi's protagonists. In *Borderline*, Farouk dreams of a new life in America and in *Outskirts*, Bob's mother fondly recalls the solidarity of World War Two. When such imaginings fail, characters like Marie and Bob fall back on drink and drugs to see them through.

As Bob's mother's nostalgia for the spirit of the Blitz suggests, Kureishi's plays echo the conviction of work like David Edgar's *The Dunkirk Spirit* (1974) and Joint Stock's *Yesterday's News* (1976) that the communitarian values identified in the popular imagination with the Second World War were rapidly breaking down in the 1970s. As with pieces as diverse as Brenton and Hare's *Brassneck* (1973) or Caryl Churchill's *Cloud Nine* (1979), this process is symbolised by Kureishi in the parlous predicament of the family, which has so often been used in post-war British culture to represent the nation.[10] Marie's neglect of her children in *The King and Me*, the petty delinquencies of Haroon's brother in *Borderline* and the parental abandonment suffered by Bob in *Outskirts* suggest in microcosm the decline of common purpose in national life as well. As in work like Brenton's *The Churchill Play* (1974), another symptom of this process which is registered in Kureishi's plays is the emergence of a much more polarised political landscape in the 1970s. In *Outskirts*, Bob typifies the drift towards extremism, declaring war on 'soft politics' and its attendant 'pussyfooting' (OOP, 64).

According to Kureishi's plays, such developments point to a deep erosion of the values identified with 'Englishness' by writers like Orwell. As Susan remarks in *Borderline*: 'I think that a certain kind of gentleness and mildness associated with English life has gone. Even I can remember a kind of tolerance, a certain respect at the heart of things' (OOP, 133). Traditional English 'decency' has not altogether disappeared, but it tends to be embodied in the older generation represented by Bob's mother. However, her advanced age and physical decline symbolise the dying out of these values. The rising tide of violence which accompanies their demise is reflected in *The King and Me*, where

Marie's husband is set upon by punks and in *Tomorrow-Today!*, where Bill and Ben live in constant fear of skinheads.

As in the work of many contemporaries, Kureishi's plays lay responsibility for these developments largely at the door of the Labour Party, which had been in power between 1964 and 1970 and again from 1974 to 1979. Itzin argues persuasively that 'fringe' was given a substantial initial impetus by the Left's realisation from 1968 onwards that Labour was content simply to manage capitalism rather than to challenge it. After Callaghan became Prime Minister in 1975, the Party seemed more preoccupied with clinging to power (it ruled for several years in alliance with minority parties) than in addressing the serious problems facing the country. In this climate, disillusion flourished. In *Birds of Passage*, the former activist David comments: 'I've done enough for the Labour Party. We'll see how they deal with the [trouble on the] estate this summer' (OOP, 190). However, the plays lay the foundations of the more fundamental critique of Left politics in his subsequent work. *Birds of Passage* represents Labour in a jaundiced light because, it suggests, a politics organised on traditional class lines was incapable of responding to other, increasingly visible, forms of exploitation and marginalisation. The influence of feminist thinking, for example, is apparent in several plays. Thus, in *Birds of Passage* David represents many of the best traditional Labour ideals. However, as Stella points out, her father is blind to his complicity in other forms of inequality in the social system which he has devoted so much energy to challenging: 'All the time you were reading Jack London upstairs or shouting in here about differentials with your square-shouldered Stalinist cronies, where was Mum?' (OOP, 193).[11]

Set against the dispiriting realities of so many aspects of British life in the 1970s, such cultural/political shifts are presented as grounds for hope; and other factors prevent the plays' vision from being entirely pessimistic. For one thing, they are too funny to be wholly dispiriting, containing some wonderful situational comedy. In *Borderline*, for example, Ravi evades the police by persuading them that his British-Asian boss's son (a perfectly respectable citizen) is the 'illegal' they are after. All the plays offer examples of Kureishi's trademark laconic wit. In *Outskirts*, for instance, Bob boasts about his first job to Del, who is still at school: '£8 a week. That's basic'. To which Del replies: 'It is' (OOP, 54). The plays also recurrently suggest Kureishi's conviction that the individual – irrespective of class, gender and ethnicity – can change his/her life through courage and application. In *Outskirts*, Del breaks away from his impoverished South London background to become a teacher and in *Birds Of Passage* Stella is off to a new life in New York. In *Borderline*, Amina rejects the life of 'a quiet ghost' (OOP, 99) and Haroon pursues his ambitions to study and become a novelist, establishing a pattern which recurs in *Laundrette*, *The Buddha* and *The Black Album*.

Even those who do not manage to change their lives are not necessarily simply victims and, like many other 'fringe' playwrights, Kureishi is in part concerned to celebrate the courage of 'small people'. In *Outskirts*, for example, Bob retains an independence of mind which shows up the timidity and conformity of the ostensibly more empowered Del: 'Won't give in. It's all bloody-minded defiance now. They've buggered me long enough' (OOP, 73). Simple durability is another common quality. After Bill's failure in *The King and Me*, Marie declares: 'I'll be all right. I always am' (OOP, 15). The harsh conditions in which many of Kureishi's characters live are, moreover, often mitigated by the solidarity which they feel towards each other. In *Tomorrow-Today!*, for example, this is expressed poignantly when Ben touches Bill's face and supports him after their drinking spree and, whatever their other defects, the relationships between couples like Marie and Bill or Bob and Maureen are enduring.

Ethnicity, racism and liberalism

In all these respects, there is nothing which radically distinguishes Kureishi's plays from a host of other examples of 'fringe' theatre and they can easily be read alongside the work of 'no future' dramatists of the 1970s like Barry Keeffe (the dominant figure at the Soho Poly, where *The King and Me* and *Outskirts* were to be performed) and Steven Berkoff (for whom Kureishi worked intermittently as an assistant stage manager after leaving college). Indeed, as one might expect of an apprentice playwright, there are strong echoes of these more established voices in his plays. The incident in *Tomorrow-Today!* where Ben threatens to set light to Bill recalls Keeffe's *Gotcha* (1976), in which the protagonist threatens to set fire to a teacher. The boys' catch-phrase, 'Gis a fag', invokes the 'Bung us a snout' of another feckless but humorous pair of youths, Les and Mike in Berkoff's *East* (1975, first shown in London 1976). By contrast, the twelve-scene structure, the comparison of past and present to illuminate the 'condition of England' (though the time scheme is more telescoped in Kureishi's play) and the themes of guilty return, all suggest the influence of Hare's *Plenty* (1978) on *Outskirts*.

Even Kureishi's interest in issues of ethnicity and immigration was not unprecedented in 'fringe'. *East* is one play in which the relationship between 'Englishness', changing working-class identity and racism is explored and Trevor Griffiths's *The Comedians* (1975) another. Even the cross-race friendship between the two youths in *The Mother Country* is anticipated in Keeffe's *In the City* (1975), though in Kureishi's piece it does not degenerate into violence. From the early 1970s issues of race began to be tackled head-on in theatre, notably by new minoritarian companies (to be discussed below). Tunde Ikoli and Mustapha Matura had written plays on such issues for the Royal Court and in the second half of the decade 'white fringe' began to follow their lead. Examples include Michael Hastings's *Gloo Joo* (1978), *Full Frontal* (1979) and *Carnival War/Midnite at the Starlight* (1981), John Burrows's *Restless Natives* (1978) and, perhaps most notably, Keeffe's *Sus* (1979). However, it is only in David Edgar's *Destiny* (1976) and *Our Own People* (1977) that British-Asian experience gets any significant space. Even in *Destiny*, Kheera and Prakash take a back seat to white British characters like Turner, analysis of whose chauvinism seems to be Edgar's primary concern.

What is distinctive about Kureishi's drama, however, is its attempt to address the predicament of Asian Britain from the inside.[12] Whatever their interest in other aspects and sectors of British society, the early plays' engagement with the 'host' culture is largely dictated by Kureishi's desire to explore, even to try to understand, its antagonism towards Asian Britain in particular. Such hostility puts the violence faced by the characters in *Tomorrow-Today!* into perspective. In *Borderline*, for example, a Gujerati youth is shot with an airgun outside Sainsbury's, a Sikh boy is stabbed and a Bangladeshi adolescent has swastikas carved into his skin.

The Mother Country, *Outskirts* and *Birds of Passage* are the first of Kureishi's many attempts to analyse the psychology of racism, but contrary to the tendency of some 'agitprop' to make cut-and-dried political points by simplifying dramatic characters and moral issues, all are characterised by complexity and nuance in their depiction of white supremacism. In this respect, they follow the example of *Destiny*, which adopted a more traditional, naturalistic style to deal with the issue of race than was the case with the treatment of comparable social and political questions in some of Edgar's previous work like *Tederella* (1973). Thus, in *Birds of Passage* Ted may switch off his TV whenever a black face appears, yet this is also a man tortured by a sense of responsibility towards the workers he has had to lay off. Similarly, *Outskirts* makes clear that Bob is himself largely responsible for his parlous situation, a responsibility which begins with his refusal to grasp the opportunities for emancipation that his friend Del recognises are represented by education. The play leaves one in no doubt that he is deluded in defending neo-Nazism on the basis that: 'This country, if anything, that's the ill one; not me' (OOP, 63). Set against Bob's political brutishness, however, is the enormous tenderness which he shows towards his ailing mother and, despite the obvious strains in their relationship, his love for Maureen.

Perhaps most indicative of Kureishi's nuanced approach to the issue of racism is the fact that Bob's political views are shown to be intimately bound up with the sense of frustration he feels as a member of a white 'under-class' which was emerging in the wake of the recessions of the 1970s (as well as being unemployed himself, Bob's mother has been laid off and his sister has been forced to emigrate). Bob explains the make-up of his neo-Nazi group in the following terms: 'Men worn down by waiting. Abused men. Men with no work. Our parents made redundant. Now us. No joke. Wandering round the place, like people stranded on holiday' (OOP, 64). To this extent, Bob is depicted as the victim of enormously powerful currents of social and historical change. His attachment to the far Right, with its attempt to make immigrants into scapegoats for developments of which they are a symptom and not the cause, is testimony to the disruptions generated by the long-term decline of a working-class sense of security, identity and community.[13] It is for this reason that Bob's claim to have the support of ordinary (white) people in the area has credibility and why he – and the class fraction that he represents – are depicted with some sympathy. As Del comments to his friend's exasperated wife: 'There's a whole machinery down on him, Mo. You've got to see that' (OOP, 82).

If the hostility of Bob to what he sees as an 'invasion' of immigrants derives to a substantial degree from a failure of political understanding, however, it is also generated by his insularity and ignorance of other cultures, a tendency which Kureishi discerns even among less disadvantaged fractions of the 'host' culture. In *Birds of Passage*, for example, Eva good-naturedly scurries to make Asif a sandwich with the remark: 'Corned beef's all right for Pakis, isn't it?' (OOP, 178). At one level, Kureishi's early plays can be understood as an attempt to confront a number of stereotypical misconceptions about British-Asian culture. For example, both *Outskirts* and *Border-line* challenge the widespread perception in mainstream society, especially at the time they were written, of British Asians as helpless and passive – even cowardly – victims of racism. Thus, in the former play, the young Bob and Del are surprised by an Indian who vigorously fights back against his assailants. (In this incident Kureishi also neatly reverses the increasingly influential assumption in the popular media of the time that 'mugging' was something done *by* members of the ethnic minorities *to* members of the host society.)[14] As Bob complains: 'I weren't expecting him to crack me round the ear with his suitcase. I didn't predict that did I?' (OOP, 75). *Borderline* presents a variety of modes of minoritarian resistance, from the quiet determination of both Amjad and Banoo not to be bullied into moving away by the bricks which are thrown through their windows, to Anwar and Yasmin's Asian Youth Movement, which seeks to fight racism by organised direct action. These are the first symptoms of Kureishi's consistent effort throughout his work not to represent minorities as *simply* victims within British society. Thus Anwar warns Susan against turning the British-Asian subjects of her documentary into victims and Yasmin refuses to participate in the film, on the grounds that 'white people would like an exhibition of my misery' (OOP, 141). More specifically, Kureishi's representation of increasingly self-assertive and politically engaged young British-Asian women like Amina and Yasmin challenges the common perception in mainstream society that such women passively accept their apparent status as the most oppressed members of an oppressed constituency.

Nonetheless, Kureishi's attempt to rebut the host culture's misconceptions about Asian Britain does not entail the production of a series of naively celebratory and compensatory counterimages of 'his' community. Kureishi has always been dismissive of such demands for 'positive images' of ethnicity: '[I]t requires useful lies and cheering fictions: the writer as public relations officer, as hired liar' (SR, 64). The early plays anticipate the more direct challenges in Kureishi's later work to sentimental visions of racial minorities, whether these are held by whites or immigrants themselves. In *Borderline*, for example, the supposedly greater sense of community amongst such groups is contradicted by Anil's dismissive attitude to his former childhood friend when the latter arrives from India. Indeed, in order to get rid of him, Anil denounces Ravi to the authorities as an 'illegal'. The latter's experience of working in Haroon's father's restaurant is treated with equal realism. Haroon's father is only the first of many ruthless British-Asian bosses in Kureishi's work; his decision to employ Ravi is not so much a question of giving a fellow-countryman his chance in life as of keeping costs down, for 'illegals' can be paid lower wages. Indeed, the Asian Youth Movement devotes as much energy to picketing the restaurant in protest against such exploitation as it does to picketing the hall where the neo-Nazis are to hold their meeting. Meanwhile, the obviously flawed Haroon incites the same ambivalent responses as many of Kureishi's later protagonists, such as Omar in *Laundrette*, even Karim in *The Buddha*. By resisting the temptation to create positive stereotypes, Kureishi largely succeeds in presenting his British-Asian and migrant characters as ordinary human beings, with the same kind of individuality and complexity as Bob is given in *Outskirts*. In doing so, however, he directly challenges the racist idea that other races than the one to which the racist belongs are ultimately lower forms of life. As Banoo comments in *Borderline*: 'For them we are not human, Susan' (OOP, 124). To this extent, the ambivalence of his British-Asian characters is politically as well as dramatically effective.[15]

Equally, despite their disgust at racism in contemporary Britain, Kureishi's plays stress the many positive features of the 'host' society. While Ravi in *Borderline* may be disappointed in his expectations, both Amjad and Haroon's father largely fulfil the migrant dream: each of them establishes his own business and achieves prosperity. In *Birds of Passage* Asif is notably optimistic about his prospects: 'I think there's plenty of opportunity for Asians in this country' (OOP, 198). In both works, the appeal of Britain is reinforced by reference to the subcontinent. While Banoo in *Borderline* may yearn for Pakistan (and Amina blames life in England for precipitating her father's decline), neither Amjad himself nor Kureishi's drama as a whole corroborates her rose-tinted vision of her homeland. Aside from the lack of job opportunity and poor social provision, India and Pakistan are represented in the drama, as in later work like *Sammy and Rosie* or *My Son the Fanatic*, as comparatively deficient in the rule of law and political stability. In *Birds of*

Passage Asif comments darkly on countries 'where nothing works; places where you go into prison and never come out if you don't bribe the right person' (OOP, 185). In his eyes, a further crucial attraction of Britain is its relative freedom of expression and an unprejudiced interest in ideas. In Pakistan, he asserts, 'if you read a book by Bertrand Russell they think you're homosexual' (OOP, 207).

The deficiencies of the 'host' culture are offset in other ways. For a start, the early plays suggest that ignorance of and condescension to other cultures is not confined to the West. In *Borderline*, Amjad warns his daughter off margarine on the grounds that it contains pig's fat, and in *Birds of Passage* Asif comments that his father sometimes 'won't sit next to whites ... You mustn't look for rationality' (OOP, 185). In fact, the early plays corroborate the implication of some parts of Homi Bhabha's work that stereotyping of other communities and cultures is common to all societies.[16] Thus, in *Borderline* Ravi's ludicrous and offensive views about western women reverse but do not displace what Edward Said has described as the tendency in western discourse to eroticise oriental women and see them as available for kinds of sexual experience not available 'at home'.[17] Anil has quite different, but equally demeaning attitudes: 'English women are stuck-up, cold, racist, common and – ' (OOP, 109), a diatribe cut short hilariously by the sudden sound of his white mistress approaching from off-stage. Nor is such stereotyping confined to different races' perceptions of each other. For example, Ravi is prone to generalised animadversions against certain groups of migrants from the subcontinent: 'My wallet was stolen in a takeaway by a bastard Sikhara. You can't trust them' (OOP, 145). Perhaps most radically, in Kureishi's *The Mother Country* the shopkeeper Hussein sees the racial riot in London as comparable to the communalist violence which he remembers from his younger days. As the mob approaches, he comments: 'I've heard that sound in India.'[18]

Finally, Kureishi does not view the 'host' culture as onto-logically prone to racism. In *The Mother Country*, foreshadow-ing *Laundrette* (where Johnny is brutally beaten saving Salim

from the thugs), Imran's closest friend is a local white man
called Joe. In *Outskirts*, Bob's mother has no time for his
extremist politics. Nor could there be a warmer welcome than
the one which Audrey extends to Asif in *Birds of Passage*:
'You're my new son' (OOP, 182). Moreover, in tracing her real
son Paul's conversion from apathy to engagement in the politics
of anti-racism, Kureishi implies that, in theory at least, any
member of the dominant society can be educated into a more
positive conception of intercultural relations. *Borderline* acknowledges the sympathetic nature of Susan's identification with the
ethnic minorities she is researching into. She shows a genuine
interest in and care for Ravi, especially after his abandonment at
the hands of Anil. She is able to gain the trust and confidence of
Amjad's family and is received with particular cordiality by
Banoo and Amina, who increasingly come to rely on her.

Nonetheless, Kureishi's early plays – like so much of his
later work – are sharply alert to the paradoxes which such 'benevolence' sometimes involves. This is evident as early as *The
Mother Country*, in the emphasis given to Joe's paternalistic
attitude to Imran. He wishes to protect Imran from racial violence; but the price of this is attempted interference in many
areas of the latter's life. The issue is taken up again in *Outskirts*'s ambivalent representation of the 'liberal' Del who, as a
'progressive' teacher in an ethnically-mixed Islington school,
advocates reason and tolerance as the only effective antidotes to
racism. However, the embarrassing – and dramatically highly
effective – revelation of the adolescent Del's participation in a
racially-motivated assault calls his good faith into question.
When Bob recalls the incident, Del is at first unable to face up to
his past and tries to escape back to London. As a youth, it
transpires, Del was as liable to casual racism as Bob; for example,
he refers to the bomb site where the pair habitually meet as full
of 'rotted rubber-johnnies that the niggers suck, pulling them
out of the mud, I've heard' (OOP, 37). Although Del's shame is
a positive indication of his subsequent moral development, this
history haunts his attempts to educate Bob out of his extremist
attitudes. As the latter comments: 'Can't understand how you

can have yer moral orgasm with me. After what you've done'
(OOP, 49).

This critique of liberalism is substantially developed in
Borderline. While Susan is in many ways an admirable figure,
the play suggests that her good intentions are compromised in a
number of ways. The first time she is seen, on her return from
India, Susan is reading James Morris's *Farewell the Trumpets*, a
somewhat nostalgic paean to the vanished British empire. Nor is
her attitude to Ravi entirely disinterested, as she makes clear:
'I'll help you if you help me' (OOP, 122). Indeed, her at times
patronising interest in him (at one point she wants to show Ravi
off at a party) seems to rearticulate certain elements of the
imperial mission as understood in Morris's text. Morris interprets the moral character of the British empire generously,
stressing its role in protecting and 'raising up' the colonised (and
like a benevolent missionary, Susan lends Amina works of
western literature as part of her project of emancipating her new
friend). Susan's desire for Anwar is a further manifestation of
her love of the exotic, a factor which undoubtedly complicates
her investment in his political projects.

Anwar himself questions whether Susan's programme is
not an appropriation of the voice of his community, a danger to
which he suggests that interventions 'from outside', however
benevolently motivated, are perhaps inevitably liable: 'I've said
you take our voice. Use our voice. Annexe our cause. Because
you like a cause don't you, a good solid cause to tie yourself
behind ... Now for a few days you've borrowed our little worry'
(OOP, 132). Kureishi's treatment of Susan metacritically and
self-referentially questions the ethics underpinning the interest
of radical theatre groups like Joint Stock (which commissioned
Borderline) in the politics of race, which might be deemed to run
the same kind of risks as Susan's investigative project. To this
extent, it also anticipates the arguments of Gayatri Spivak about
the unfortunate effects of certain kinds of 'radical' western
intellectual work on behalf of the 'subaltern'. Spivak has taken
the post-structuralist philosophers Michel Foucault and Gilles
Deleuze to task for assuming that their interventions on behalf

of the oppressed are 'transparent', in other words that they can represent the views – and interests – of the marginalised without at the same time 'standing in' for these constituencies, thereby perpetuating their subordination (not least by converting their material struggle into a pitch for authority within the western cultural establishment).[19]

However, it cannot be said that *Borderline* definitively resolves the issues raised here. Susan defends herself vigorously on the basis that it is not necessary to have personal experience of a particular oppression to want to oppose it. Also, in response to Anwar's objections to her proposed film on Asian Britain, she seems justified in complaining that his social atypicality means that he is himself speaking for the marginalised in precisely the manner that her work supposedly does (an argument which might, indeed, be used against Spivak's condemnation of Deleuze and Foucault). The issue is further complicated by the ambiguous implications of Haroon's desire to write about Asian Britain, which inevitably invites reflection on Kureishi's own role as a writer about 'his' community. Yasmin suggests that Haroon's proposed vocation is in some sense parasitic upon the very people from whom he affects to want to distance himself. She caricatures his novel as follows: 'It's full of feeling, I've heard. It's subtle with suffering. Whose suffering, Haroon?' (OOP, 148). One inference to be drawn from this debate is that a shared ethnicity or roots in a particular marginalised community grants no *a priori* privileges to the intellectual or artist in the context of the question of the right to represent that community's oppressions.[20] On the other hand, it is at times difficult to distinguish Haroon's strategy of writerly detachment *vis-à-vis* the pressing socio-political issues surrounding him from an apparently self-centred pursuit of personal and professional fulfilment. From one angle, Haroon's primary motivation seems to be a desire to abandon his community of origin and escape as quickly as possible to somewhere where the problems of race are less immediate.

Perhaps the most pressing theme raised in Kureishi's drama – and, indeed, in his work as a whole up to 1995 – concerns how immigrants should adapt to their new life in Britain. *Borderline*, which of all the plays engages most fully with this problem, sets up a number of alternatives. The first is represented by Haroon's father and, in a more complicated way, by Amjad, who both belong to the older generation which has not been born in Britain. Their emphasis is on assimilation to the norms of mainstream British society, at least in respect of the 'public sphere' of life outside the home. In terms of the problem of racism, more specifically, their response is largely apolitical. Both Haroon's father and Amjad continue to trust in basic British decency and, when this fails, they look to the established institutions of law and order to deal with provocations. Such characters (another is Hussein in *The Mother Country*) tend to see the economic sphere as the key both to integration and to empowerment in contemporary British society. Haroon explains his father's attitude as follows: 'He says "What I want to see in England is a day when you won't find a single Pakistani on the shop-floor. You never see Jews in overalls. We've got to develop our businesses, our power"' (OOP, 138).

However, *Borderline* suggests a number of problems with the strategy of the older generation. Their belief that assimilation in the 'public sphere' can be squared with the continuing sway of custom and tradition in the domestic domain is predicated on the belief that the two spaces can be kept entirely separate. Thus, Amjad can claim: 'Our Amina was born here, as you know. But she's Pakistani through and through' (OOP, 153). As his daughter's experience suggests, however, this division of roles and spheres is hard to sustain. Inevitably, her immersion in the outside world of education and work prompts discontent with the expectations which her parents have for her as a daughter at home. In any case, the play suggests, custom and tradition are nothing if not social in origin and to the extent that they therefore inevitably involve questions of social power, *Borderline*, like *Birds of Passage*, corroborates the argument of 1970s feminism that 'the personal *is* the political'. Moreover, the older generation's misplaced faith in the institutions of the the 'public sphere' to deliver social justice is highlighted in a number of ways. As Yasmin points out, material prosperity provides no safeguards against racism – as is made evident by the terrifying experience of Haroon's parents during the Southall riots and, as Amjad's ordeal at the police station when he complains about harassment also makes clear, the forces of law and order can be as much part of the problem of racism as of its solution. His trust in British decency is further called into question by the fact that everyone in the play agrees that violence against migrants is actually on the increase.

This dispiriting reality lends weight to an alternative mode of response which *Borderline* explores. This is fairly symmetrically opposed to the strategy of the older generation insofar as the younger British Asians in this play (unlike in some later work like *The Black Album* or the film *My Son the Fanatic*) tend to be much more assimilated to everyday life in Britain than their parents and consequently have a great deal less attachment to cultural tradition, especially as regards their private lives. Haroon, for example, comments scathingly on the 'out-of-date ways. That ridiculous religion', and he is particularly harsh on arranged marriages, which he dismisses as 'just prostitution' (OOP, 137). The Asian Youth Movement is represented positively insofar as it opposes such practices and helps to facilitate British-Asian women's admission to education, work and politics (though the relationship between Anwar and Yasmin suggests that, as in many comparable radical organisations of the time, a patriarchal hierarchy is in fact preserved in their group). As this suggests, at this stage of his career Kureishi is more concerned with access to equal rights and opportunities than with respect for the principle of cultural difference. Equally, the way that the younger generation deals with racism differs sharply from its parents' policy of measured response (which the young people equate with appeasement). Yasmin initially argues for the necessity of political organisation and, if necessary, of a militant response to provocations on the basis that 'we can't wait for the race relations board to prosecute someone. People are being burnt to death' (OOP, 148).

To the extent that *Borderline* represents Asian Britain as an embattled community, such arguments carry considerable weight. However, while there is much to admire in characters like Anwar and Yasmin, and the group which they organise, the play suggests that in the end their tactics too closely mirror those of their immediate opponents and that violence only perpetuates the predicament in which they find themselves.[21] Moreover, Haroon argues, the seige mentality which the group cultivates runs the danger of encouraging ghettoisation and a disabling tendency to sever links with mainstream society: 'Yasmin and Anwar – they're brave. But they're separatist' (OOP, 118). Despite her criticims of Haroon, Yasmin increasingly comes to share his doubts. Half-way through the play she has come to identify a crucial weakness in the group's strategy: 'They talk of petrol bombs, they explain how to saw off a shotgun. I tell them to learn how to read and write. But they hate anything that takes longer than a night to achieve' (OOP, 141). By the end, significantly, Yasmin has changed her strategic thinking to the extent of dissuading Amina from assisting in the proposed petrol bombing of the hall where the Fascists are gathering.

Thus, *Borderline* can be interpreted as an early exploration of the possibilities of a 'third way' of responding to the worsening racial situation. This is embodied in Haroon's perspective, which on first sight seems to echo his parents' generation's quietism: 'I don't believe in street fighting. I'm going to be a lawyer' (OOP, 158). Haroon can, however, lay claim to a progressive and principled politics inasmuch as the course which he has chosen represents a way of engaging with the issues in question while at the same time transcending an unacceptable choice between the essentially apolitical position espoused by Amjad and Haroon's father on the one hand and, on the other, the destructive militancy and separatism of the Asian Youth Movement. Haroon describes himself as being at the beginning of a 'long march through the institutions. The black mole under the lawns and asphalt of England' (OOP, 159). The goals of his march are twofold; first of all, to make use of the structures of the dominant society to empower subordinate constituencies like his own and, secondly, by the very process of infiltration to change the nature of that dominant order from within. As Haroon argues to his girlfriend: 'I say we've got to get educated … and get inside things. The worm in the body, Amina' (OOP, 118). To this extent, Haroon's arguments seem to represent a politically subversive model of cultural hybridity which Kureishi's later work will repeatedly elaborate.

Kureishi's endorsement of this cultural politics of the 'in-between' position might also be inferred from a consideration of the material contexts in which his early plays were produced. From the outset the budding dramatist decided not to confine himself within the institutions of minoritarian theatre which were beginning to emerge in the 1970s. Dark and Light Theatre, Temba and Black Theatre Co-operative were all established during the decade and Tara Arts, the first British-Asian theatre group, was founded in 1976. Such groups were initially geared to constructing a theatrical audience *within* the ethnic communities and sought to give opportunities to writers, actors, directors and production staff from such communities who were finding limited opportunities to express their talents, whether in mainstream or in 'fringe' theatre. Kureishi certainly shared the ambition of such groups to give a cultural voice to ethnic minorities, and *The Buddha* corroborates many of their complaints about the institutionally racist nature of British theatre, including its radical wings. Here the suicide of Eleanor's former lover, the black actor Gene, is explained as follows: '[H]e never got the work he deserved. He emptied bed-pans in hospital programmes. He played criminals and taxi-drivers' (BS, 201). Nevertheless, as Chapter 1 suggested, Kureishi has always insisted that the solution to the problems which migrant communities face lies not just in fostering a more confident sense of their own identity, but in educating the 'host' society about its shortcomings in adjusting to the ethical and political challenges posed by the changing cultural and demographic make-up of modern Britain. To this extent, Kureishi's decision to work in 'fringe' can be understood as an attempt to plant the 'ethnic worm' in the body of 'white' theatre. Catherine Itzin has described Hampstead Theatre, where *Birds of Passage* opened, as 'a fringe theatre on the edge of the establishment with regular transfers to the West End'.[22] This illuminates the way that such venues could act as a 'third space' between mainstream and minoritarian theatre, enabling Kureishi to address the majority ethnicity without – in theory – exluding a minority audience.

Dramatic styles and intertexts

Kureishi's plays testify to an unstable and eclectic range of dramaturgical influences. Indeed, his disaffection with theatre after 1983 may partly be related to his inability to synthesise these influences sufficiently and impose his own voice on them. Most obviously, the preoccupation with sometimes highly localised, real-life problems and events (for instance, Kureishi encountered an organisation called the Asian Youth Movement in Bradford), approached from an explicitly political rather than moral perspective, links much of Kureishi's drama directly to the agitprop branch of 'fringe'. Kureishi has described such work as 'a mixture of information about the state of things, polemical journalism and theatre' (OOP, xviii). Like many of his contemporaries, the major influence in this respect was Brecht, whom he has described as the 'central figure of the age' (MBL, 115). Kureishi was first introduced to him through the work of Edward Bond, one of the leading dramatists at the Royal Court in the 1970s. He read Brecht's dramaturgical theory voraciously and eventually wrote a version of *Mother Courage* for the RSC in 1984.[23]

Brecht's stylistic influence is clearest in *Borderline*, which Kureishi has described as an attempt at 'epic' theatre (HK). It closely approximates to the structure of Brechtian drama, which has been described by William Gaskill as 'a demonstration of thesis, antithesis and synthesis'.[24] Thus, the response of the older generation to the problems of racism is compared with, and challenged by, the perspectives of the Asian Youth Movement; out of this contest emerges the 'third way' which is offered by Haroon. These different political strategies and goals are argued for by characters whose 'shape' is in part determined by their function in the elaboration of such debates. Thus, Yasmin's role is initially limited to making the most explicit kinds of political pronouncements:

> It's this Tory government that's down on us. That's the issue ... I think the Tories are working towards giving us only guest-worker status here. With no proper rights. That'll bring us into line with some EEC countries. At the same time they're pumping money into the race relations industry. It's probably the only growth area in the country, like hospitals in a war. (OOP, 115)

If Yasmin best exemplifies the use of 'caricature' which Kureishi has identified as one of the principal techniques of Brechtian forms of agitprop (OOP, xv), even more complexly-drawn characters, like Haroon, are always also 'ideal-types' of particular social predicaments or political positions.

However, like many of his contemporaries, Kureishi's conception of 'fringe' was also strongly influenced by Jerzy Grotowski's concept of a 'poor theatre', Peter Brook's ideas about 'the empty space' and Keith Johnstone's work on improvisation (HK). Their imprint is clear on *Borderline*'s mode of production. Kureishi recalls that in conformity with the collective ethos of Joint Stock, the ensemble founded by David Hare and William Gaskill (among others) and based at the Royal Court,[25] the script of *Borderline* was elaborated 'from the bottom up' by the whole group, with his role reduced to that of an amenuensis who had no final say over the script as it emerged (Kureishi was in fact already working towards this collaborative mode in *The King and Me*. Thus, the stage directions to Scene Two offer the following invitation: 'Various asides and jokes during this scene could be improvised both in rehearsal and during the actual playing of it.') Secondly, *Borderline* was staged in accordance with the norms of 'poor theatre', using minimal staging and lighting and conjuring up its physical locations in a very stylised manner (Vincent Ebrahim, who played Haroon/Farook, remembers the use of scaffolding poles to signify trees, for example). Kureishi has recalled that, when the play reached a new venue on tour, he and the director Max Stafford-Clark would debate whether it was spacious enough to 'support a four-chair or five-chair production' (HK).

However, in comparison with a lot of 'fringe', Kureishi's plays are never radically experimental in terms of form. They employ few of the more obvious hallmarks of Brechtian theatre, such as placards or an intrusive narrator; nor are the techniques of Dadaist 'fringe' much in evidence, despite Kureishi's awareness of the dramaturgical theory of Artaud (to which he was introduced by Steven Berkoff). None of his plays fully respond to Howard Barker's injunction to 'chuck overboard any concern with unities and pillage the entire stock of forms and conventions',[26] although the intercutting of scenes from past and present in *Outskirts* complicates the chronology – and increases the drama of – the revelations about Bob's past. Following the example of groups like Roland Muldoon's CAST, pop music is used occasionally, most notably in *The King and Me*. At the end of Scene One, for example, the playing of Elvis's 'In the Ghetto' somewhat obviously reflects on the situation of a couple anchored at the bottom of the social ladder. While physical violence and sexually explicit acts of the kind commonly used by dramatists like Bond, Barker or Brenton to provoke their audiences are largely absent from Kureishi's plays, profanity is used in many of them and sometimes succeeds in providing a salutary shock. For example, when Yasmin makes statements like 'I think I should fuck more' (OOP, 141), Kureishi effectively disrupted conventional assumptions about the sexually passive and demure nature of British-Asian women in both majority and minority society (though from a current perspective such tactics seem more questionable). Indeed, Kureishi has linked the fact that *Borderline* never played in Southall, as had been planned, to threats from local activists who were outraged at his boldness in this regard.[27] Perhaps the most effective single instance of defamiliarisation in Kureishi's plays is the use of white actors to play Asian roles and vice versa in *Borderline*. The same experiment had been used with great effect in an earlier Joint Stock production, David Lan's *Sergeant Ola and His*

Followers (1979; compare Caryl Churchill's *Cloud Nine* in the same year, in which men played women's roles and vice versa.) In this way Kureishi and the members of Joint Stock successfully challenged the audience's (and, according to Vincent Ebrahim, their own) received perceptions and expectations about ethnic difference.

Moreover, as might have been inferred from the earlier comments on characterisation in *Outskirts* and *Birds of Passage*, there is a recurrent tension in Kureishi's drama between the agitprop elements of 'fringe' and the desire to produce a more 'writerly' kind of theatre. In the 'Introduction' to *Outskirts and Other Plays*, Kureishi describes how he made Beckett's acquaintance while the latter was rehearsing *Footfalls* at the Royal Court and how Beckett lent him £50 towards the cost of a drama course.[28] At the level of theme, the influence of Beckett is evident in a number of areas: the feelings of entrapment, whether in physical environments like the flat in *The King and Me*, imprisoning cultural/geographical locations like South London, or in relationships, which Kureishi's characters so often prove unable to escape from, however much they may at times desire to; the problems of non- or failing communication between characters; the burden on them of the unfulfilling present (and its evasion through fantasy or nostalgia); the endless waiting (or 'hanging about'); the at times almost unendurably repetitive and ritualistic nature of life. If all these are staples of both writers' work (and some of the characters in Kureishi's earliest plays, especially, inhabit a universe nearly as 'absurd' as that in Beckett's drama), so are the positive elements which prevent either writer's vision from collapsing into mere bleakness: the humour, the solidarity between characters and the stubborn will to endure.

At the level of form, Beckett's imprint is most clear in *Tomorrow-Today!*, another play in which, to adapt Vivien Mercier's description of *Waiting for Godot*, 'nothing happens twice'.[29] The two-scene division, in which many of the themes and situations in the second half of the play mirror those in the first, repeats the structure of *Waiting for Godot*. Scene Two of

Kureishi's play begins with the stage direction 'Next day. Same place. Same time.' This is a minor variation on the one which prefaces Act Two of Beckett's play. The setting of *Tomorrow-Today!*, adjoining a motorway, recalls the road beside which Vladimir and Estragon are marooned. The percussive, truncated dialogue; the curious anonymity and interchangeability of the characters and the shifting power relations between them; the comparative lack of dramatic action and plot; the exclusively male gender economy; the routines which the characters perform to amuse each other and pass the time; the allusions to tramps and boots; the apocalyptic atmosphere (the frustration and impotence – as well as the gallows humour – of Bill and Ben is partly a response to their anxieties about nuclear catastrophe of the kind which are implicit in *Waiting for Godot*); the circularity of the play and its inconclusive, anti-climactic ending – all suggest the degree to which Kureishi's representation of alienated urban youth in the 1970s is mediated through conventions associated with his predecessor.

Another major model was Joe Orton, whose interest for Kureishi lay in the attempt to adapt elements of the absurd to a more explicit exploration of questions of social justice and morality than is characteristic of Beckett. Kureishi was much impressed by his first contact with Orton's work, which came in the form of Silvio Norizzano's film of *Loot* (1970). At a personal level, Kureishi identified not just with Orton's impressively scandalous lifestyle, but with his lower-middle-class origins and the fact that Orton had come to prominence in the London theatre world from an unpromisingly provincial milieu (Leicester). Consequently, when Kureishi was looking for someone to represent him, his first approach was to Orton's agent, Margaret (Peggy) Ramsay (who declined).[30] In 1975, the Royal Court mounted an Orton festival, some of which Kureishi attended (HK), including the revivals of *Entertaining Mr Sloane* (1964), *Loot* (1966) and *What the Butler Saw* (1969).

The influence of Orton is evident in several of Kureishi's early plays (and extends to the recent *Sleep With Me*), particularly *Birds of Passage* which, like *Entertaining Mr Sloane*, revolves around a lodger who progressively usurps the 'host' family.[31] Just as Kath welcomes Sloane as a replacement for the son she has lost, so Audrey greets Asif as a 'new son'. Just as Kath and Sloane become lovers, so do Asif and Audrey's sister Eva in Kureishi's play. Kemp expresses similar kinds of racist sentiment to Eva's husband Ted. Sloane's relations with Ed are at first conflictual, with each struggling for ascendancy, before the relationship settles into a co-operative one of mutual benefit, a pattern largely followed in Asif and Ted's relationship. Like Sloane, Asif is without apparent shame or guilt for the way he behaves in his private life. Stylistically, the debt is most evident in Kureishi's dramatic language, which in many of his plays echoes Orton's somewhat mannered and aphoristic phrasing as well as his colloquial register.

Birds of Passage, which Kureishi has described as 'an old-fashioned play, in some ways' (OOP, xx), also testifies to the influence of two playwrights whose careers long predate the revolution on the British stage in the late 1960s. The first, Ibsen, has always been one of the dramatists most admired by Kureishi (HK). In 1993, he began work on a version of *Pillars of the Community* (1877) for the National Theatre – though the project never came to fruition. The naturalistic conception of character, stage time and structural development in *Birds of Passage*, and its interest in moral as much as social issues, especially the conflict, repression, hypocrisy and secrets characteristic of family life, all suggest Ibsen's influence. An even more important source for *Birds of Passage* is Chekhov. The link is signposted by Asif, who asks Stella what she thinks of the Russian dramatist (OOP, 216).[32] *The Cherry Orchard* (1904) is the key intertext here in terms of character, action and theme. Thus, Paul's conviction that 'Sydenham's a leaving place' (OOP, 173) echoes Yasha's desire to quit the backwoods for the metropolis. Just as David and Audrey long for a life of contemplation in Wales, Varia yearns to improve herself in 'holy places'. Gayev has the same kind of 'progressive' attitudes as David, and their politics, about which each likes to hold forth at length, are represented as equally out of date. Kureishi combines the roles of the student Trofimov and the businessman Lopakhin in Asif. Audrey greets Asif as her new son, just as Liuba sees Trofimov as a surrogate for Grisha. Both Asif and Lopakhin are represented ambiguously, insofar as their energy and ambition is admired while their disdain for traditional moral values is decried. Like Asif, Trofimov is a restless 'bird of passage'. Like Liuba, Stella returns home after a period away, with a dark secret which is uncovered in the play. As with Liuba and Gayev, her parents are afflicted by feelings of failure and the sense that their best days are behind them. This grounds the main social issue of both plays, the exploration of the decline of the class which these respective pairs of parents represent. Just as Lopakhin, whose parents were family serfs, takes over Liuba's house, so Asif, whose parents were colonised subjects, takes over David's.

However, while *Birds of Passage* certainly reiterates Kureishi's interest in social issues, the play can also be read as an analysis of self-deception, yearning, failed ambitions and frustrated talent. The same is true of *The Cherry Orchard*. Chekhov's concern for social justice is clearly evident in the figure of the tramp and the themes of urbanisation, new forms of philosophical thinking and democracy are central to the play. Yet these interests do not outweigh a traditional humanist interest in the dramatic exploration and revelation of moral attitude and character. While the earthiness of Kureishi's humour and the characteristic coarseness of his principal protagonist prevent his play from attaining the refined poignancy and bitter-sweet timbre of Chekhov's, there are undoubted hints of an attempt to produce a similar sense of the pathos (and dignity) of human life and relations within the quite different social contexts of late twentieth-century, multi-racial, Britain.

Conclusion

By the early 1980s, Kureishi seemed set to become one of the most successful new playwrights of his generation (looking back from 1998, Max Stafford-Clark stated that he was one of the two or three most promising playwrights he had ever worked with).[33] In 1980, he won a Thames Television Playwright Award for *The Mother Country*, and the following year was appointed Writer-in-Residence at the Royal Court, where he subsequently won the George Devine Award for *Outskirts*. In 1982, *Border-line* was judged the best play in Thames Television's Bursary scheme. Kureishi's success can be measured not just in terms of such awards, but also in terms of the companies (the RSC and Joint Stock) and directors (Howard Davies and Stafford-Clark) he worked with, the prestige of the venues at which his work was shown (which included the Royal Court, RSC Warehouse and Hampstead Theatre) and the status of his publishers (John Calder, Methuen and – since the mid-1980s – Faber.) His plays were also generally well received by the public and reviewing establishment. Typical of the general tone was the *TLS* notice of *Borderline*, which described its depiction 'of the diverse and contradictory values of the immigrant community [as] a fine example of the possibilities of investigative theatre'.[34]

Despite such success, however, Kureishi was becoming increasingly disillusioned with theatre. After *Birds of Passage*, which opened in September 1983, he recalls:

> I stopped being able to find a tone or style to accommodate my voice or themes. I didn't feel comfortable writing plays any more: I didn't know what sort of plays they should be; and the challenge of that doubt didn't stimulate me. (OOP, xx)

In 1984 Kureishi began to contemplate the script of *Laundrette*, inaugurating a period of several years in which film became his prime interest. There were, in fact, many reasons behind his decision to abandon drama, several of which reflect the crisis into which 'progressive' theatre had fallen by the early 1980s. Despite the success of the Theatre Writers' Union in 1979 in enforcing a minimum standard contract for writers (in 1976, the National had paid Howard Brenton a mere £350 for *Weapons of Happiness*),[35] only a handful of playwrights earned sufficient to do more than scrape by. This situation was exacerbated once subsidies to all forms of theatre began to be cut systematically after Thatcher's election victory in 1979. As the material base of 'fringe' began to shrink, so inevitably did opportunities for writers. Ambition and the desire for greater financial rewards and security were, then, an important factor in Kureishi's abandonment of theatre.

More importantly, perhaps, the visual media provided the chance to reach much larger audiences than those achievable even at well-established subsidised theatres like the Royal Court and the RSC Warehouse, let alone tiny venues like the Soho Poly. Kureishi was increasingly frustrated by the failure of radical theatre to fulfill its ambition to reach new audiences, least of all amongst the marginalised sections of society on whose behalf it was ostensibly so concerned to intervene. To the extent that its audience remained confined to a narrow constituency of generally well-educated, relatively affluent left-liberal consumers, Kureishi argues, 'fringe' 'was even more elitist and esoteric than conventional theatre' (OOP, xv). In this respect, he echoed the views of many of his contemporaries. David Edgar acknowledged that 'fringe''s principal audience was 'radically-inclined middle-class people' and Trevor Griffiths became fed up with 'talking to thirty-eight university graduates in a cellar in Soho'.[36] Despite some good British-Asian audiences on tour and at the Royal Court, the furore over *Borderline* in Southall, which prevented the play from being shown in one of the community's heartlands, helped persuade Kureishi that a minoritarian audience might be more effectively reached via the visual media.[37]

The problem of audiences exacerbated Kureishi's growing scepticism about the political efficacy of 'fringe' theatre, an attitude which was also increasingly apparent amongst Kureishi's contemporaries. Indeed, as early as 1974 Howard Brenton was arguing that 'fringe' had failed in its political mission, and in 1978 Ed Berman, who had been instrumental in the emergence of alternative theatre a decade earlier, commented: 'I wonder if political theatre has ever changed anyone's opinion on anything or whether it has just corroborated and consolidated.'[38] *Birds of Passage* suggests that by the early 1980s the politics on which 'fringe' was characteristically predicated had been overtaken by major realignments in British political culture (a few months before the play opened, Labour suffered its worst defeat in post-war electoral history in the course of a second successive triumph for the Tories). By means of the weapon of mass unemployment, the play suggests, Thatcherism had routed its traditional opponents, especially the unions to which David has devoted so much of his life. David's retreat to Wales perhaps expresses the new mood of quietism on the Left as the realisation spread that, far from collapsing – as had so confidently been predicted in the 1970s – 'late capitalism' had proved capable of vigorously reconstituting itself. If, as David sneeringly suggests, 'political and moral radicalism is [now] a dead duck at the polls' (OOP, 217), the inescapable implication of *Birds of Passage* was that 'progressive' theatre, too, was becoming an anachronism.[39]

Interestingly, such developments are by no means presented as wholly regrettable. Despite the anguish at the failures of the Welfare State, there are also moments in several plays when 'welfarism' and the habit of looking to the state to solve every social problem are themselves isolated as key factors in the parlous state to which Britain had been reduced by the 1970s. In *Birds of Passage*, David complains of his children's shiftlessness: 'And do you think the tax-payer educated you just to enjoy films with sub-titles?' (OOP, 194). Most strikingly, Asif endorses the self-help ethic and entrepreneurialism of his Tory foe Ted as the best means for migrants to achieve social justice. Condemning the 'shouting and stone throwing' tactics (OOP, 200) of Paul's anti-racist group, Asif offers a conception of the 'third way' to Haroon's in *Borderline*, which, although superficially similar, is more difficult to distinguish from assimilation to the dominant values: 'We'll protect ourselves against boots with our brains. We won't be on the street because we'll be in cars. We won't be throwing bricks because we'll be building houses with them. They won't abuse us in factories because we'll own the factories and we'll sack people' (OOP, 215). To this extent, the play expressed elements of a popular (rather than radical-Left) disenchantment with Labourism which few other 'fringe' playwrights (or Left cultural critics) were as yet able or willing to articulate.[40]

By the early 1980s, moreover, Kureishi was also plainly becoming exasperated by the internal politics of 'fringe', a factor which animates the scathing satire of radical theatreland in *The Buddha*. From the outset of his involvement with the Royal Court, in fact, Kureishi appears to have been unfavourably struck by the extent of the 'factions and quarrels' in 'fringe' theatre and the 'spite and biliousness' which accompanied them (OOP, viii–ix; compare BS, 168, 221). More important, perhaps, he was increasingly uneasy with what he identified as a strongly authoritarian streak within the milieu. In the 'Introduction' to *Outskirts and Other Plays*, he recalls being castigated for admiring writers like Tom Stoppard, whose politics were deemed to be 'incorrect'. For Kureishi, such behaviour was emblematic of a tendency towards 'categorization, exclusion and contempt' (OOP, viii) and a clear perversion of the laudable ideal that 'the democratic will of the company was sovereign' (OOP, xix) in ensembles like Joint Stock.

As implied earlier, Kureishi was also increasingly dissatisfied by the characteristic subordination of aesthetic form to political content in agitprop especially. Kureishi's disaffection in this respect came to a head in the context of *Borderline*, of which he comments that it 'was using a method, journalism, as the tool for a different form, art or theatre … A play is not an article in a newspaper' (OOP, xix). Again, this was a common development amongst his contemporaries. In 1981 David Hare looked back ruefully on his approach to drama in 1969: 'I had no patience for the question of how well written a play was. I was only concerned with how urgent its subject matter was, how it related to the world outside.'[41] To a considerable degree, Kureishi's negative estimation of his plays at the launch of *Love in a Blue Time* was bound up with his recognition that interventions in immediately contemporary events (for example, *Borderline*'s engagement with the Southall riots of 1981) involves the risk that the work in question will be merely ephemeral in its interest. Moreover, aesthetic distance is clearly hard to achieve when the articulation of 'politically correct' analyses and 'solutions' of the problems under discussion is held to be paramount. Kureishi has commented of 'progressive' theatre that: 'You could sit through some terrible evening and hear the writer or director say in the pub afterwards, "At least the point was worth making", confirming a leftish audience in its prejudices just as much as a bourgeois audience was confirmed in its own' (OOP, xv). Interestingly, though perhaps paradoxically, Kureishi has suggested that to reach the much larger and less politically sophisticated audiences characteristic of film and television required greater emphasis on issues of form and aesthetic shape, a challenge which he warmly welcomed (HK).

The films

Introduction: from drama to film

While his move into visual media represented a clear change of direction for Kureishi, there are nonetheless many continuities between the first two phases of his career. Perhaps unsurprisingly, *My Beautiful Laundrette*, his first film script, was initially developed like a play (MBL, 3). Kureishi's description of *Sammy and Rosie Get Laid* as an example of a 'poor and rough cinema rich in ideas and imagination' (SR, 71) indicates that his conception of the medium was influenced by the dramaturgical theory of 'fringe' gurus like Grotowski. His first three films all attempt to make a virtue of limited resources in the same way as 'fringe',[1] and are representative of much new-wave British cinema in the early 1980s in being 'low-budget films made quickly and sometimes quite roughly' (SR, 63). Once in production, moreover, they at times evolved in the improvisatory manner of 'fringe'. Thus, on the sets of *Laundrette* Kureishi often found himself adding dialogue *ad hoc* with the actors, and regularly had to rewrite the script of *Sammy and Rosie* at the behest of the director Stephen Frears. Kureishi recalls that the editing of this film was 'like a structured improvisation', as writer and director struggled to impose shape on the mass of footage they had accumulated (SR, 120). Even *London Kills Me*, over which Kureishi had greater control insofar as he was its director as well as writer, evolved in a similar fashion: 'Some scenes ... developed as we rehearsed. Some just changed in front of the camera. A certain amount of the dialogue was made up by the actors' (LKM, x).

Secondly, Kureishi's drama is repeatedly raided for motifs, themes and character types for his films. In *Laundrette*, the central relationship reworks Imran and Joe's in the unpublished play, *The Mother Country*, as well as elements of Del and Bob's friendship in *Outskirts*. One source for *Sammy and Rosie*, Kureishi tells us in 'Some Time With Stephen' (SR), his diary of the making of the film, was another early, unfinished, play about an exiled Asian politician living in London. Both Rosie and Headley, the exploitative liberal in *London Kills Me*, have parallels with Susan in *Borderline*. In her role as an investigative reporter, moreover, Susan prefigures the American photo-journalist Anna in *Sammy and Rosie*. The clashes between host society and immigrant communities, the conflict between different generations of Asian Britain, the predicament of alienated young people, issues of gender and the exploration of father–son relationships are all examples of preoccupations in Kureishi's drama which are recycled and rethought.

Kureishi's career in the theatre also provided him with a network of contacts on which he could draw in making his films. Rita Wolf, who played Amina in *Borderline*, reappears as Tania in *Laundrette* and both Frances Barber and Meera Syal (Rosie and Rani in *Sammy and Rosie*) had acted at the Royal Court during Kureishi's association with it. Tunde Ikoli, the tramp in *London Kills Me*, had been a writer there and, most important perhaps, Stephen Frears, who directed Kureishi's first two films, was Lindsay Anderson's assistant at the Court (as well as directing some of the TV plays which Kureishi most admired, including work by Alan Bennett, Dennis Potter and David Mercer). As Kureishi commented of the team behind *Sammy and Rosie*, 'it was like the Royal Court in exile' (SR, 71). (When *The Buddha of Suburbia* was made into a BBC TV series in 1993, another Court contact, Roger Michell, was chosen as director.)

Lastly, Kureishi transposed some of the characteristic stylistic features of 'fringe' into his films. For example, the crucial moment at the opening of Omar's laundrette, when Omar and Johnny are overlaid onto Nasser and Rachel by means of the two-way mirror, recalls the use of back-projection in 'fringe'. In *Sammy and Rosie* such links are extensive, notably in its generic incongruities. Kureishi's description of the film as a 'mixture of realism and surrealism, seriousness and comedy, art and gratuitous sex' (SR, 64) would apply to a great deal of 'alternative' theatre of the 1960s and 1970s. Some of the shock tactics employed evoke the desire of 'fringe' to assault its audience's sense of decorum. These include the very title (which plays the derogatory label 'Sambo' off a traditional icon of 'Englishness' and English womanhood in particular), the sudden cut from the shooting of the black woman to Anna's buttocks, and the scene of Sammy masturbating over a porn magazine while simultaneously snorting coke and eating a hamburger. The sometimes schematic characterisation (for example, the Tory property developer), and the subordination of plot to set-piece didactic speeches and debates which interrupt the developing action, both recall the primacy given to communication of political ideas in agitprop. Like many instances of 'fringe', moreover, *Sammy and Rosie* sometimes has a documentary and of-the-moment quality, notably in the sequences shot with a hand-held camera. The shooting at the start of the film is explicitly modelled on contemporary incidents like the killings of Cherry Groce and Cynthia Jarrett by the Metropolitan Police and the riots obviously recall events in so many British cities in the early 1980s.

As this implies, despite his desire to work in a medium which he felt would be more conducive to his 'writerly' ambitions, Kureishi's films also resemble 'fringe' theatre in terms of their engagement with social issues (indeed, Kureishi has described *Sammy and Rosie* as 'a sort of agitprop film').[2] In common with much of the new British cinema of the 1980s, Kureishi's films are primarily concerned with 'the exploration of areas of British life not touched on before' (SR, 63) and, more particularly, with the experience of marginalised social groups. His description of such interests as material 'that wouldn't be acceptable to the mainstream commercial world' (SR, 66) recalls 'fringe's' ambition to provide an alternative vision of society to that of commercial theatre. Most obviously, Kureishi's films attempt to make Asian Britain the subject of representation, redressing an obvious lacuna in post-war British cinema. The first two films, in particular, are remarkable for the restricted number and nature of the roles given to white British characters. In *Sammy and Rosie*, especially, male white Britons, more specifically, occupy only marginal positions. One significant development *vis-à-vis* Kureishi's plays is that as well as analysing the consolidation of 'underclass' Britain,[3] the films also attend to gay and lesbian sexualities and the emergence of other kinds of sub-cultural community.

In these respects, Kureishi's films look back not just to 'fringe', but to a long TV tradition of imaginative social investigation. From the late 1950s, issue-oriented theatre and TV drama had fed off and stimulated each other. Just as 'kitchen-sink' plays helped to make possible ITV's *Armchair Theatre* and the BBC's *Wednesday Play*, so these in turn helped to create an audience for the more politicised theatre which emerged in the later 1960s. Series like *Play for Today* had, in Kureishi's view, made the BBC drama department one of the three key British cultural institutions when he was growing up (MBL, 109; and he describes his most recent film, *My Son the Fanatic*, as a 'Play for Today' for the late 1990s).[4] This tradition was in decline by the early 1980s, however. One symptom of the lurch to the right under Thatcher was a systematic attack on the supposedly left-wing bias of the BBC which led the Corporation to be much more circumspect about offering work like *Boys From the Blackstuff* (1982), an acclaimed drama series anatomising the impact of Thatcherism, which was strenuously denounced by the New Right. By mid-decade, in Kureishi's view, a demoralised BBC – threatened with privatisation and beset by anxiety over the renewal of its Charter – had caved in. When Frears suggested approaching it to help fund *Sammy and Rosie*, Kureishi was horrified: 'I counter by saying they've become too reactionary … [and] cowed by censors. If you want to show an arse on the BBC, they behave as if their entire licence fee were at stake' (SR, 64).

However, the opening of Channel 4 in late 1982 provided an

important counterweight to these dispiriting developments. Through its film-making subsidiary, Film Four International, Channel 4 invested heavily in features for both cinema and TV release and was, in consequence, a major contributor to the mini-renaissance in British film-making in the 1980s. It was happy to use some of its substantial subsidy (which came from both central government and ITV) for 'progressive' ends. As Kureishi records, Channel 4 took on the BBC's former mandate in 'presenting serious contemporary drama ... to a wide audience' (MBL, 3). Like 'fringe', Channel 4 encouraged those who had not traditionally had easy access to the medium, especially women and minority film-makers, first-time directors and writers. The relative freedoms offered by Channel 4 also evoked the democratic atmosphere of 'fringe'. Kureishi remembers enthusiastically being given the opportunity to make films 'outside the system of studios and big film companies, films that the people involved in can control themselves' (SR, 63).

Just as Kureishi's plays focus primarily on the 'condition of England' in the late 1970s, so his films move on to consider the state of the nation in the following decade, which he has described as 'the authoritarian eighties' (MBL, 80). In Kureishi's view, Thatcherism constituted a revolutionary attempt to overturn many of the assumptions which had governed British society since 1945 and, more particularly, the values of the counter-cultural 1960s. As he notes, Thatcher's close associate Norman Tebbitt famously anathematised upon 'the insufferable, smug, sanctimonious, naive, guilt-ridden, wet, pink orthodoxy of that sunset home of the third-rate minds of that third-rate decade' (MBL, 116).[5] Indeed, the shrill invocation of 'Victorian values' in Thatcherite discourse suggested that, as far as the 'New Right' was concerned, the rot had set in many decades earlier. The ensuing struggle over the direction that Britain should take, and the meanings of national identity and tradition, was fought out not just in the political domain but in the field of culture too. In every medium, including TV and film, a 'battle of representations' ensued, producing some of the most distinctive cultural work of the decade.

As interventions in this ideological struggle, Kureishi's films can be approached in the first instance in terms of their engagements with two strands in Britain's visual media (each of which, ironically, Channel 4 was also heavily involved in developing). Consciously or not, both seemed to support – or at least give comfort to – the New Right's vision of the need for a new national mission which would redirect a stricken Britain back to the path from which it had been seduced by welfare socialism. Following Salman Rushdie's scathing account in *Imaginary Homelands*,[6] the first strand can been categorised as 'Raj Revival' cinema and includes Richard Attenborough's *Gandhi* (1982) and David Lean's *A Passage to India* (1984). The second strand has been described as 'Heritage' cinema; notable examples are Hugh Hudson's *Chariots of Fire* (1981) and – in a more subtle vein – James Ivory's *A Room with a View* (1986). It is in relation to these four films primarily that Kureishi's will be considered.

In some obvious ways, of course, 'Raj Revival' and 'Heritage' films are quite distinct genres, notably in their settings and those aspects of the nation's histories on which they focus. However, in Kureishi's mind the two strands had common ideological purposes and effects, as he makes plain in his account of an exchange with an American reviewer who had been critical of the backward-looking nature of recent British cinema:

> The journalist's view isn't entirely surprising since a lot of English 'art' … dwells, gloats on and relives nostalgic scenarios of wealth and superiority. It's easy therefore for Americans to see Britain as just an old country, as a kind of museum, as a factory for producing versions of lost greatness. After all, many British films do reflect this: *Chariots of Fire*, *A Room with a View*, the Raj epics, and the serials *Brideshead Revisited* and *The Jewel in the Crown*. (SR, 82)

Constitutive of such works' vision of national identity and cultural tradition are a number of what Kureishi calls 'saleable myths' (SR, 82) which his own films vigorously contest.

Kureishi and the 'Raj Revival'

Kureishi's films engage explicitly with 'Raj Revival' cinema, which enjoyed great commercial and critical success in the 1980s. *A Passage to India*, winner of two Oscars, was the culmination of the career of one of Britain's greatest post-war directors, David Lean, whose earlier successes included *Lawrence of Arabia* (1962) and *Dr Zhivago*, (1968). Meanwhile *Gandhi* received no less than eight Oscars. Kureishi was deeply irritated by such work:

> I was tired of seeing lavish films set in exotic locations; it seemed to me that anyone could make such films, providing they had an old book, a hot country, new technology and were capable of aiming the camera at an attractive landscape in the hot country in front of which stood a star in a perfectly clean costume delivering lines from the old book. (MBL, 5)

The reference to 'old books' suggests a number of possible targets for Kureishi's wrath aside from Lean's version of Forster's novel. These include Sidney Pollack's *Out of Africa* (1985), based on Karen Blixen's 1937 memoir; John Huston's *The Man Who Would Be King* (1975), adapted from Kipling's short story of that name; and Channel 4's own major series *The Jewel in the Crown* (1984), adapted from Paul Scott's *Raj Quartet* (1966-75). Comparable work included Mike Radford's *White Mischief* (1987) and Peter Duffell's *The Far Pavilions* (1984), adapted for TV from M. M. Kaye's novel of 1978. Kureishi saw both *The Raj Quartet* and *The Far Pavilions* on video during a visit to Pakistan when *Laundrette* was beginning to take shape in his mind.

To the extent that such intertexts inform Kureishi's films, they suggest his concern to subvert a number of tropes in literary forms of colonial discourse which had an afterlife in recent British cinema.[7] Thus, in contrast to the relationship between Fielding and Aziz in *A Passage to India*, in *Laundrette*, Omar is the dominant partner. Johnny's dependence on Omar plays off the colonialist trope of 'the faithful servant'; and in providing Johnny with work, Omar contributes to his friend's moral regeneration in a way that parodically recalls the colonialist project of 'civilising' the brutal natives. Instead of the white colonial male enjoying the native female, as occurs in *The Man Who Would Be King*, the non-white Omar enjoys the native British man. *Gandhi* is invoked on several occasions in Kureishi's films, most notably in *Sammy and Rosie*, when Danny seeks advice from Rafi on whether non-violent methods are likely to provide effective resistance to domestic racism (there is also a poster of Gandhi on his caravan wall). And the American photo-journalist Anna perhaps inevitably recalls the *Time* photographer Margaret Bourke-White, who covers the later stages of Gandhi's campaign against the British. In *London Kills Me* Dr Bubba is suggestive of a parodic reworking of the saintly Gandhi – and, indeed, of Godbole in *A Passage to India* (As a character in *Gandhi* comments: 'We westerners have a weakness for these spiritually-inclined men from India.') The links between Kureishi's films and 'Raj Revival' cinema are strengthened by his use of some of its leading Indian actors, particularly in *Laundrette*. Roshan Seth (Hussein) and Saeed Jaffrey (Nasser) had appeared in both Lean and Attenborough's films and Daniel Day-Lewis (the former skinhead Johnny) played a racist thug in the opening sequences of *Gandhi.*

As was pointed out in Chapter 1, Kureishi's aunt berated *Laundrette* for its supposedly negative vision of Pakistani immigrants and did so partly through comparing it unfavourably with *Gandhi*, which she described as a 'top quality' work (SR, 64). In Kureishi's mind, whatever their presumed quality, many such films could be linked to an earlier film tradition which glorified Britain's imperial past and, more particularly, lauded its military and even racial virtues. Typical of such work was Cy Enfield's *Zulu* (1964), which Kureishi saw 'several times' as a boy (MBL, 74; the film also makes a big impression on the young Imran in the unpublished play *The Mother Country*). As is also suggested by his reference to the place given to C. S. Forester, the creator of Hornblower, on his school syllabus (MBL, 108), Kureishi felt himself to be growing up in a national culture which still took deep pride in its history of conquest and domination overseas, long after decolonisation. Like the plays, then, Kureishi's films were partly aimed at puncturing glamorising visions of Britain's imperial past.

Even in the more critical examples of 'Raj Revival', there is certainly evidence to support Kureishi's suspicions. For example, Gandhi himself never takes up a militantly anti-British stance in Attenborough's film: 'We've come a long way with the British. We want to see them off as friends.' Of certain colonial officials, he comments approvingly: 'Just like proper English gentlemen. I'm proud of them.' Indeed, at the outset, a curiously anachronistic 'multi-cultural' conception of *British* citizenship animates Gandhi's early struggle. In the South African sequences of the film, it is the Afrikaners who abuse him, both verbally and physically. Indeed, Attenborough manages to suggest that it was only on the accession of General Smuts as Prime Minister that overtly oppressive race regulations came into force (whereas, of course, it was the British who laid the foundations for the system which eventually developed into apartheid).

Moreover, the domestic British audience is paradoxically encouraged to take pride in its imperial past insofar as many of their countrymen are represented as actively opposing colonialism. In *Gandhi*, the Rev. Charlie (Ian Charleson, who also played the future missionary Liddell in *Chariots of Fire*) is an aide of Gandhi's and Dr Kallumbach a sympathiser. Mirabehn – the former Miss Slade – is actually part of Gandhi's household, taking over many of Mrs Gandhi's functions after her death. Such figures represent the liberal attitudes of the home population in Britain, with which the cinema audience is aligned, where children write admiring essays about Gandhi and ordinary cloth workers sympathise with his call for a boycott of their product. By contrast, officials like Dyer (who is clearly repudiated for his part in the Amritsar massacre) are dinosaurs, part of an obstructive minority which is out of touch, not just with the wishes of the Indian people, but with government in Westminster.

Both *A Passage to India* and *Gandhi* are primarily moral, rather than political, critiques of Britain's presence in India. Thus, in *Gandhi* there is relatively little attention to the protagonist's 'Quit India' agitation. The moral mission of imperialism, while certainly discredited in some respects, particularly in the latter film, is also partly recuperated through an insistence on the essential rectitude of the British national character in each piece. While a serious injustice is, indeed, nearly committed in *A Passage to India*, it is prevented not by the brilliance of the Indian defence lawyer, but by the conscience of Adela, who comes good in the end, and by Fielding, whose quest for justice makes him, and not Aziz, the hero of the film. Just as Liddell is a 'true man of principle' in *Chariots of Fire* and therefore peculiarly fitted for his future imperial role in China, so Fielding's intervention reinforces the customary equation of British rule with 'fair play'. Indeed, Fielding is the hero of Lean's film in part because, like Forster before him, Lean represents Aziz as obsequious, cowardly and over-sensitive (a fault he shares with the 'Oriental' Abrahams at the beginning of *Chariots of Fire*). Whereas Attenborough clearly sentimentalises Gandhi, the more obviously 'political' Jinnah is an antipathetic figure, cold, rigid, aloof and cunning, who compares badly not just with his rival but with many of the British officials.

Some 'Raj Revival' films massage the *amour propre* of their British audiences in less obvious ways, for example by their primary focus on white characters.[8] Of most relevance to Kureishi's films in this respect, however, is the implication that their subject is 'properly' historical. Characteristically they pay no attention to the legacies or aftermath of empire. By contrast, all of Kureishi's films insist that Britain's imperial past continues to shape the modern nation in important ways. Perhaps most obviously, the significant presence of Black-British and British-Asian characters in all three works – quite unusual in British cinema, even as recently as the 1980s[9] – testifies to the continuing imbrication of contemporary Britain with countries which it formerly dominated. Moreover, the negative response to such characters from many sections of the host nation suggests the continuing influence of attitudes to race and cultural difference which were characteristic of the period of formal empire. Thus in *Laundrette* Genghiz's gang is disgusted by Johnny and Omar's contravention of the 'natural' order of things, in which non-whites should serve whites. In *Sammy and Rosie* Danny provides the most powerful rebuttal of the implication that imperialism is now a safely historical issue (and one which can therefore be evoked nostalgically), by describing the predicament of Britain's ethnic minorities as 'a kind of domestic colonialism' (SR, 21). As even the mild Hussein (Papa) complains in *Laundrette*: 'We are under seige by the white man' (MBL, 18). In *Sammy and Rosie* the police brutality seen in the salt-march sequences of *Gandhi* returns in the uniform of the Metropolitan Police, which behaves like an occupying army in areas where the descendants of the colonised populations are concentrated.

Kureishi's insistence on the importance of recognising continuities between the colonial past and the neocolonial present is further evident in his films' engagement with contemporary Pakistan, notably in *Sammy and Rosie*. The cabbie, whose body so graphically bears the marks of torture, is a potent reminder of the deplorable contempt for human rights which is evident in some such countries. However, the film suggests that Britain bears at least some responsibility for this lamentable state of affairs. As Rafi argues: 'I come from a land ground into dust by 200 years of imperialism. We are still dominated by the West and you reproach us for using the methods you taught us' (SR, 29). Some vindication of Rafi's views may be inferred from his very presence in London, a reminder that Britain has proved regrettably amenable to harbouring fallen Third World dictators (at least until the arrest of the former Chilean dictator Pinochet in 1998). The complicity between the old imperial order and its corrupt successor, the 'national bourgeoisie', is symbolised most obviously in the relationship between the aggressively Anglophile Rafi, with his Savile Row suits and nostalgia for the kind of Britain celebrated in 'Heritage' films, and the colonial-born Alice. In her mind, the end of empire is a key stage in the collapse of 'that old world of certainty and stability' (SR, 36), for which Rafi is as nostalgic as she is.

Kureishi and 'Heritage' cinema: envisioning a New Britain

The engagement of Kureishi's films with 'Heritage' cinema is even more extensive than is the case with 'Raj Revival' work. At the 1987 Oscar ceremonies he was aware of intense lobbying on behalf of *A Room with a View* (it was nominated for eight awards) and clearly had Ivory's film in mind during the gestation of *Sammy and Rosie*. In 'Sometime With Stephen', it is compared with *Laundrette* in terms of narrative structure (SR, 111) and is invoked in *Sammy and Rosie* on at least two occasions. First, there are clear parallels between Rafi's threatening journey through the streets of London, from which Danny rescues him, and Lucy's unnerving trip into central Florence, from which George rescues her. A more explicit allusion occurs when Sammy pulls back the curtains in Rafi's bedroom to reveal the street riots below: 'We thought we'd give you a room with a view' (SR, 12). References to the Oscar-winning *Chariots of Fire* are more oblique. The Cambridge-educated Rafi's first words in *Sammy and Rosie*, 'For me England is hot buttered toast on a fork in front of an open fire' (SR, 4), invoke the scene in Caius where the future Olympian Harold Abrahams is toasting teacakes while he meditates on the meanings of 'Englishness'.[10] Equally, the inclusion of the radical Eva on the fringes of Sammy and Rosie's semi-commune may be a riposte to Hudson's use of Abrahams's Jewish identity to support a narrow kind of assimilationism.

The mythopoeic nature of 'Heritage' Britain derives from a composite of qualities and values which it is necessary to disentangle in order to appreciate fully the meanings and effects of Kureishi's films.[11] In the first place, 'Heritage' cinema, like the 'Raj Revival', (ostensibly) focuses on the past; this enables the nation to be represented as a great international power, with all the glamour and prosperity which this entails. *Chariots of Fire* uses the metaphor of the Olympic games to represent Britain as a nation of world-beaters (Abrahams and Liddell both win gold). The superiority of the British is evident not just from their possession of a vast empire, to which Liddell will in due course devote his life, but through comparison with other western nations. The moral inferiority of the French is first suggested early in the film, when one of their athletes shoves Liddell off the track. On the eve of the Olympics, during negotiations with his hosts to reschedule events in order to accommodate Liddell's religious beliefs, Lord Birkenhead warns: 'They're not a very principled lot, the Frogs.' *A Room with a View* works more subtly in this respect. If the Italians are certainly represented sympathetically, the intrinsic oddity of foreigners is registered in their ludicrously stereotyped accents; moreover, their role is primarily as servants to the English. And while the Rev. Beebe confesses that his whole circle is 'drawn to things Italian', such cosmopolitanism can clearly be taken too far. Cecil Vyse's description of himself as an 'inglese italianato' is one marker of his impressive pretentiousness.[12]

However, in contrast to 'Raj Revival' films, 'Heritage' cinema allegorically implies the continuing relevance of its vision of the national past for contemporary Britain. *Chariots of Fire*, in particular, abetted Thatcherite revivalism, which trumpeted its determination to restore the kind of glories celebrated by Hudson's film. (Thus, if the film plays on the nation's historic rivalry with France, it also mobilises the audience behind Thatcherism's hostility to a French-dominated Europe.) If *A Room with a View* is less obviously 'patriotic', it nonetheless reinforces the image in *Chariots of Fire* of early twentieth-century Britain as a civilisation to be admired and, by implication, imitated. (Hudson's film is more obviously manipulative, given that the period in which it is set, 1919-24, were in reality years of deep economic depression, political division and social unrest.)[13]

Whereas they insist that the imperial past explored in 'Raj Revival' is *not* safely historical, but continues to shape today's Britain, Kureishi's films are concerned to challenge the implication of 'Heritage' cinema that the highly selective national past it celebrates has any relevance to the modern nation. To this end, they are all aggressively contemporary in their focus and make no reference to the 'guidebook' Britain constructed in

'Heritage' cinema. In the 'Introduction' to *London Kills Me*, Kureishi offers useful clues about the thrust of his own work in an approving citation of the novelist Colin MacInnes, writing in 1959: '[A]s one blinks unbelievingly at 'British' films, it is amazing – it really is – how very little one can learn about life in England here and now' (LKM, ix). As in his plays, the 'here and now' in Kureishi's films is emphatically diminished in comparison with the Britain of 'Heritage' cinema. Thus, for Cherry in *Laundrette*, Pakistan, for all its problems, compares well with what she calls 'this silly little island off Europe' (MBL, 19). London is presented not in terms of its great monuments, famous shopping streets or fashionable residential quarters but of its decaying inner-city districts.[14] Papa's flat looks onto a grim vista of railway tracks in Vauxhall and Johnny lives in 'a street of desolate semi-detached houses in bad condition' (MBL, 38). Much of *London Kills Me* takes place on the streets and in a squat and *Sammy and Rosie*'s excursion to affluent Cockfosters (the sequences were actually shot in Kew) merely emphasises the deprivation suffered in the heart of the capital. Approaching Danny's caravan site, Rafi walks through 'desolate tunnels and grim streets', pausing 'under a railway bridge where other wretched rejects are sheltering – the poor, the senile, the insane, the disabled' (SR, 50).[15]

Such images also challenge the representation of Britain in 'Heritage' cinema as an impressively unified and harmonious nation, symbolised by the cosy village in *A Room with a View*. In *Chariots of Fire* this unity is constructed through a constant emphasis on 'team spirit', which assimilates athletes of varied backgrounds to the shared purpose of representing the nation. Thus, at the end of the film the Prince of Wales welcomes the Scotsman Liddell with the words: 'Nice to have you on the same side at last.' The Union Jack functions throughout as the inspiriting symbol of what the Prince calls 'common heritage, common bond, common loyalty'. More perniciously, the unity of 'Heritage' Britain is predicated on the principle of ethnic homogeneity. Whereas *A Room with a View* presents this homogeneity as a 'natural' matter of course, *Chariots of Fire* is more programmatic in its monoculturalism. While the American and French Olympic teams contain black athletes, the British one, despite its imperial possessions, does not. More perniciously still, Abrahams learns to use his running as 'a weapon against being Jewish' (his father is from Lithuania) and his marriage to a non-Jew is represented as an unambiguous good insofar as it constitutes his final absorption into 'Englishness'. Meanwhile, his more obviously 'foreign' coach, the half-Arab Missabini, is excluded from the team despite his crucial role in Abrahams's triumph.

In strong contrast, Kureishi's Britain is one of often violent divisions which threaten anarchy. Indeed, in *Sammy and Rosie* the situation is one of incipient civil war, as the references to Beirut suggest. Thatcher's stated desire to restore a sense of national unity, symbolised by her quotations from St Francis of Assisi immediately after her victory in 1979, which are relayed as the film begins, is juxtaposed ironically with the social fragmentation which her policies in reality exacerbated. In this regard, the system of 'domestic colonialism' is the major factor, but it is not the only form of social division, as the mixed racial composition of the rioters in *Sammy and Rosie* suggests. In *Laundrette*, as in *Outskirts*, the rise of racist politics is linked to the battering which the urban working classes receive as economic restructuring strips away traditional modes of social identification and employment opportunities. In *London Kills Me*, it is disaffected and disadvantaged youth which, as in *Tomorrow-Today!*, most preoccupies Kureishi.

Kureishi's first three films suggest that recourse to an ethnically-grounded monoculturalism as the principal guarantee of a common national identity plays a major role in fostering conflict and exclusion in contemporary Britain. The colonial-born Alice in *Sammy and Rosie* most explicitly rearticulates the key assumption of 'Heritage' cinema: 'Being British has to mean an identification with other, similar people' (SR, 48). As the Powellite inflection of Alice's comment indicates, Kureishi's films posit a direct continuity between some seemingly 'liberal' conceptions of 'Englishness' and the emphasis of contemporary extremists on racial 'purity' as a precondition of national belonging. In *Laundrette*, Hussein's depression and (in the script) his wife's suicide,[16] are directly linked to the harrassment which they have suffered as a mixed-race couple. The significant stress on inter-racial desire in Kureishi's films strikes at the very heart of monoculturalist ideology. The latter's more-or-less explicit equation of the preservation of racial hierarchy and cultural purity with the sexual segregation of the races is symbolised when Rosie gets off the pillion of Danny's motor bike and the 'police in the street look on in disgust' (SR, 46).

The social harmony and ethnic homogeneity of 'Heritage' Britain is reinforced by its construction of the nation as a rural, non-industrial culture.[17] Neither London nor any other major city registers in any consequential way in *Chariots of Fire*. A *Room with a View* also emphasises what Mr Emerson calls 'the sweetness of the English countryside', which is disturbed only by bicycles and 'phaetons'. While 'the squalor of London' is mentioned in the second scene of the film, it is never shown. Of the industrial working classes, little is seen in either film. In *Chariots of Fire* there is a glimpse of sooty faces, probably miners (or are they the 'great unwashed' more generally?) at the rugby international early in the film. In the determinedly idyllic *A Room with a View*, the 'lower orders' are also almost completely written out of 'England's story', unless as domestic servants, an absence all the more striking for the prominent role given to the (heavily sentimentalised) Italian peasantry in the early part of the film. Such films chime in neatly with the post-industrial future which Thatcherism planned for the nation through a massive reduction of the traditional heavy industries on which Britain's economy still primarily depended as late as the 1970s (together with an erosion of the political power of the classes on whose labour the industrial base depended).

In contrast to this, as suggested earlier, the principal setting of Kureishi's first three films is London. Only *London Kills Me* ventures further afield than the suburbs of northern Kent and then only because Clint knows 'a good place where there's not too many farmers' (LKM, 42). Instead of a reverential visit to some gorgeous country house of the kind Lord Lindsay inhabits in *Chariots of Fire*, Clint's excursion ends at a modest brick cottage of the type formerly inhabited by the rural labourers who are largely invisible in 'Heritage' cinema. For most of Kureishi's characters, non-metropolitan England is a foreign land. In *Laundrette*, Johnny declares: 'I don't like the country. The snakes make me nervous' (MBL, 61). For Danny in *Sammy and Rosie* even relatively green, outer-London districts like Cockfosters are alarming, potentially 'dangerous' (SR, 20).

There is, however, more than easy satire of the enervating nostalgia for 'chocolate-box' England at stake in Kureishi's focus on London. One corollary of 'Heritage' cinema's obsession with rural Britain is the implication that the culturally and demo-graphically hybrid nature of major cities like London disqualify them from being appropriate sites through which to represent the nation. By contrast, as was suggested in Chapter 1, London is given such an emphatic place in Kureishi's films precisely because it represents a space in which new, non-hierarchical and pluralistic kinds of individual and national identity which reflect the reality of modern Britain's increasing cultural diversity can potentially be forged. The reasoning behind Kureishi's turn to the conurbation as a site through which to explore a more flex-ible and adequate model of 'nation-ness' is most interestingly explored in 'Bradford', where the northern, (post-)industrial city is seen as 'a microcosm of a larger British society that was struggling to find a sense of itself, even as it was undergoing radical change' (MBL, 124). Some measure of that struggle – and its direction – is indicated in Kureishi's meditation on one of the key commentaries on 'Englishness' in the inter-war period.

In 1993 [*sic*], when J. B. Priestley was preparing his *English Journey*, he found three Englands. There was guide-book England, of palaces and forests [the England which 'Heritage' films focus on]; nineteenth-century industrial England of factories and suburbs; and contemporary England of by-passes and suburbs. [*sic*] Now, half a century later, there is another England as well: the inner city. (MBL, 129)

As was also indicated in Chapter 1, other minoritarian commentators on contemporary Britain have seconded Kureishi's sense that the major (post-)industrial cities are perhaps the best (and often the only) site through which ethnic minorities can gain access to a sense of 'national' identity that respects their cultural differences *vis-à-vis* mainstream society. For instance, Yasmin Alibhai-Brown has argued that:

> The civic pride felt in these places is around the notion of diversity. If we blacks are going to be locked out emotionally from Wales, Scotland and England, I wish to claim London for us and those who think like us. Here we will preserve that historical fudge - a Britishness which is a civic device to bind people together without recourse to ethnicity.[18]

Such ideas are repeatedly endorsed in Kureishi's films. For example, Sammy concludes his paean to London in *Sammy and Rosie* with the assertion: 'We love our city and we belong to it. Neither of us are English, we're Londoners you see' (SR, 33). Such sentiments clearly echo Kureishi's own feelings: 'I'm no Britisher, but a Londoner.' (SR, 75)[19]

However, Kureishi's films suggest that the cultural diversity of modern Britain, and of its great cities more particularly, does not derive from the nation's increasing ethnic variety alone. 'Bradford' once more provides his manifesto:

> Among all the talk of unity on the New Right, there is no sense of the vast differences in attitude, life-style and belief, or in class, race and sexual preference, that *already* exist in British society: the differences between those in work and those out of it; between those who have families and those who don't; and, important, between those who live in the North and those in the South. (MBL, 143)

For Kureishi, the unity aimed at by Thatcherism was spurious to the extent that it was predicated on the suppression of such difference. In his view, her administrations spelled the end of the counter-cultural dream of the 1960s 'that our society would become more adjusted to the needs of all the people who live in it … [and] less intent on excluding various groups from the domain of the human' (SR, 125). One obvious further way in which Kureishi's films contest the repressive thrust of Thatcherism – and in doing so, dispute the vision of the nation in 'Heritage' films – is through their emphasis on gender and sexual difference.

The homogeneity (and social harmony) of 'Heritage' Britain is reinforced by its treatment of such issues. In the context of the New Right's rejection of feminism and the drive for equality promoted by the Women's Movement which emerged in the 1960s, the female characters in *Chariots of Fire* are deeply significant. In the first place, the focus on Cambridge and the world of athletics tends to diminish the role of women altogether. (Nor is there any sign of the British women's team at the Paris Olympics.) The two principal female roles – Abrahams's fiancee Sybil and Liddell's sister Jenny – are subordinate ones, not only in terms of the film time they are given, but insofar as each functions strictly in relation to the men in their lives. *A Room with a View* is equally conservative in implication. Thus, while Lucy finally throws over Cecil Vyse, the film does little to subvert Forster's own oppressive gender economy.[20] Here, as in *Chariots of Fire*, the function of women is to support their menfolk in return for the kind of protection which George offers Lucy after the stabbing in Florence. The triumph of true love between Lucy and George, then, serves to reinforce the established hierarchies rather than to challenge them.

'Heritage' cinema also gave comfort to the New Right in its treatment of sexuality. Heterosexuality is unambiguously the norm in such films and 'manliness', marriage and the family are strongly endorsed. Single women, like Miss Lavish in *A Room with a View*, are figures of mild ridicule or slightly fierce and puritanical, as is the case with Jenny in *Chariots of Fire*. But active sexuality is always very discreet. Abrahams's relationship with Sybil is remarkably chaste, to the point that when they first kiss, she pulls her hat forward as a screen in front of the camera. This self-consciously symbolises a reassertion of the autonomy of the private sphere which had been so strongly challenged by feminism (as Chapter 2 suggested, one of its most famous slogans was 'the personal is the political'). *A Room with a View* is equally passionless, at least where the English characters are concerned, a kiss in a cornfield being the most explicit treatment of the physical attraction between George and Lucy. Homosexuality is even more tangential in such films. There is plenty of emphasis in *Chariots of Fire* on male bonding, which is complemented by much footage of the perfectly-formed bodies of exquisite young men, sometimes half-naked on the massage table or clad in wet-look training shifts. In keeping with the New Right's hostility to 'permissiveness' and its emphasis on 'family values', however, such representations are – ostensibly – 'innocent' and the possibility of actual 'deviance' is never entertained (compare the suppression of the homo-eroticism of Forster's novel in Lean's *A Passage to India*.). Despite one of Britain's best-known gay actors, Simon Callow, playing the Rev. Beebe, and making much comic capital out of the naked male romp in the woods, *A Room with a View* does nothing to challenge the 'natural' order of heterosexuality. Indeed, in counterposing Cecil Vyse's verbosity and unsporty foppishness against the athletic, taciturn (and blond) George Emerson, the film endorses the masculinism and heterosexualism of *Chariots of Fire*.

Kureishi's treatment of gender and sexuality is altogether different. Thus, women are given a far greater proportion and diversity of roles and they are seen less in a dependent relation to men. In *Laundrette*, Tania's final departure into an uncertain future contrasts, on the one hand, with the subordinate, circum-scribed and seemingly predestined roles allotted to Sybil and Jenny in Hudson's film; on the other, her role compares favour-ably with the mocking treatment of Miss Lavish's spinsterism in *A Room with a View*. They are also much more alert to patriarchy than characters such as Lucy Honeychurch and more active in challenging male control. In *Sammy and Rosie*, even Alice, the most politically conservative woman in the film, wakes up to what patriarchy has done to her and joins the feminist net-work at Rosie's flat. In all these ways, Kureishi challenges the 'natural' order of heterosexism constructed in 'Heritage' cinema. Secondly, Kureishi's treatment of sexuality is far franker than 'Heritage' cinema's, and reflects his desire to remedy its exclusion of significant areas of human experience. As Alice reminds the audience, 'even' older people enjoy the kind of passions which are in any case barely expressed by characters like Abrahams in *Chariots of Fire*. Moreover, such frankness seeks explicitly to counter the backlash against the huge advance in personal/political freedoms associated with what the New Right identified as the 'permissiveness' of the 1960s.

Kureishi's treatment of gay love has broadly similar aims and effects. *Laundrette* is one of a number of films in the 1980s, including Derek Jarman's *Caravaggio* (1986) and Frears's *Prick up Your Ears* (1987), which bring out the repressed subtext of *Chariots of Fire* (and Lean's interpretation of *A Passage to India*), the issue of same-sex attraction. Kureishi's film can, however, be considered even more radical than most of these works in one respect. If miscegenation is a threat to mono-cultural models of British identity, gay relationships across the racial barrier are a yet more 'perverse' and subversive proposition. *Laundrette* is almost certainly the first British film to reach a wide audience which shows a white and a non-white man kissing, just as *Sammy and Rosie* is probably the first to give such explicit representations of inter-racial lesbian liaisons. As Radhika Mohanram argues, in such work, 'the effete homosexual body, like the racialized body, signifies a threat to the myth of ontological purity of the nation.'[21]

This aspect of Kureishi's films again reflects the realities of modern British social experience and celebrates its diversity. However, it seeks to counter a more specific manifestation of the New Right's assault on 'permissiveness', its desire to curb homosexuality. This was represented by the refusal of successive Thatcher governments to bring the homosexual age of consent in line with its heterosexual equivalent, its complicity in the representation of AIDS as a predominantly 'gay' plague and measures such as Clause 28 of the Local Government Act (1988), which forbade the 'promotion' of homosexuality. Kureishi's films can also be understood as a riposte to the New Right's more obvious attempts to censor cultural works which depicted homosexuality, perhaps the most notorious example being Mary Whitehouse's private prosecution of Howard Brenton and the National Theatre for the scenes of buggery in *The Romans in Britain* (1981).[22]

Insofar as the economy of gender and sexuality in 'Heritage' (and 'Raj Revival') cinema supports their broader endorsement of a hierarchical conception of social order, Kureishi's attention to these issues is also a key part of his determinedly democratic conception of the modern nation. 'Heritage' Britain is unashamedly anti-democratic in temper. The village in *A Room with a View*, arranged around the church and manor house, constructs Britain as an organic social structure, the gradations of which are accepted as a fact of nature by all its inhabitants. *Chariots of Fire* centres overwhelmingly on Britain's social elite, represented by the upper-middle-class Cambridge athletes. In this world, privilege is nothing to get upset about. Lord Lindsay is one of the most sympathetic figures in the film and his stately home is used to lovingly evoke the physical glories of Britain's great country houses. Aristocrats fulfil important functions in the film and, by implication, can do so again in contemporary British society. Thus Lord Birkenhead is the respected British team leader at the Olympics, where his key aide is Lord Cadogan. This happy hierarchy is, of course, capped by the monarchy, which makes its triumphant entry at the end of the film, in the form of the glamorous future King Edward VIII, a figure who perhaps inevitably invoked for a contemporary audience the present Prince of Wales in his bachelor days. As one figure comments on the Prince's arrival: 'That chap's invaluable. We couldn't do without him'. To which comes the response: 'Hear, hear. Henry V and all that.' (Little surprise, then, that the film was chosen for the Royal Film Performance in 1981.)

The conservative vision of 'Heritage' cinema is reinforced by its treatment of alternative political perspectives. In *A Room with a View*, the mildly socialist views of Mr Emerson are seen as simply another expression of his gloriously English eccentricity and do not prevent him from happily cementing his niche in the society overseen by Sir Harry Otway through George's marriage to Lucy. While Otway is not sympathetically represented, this is primarily because he is 'vulgar' and not on account of any questions about the legitimacy of the social hierarchy which he represents. The politics of *Chariots of Fire* are much more explicitly right wing. For example, at the Cambridge 'freshers' fair', the whingeing representative of the Fabian Society is interrupted by the demand: 'Where were you when your country needed you?' The fact that this rhetorical question cannot be attributed to any identifiable individual reinforces the feeling that it represents the 'voice' of the film itself.

While clearly opposed to the political thrust of much 'Heritage' cinema (*Sammy and Rosie*, in particular, is programmatically anti-Tory; for example, the property developer who ousts the 'straggly kids' is one of Thatcher's MPs and her vision of a 'new Britain' is blatantly lampooned), Kureishi's films do not, however, endorse traditional kinds of Left oppositional politics as the best means by which to challenge the hegemony of the New Right. As was seen in the last chapter, Kureishi's plays express impatience with the pieties of both 'welfarism' and traditional class politics. In the films, too, there is clear scepticism about what one might call 'old Labourism' and the radical Left alike. Hussein (who is aged, drunken and decrepit) in *Laundrette* represents the former and Eva in *Sammy and Rosie* the latter. While by no means unsympathetically conceived, their strictly limited roles, together with the self-absorption and ineffectuality of the left-leaning Rosie (she walks obliviously through the riot outside her flat), suggest Kureishi's conviction that, while socialist ideas still had some part to play in countering the New Right in 1980s Britain, Labour's repeated electoral ineffectiveness meant it could no longer be considered as the natural leader in such engagements.

Instead, Kureishi's films prioritise two other modes of opposition. The first is based on the concept of a 'rainbow coalition' of marginalised groups,[23] which includes those who are discriminated against on the grounds of gender and sexuality as well as of class and race. The principal images of this in the films are the commune of 'straggly kids' in *Sammy and Rosie*, the informal collective based round Sammy and Rosie's flat and the posse in *London Kills Me*. In this respect, Kureishi's films endorse the politics of what Chapter 1 described as the 'new social movements' which had their origins in the 1960s 'counter-culture', especially feminism, gay-rights activism and new forms of mobilisation around the issue of race.

Drawing on the work of Alain Touraine, Manuel Castells and Alberto Melucci, Paul Gilroy's *'There Ain't No Black in the Union Jack'* (published in 1987, the year *Sammy and Rosie* was shot) identifies some of the key premises of these 'new social movements', many of which inform Kureishi's representation of them in his films. In the first place, Gilroy suggests that their emergence is linked to the decline of the industrial economy and that consequently they pursue 'the issue of emancipation beyond the particularist interests of industrial workers'.[24] Secondly, such movements are not primarily interested in the conquest of state institutions; indeed, they often refuse the mediation of their demands through conventional political structures: 'Authentic politics is thought to recommence with this act of withdrawal.'[25] Thirdly, the new 'race politics', in particular, is intimately bound up with models of community which are available only in the modern city. Fourthly, the 'new social movements' focus on the body as a site of political engagement, whether in connection with issues of 'colour', sexuality or reproduction. Fifthly, such movements have a spiritual dimen- sion (perhaps hinted at in the association between Dr. Bubba and the posse in *London Kills Me*). Finally, the 'rainbow coalition' is conceived, not in terms of the desirability of a synthesis of its varied constituencies into a new whole, but of a strategic alliance based on respect for their differences. This implies the possibility of conflict between such constituencies as well as the potential for alliance, a state of affairs which is reflected in Kureishi's films. For instance, Rani clashes violently with Rafi in *Sammy and Rosie*, despite their shared ethnicity and, notwithstanding his socialist inclinations, Hussein in *Laundrette* feels no solidarity with Genghiz's working-class crew – for obvious reasons.

The second mode of opposition is based on lifestyles. Subcultural style in its various manifestations in Kureishi's films is always associated with a refusal of dominant social – and therefore ultimately political – norms.[26] Thus, the emphasis on pleasure, particularly through sex and the consumption of drugs is in clear opposition to the emphasis on 'duty' in New Right discourse. In all the films one can detect Kureishi's association of sexual with political repression, so that when Omar in *Laundrette* opines that 'much good can come of fucking' (MBL, 35), he is implicitly rebutting the association between self- and social control in 'Heritage' cinema. Equally, the eponymous characters in *Sammy and Rosie* (which Kureishi had originally wanted to call *The Fuck*) consider their 'permissive' sexuality to be subverting a bourgeois order which is characterised as much by the value it attaches to monogamy as to money and social status.

There is a double link between Kureishi's emphasis on lifestyle as a mode of potential dissent and the politics of the 'new social movements'. In the first place, Gilroy argues, 'it is precisely this sphere of autonomous self-realization which is addressed by many of the new social movements.'[27] Secondly, both attach great importance to expressive culture, whether articulated through sexuality, music or fashion. This is not only the principal means by which the social sub-formation in question constitutes itself symbolically but also the base on which it organises politically. According to Gilroy, the 'new social movements' are exercised to 'reintegrate culture with everyday life',[28] but the culture in question is to be understood not as something imposed from above, but as 'of the people'. Thus, in contrast to the 'high' cultural musical references of *Chariots of Fire* and *A Room with a View* (Lucy is a concert pianist), the subversive (and hedonistic) thrust of Kureishi's films is reinforced by a consistent reference to sub-cultural fashion (for example, the 'punk' Johnny in *Laundrette*, the 'Gothic' Sylvie and 'white Rasta' Tom-Tom in *London Kills Me*) and pop music (Danny in *Sammy and Rosie* was played by the lead singer of the quintessentially 1980s band, Fine Young Cannibals).

Thus, while Kureishi's films, like his plays, point to the nation's relative material decline *vis-à-vis* the Britain constructed in 'Heritage' cinema, at times they paradoxically echo the upbeat tone which is characteristic of a genre which they challenge in almost every other respect. Despite their often dark undertones, all his films insist on the many positive developments in post-war Britain, particularly since the 1960s. The parties in *Laundrette* and *Sammy and Rosie* are carnivalesque, celebratory symbols of the cultural diversity which is in Kureishi's mind the nation's greatest glory in the contemporary period. (The gaping country youths who follow Clint and his posse in *London Kills Me* suggest that the monocultural nation of 'Heritage' cinema in fact leads to a lack of creativity and self-confidence, to repressive conformity and conservatism.) The upbeat, even at times highly comic, register of his films also reflects Kureishi's continuing resistance of the temptation to approach the issue of ethnic diversity (or other kinds of sub-cultural difference) only in terms of a social pathology. Sammy and Rosie's mixed-race marriage is not represented as a 'problem' for them to solve. Nasser and Omar in *Laundrette* are completely at ease in Britain and Bike's presence in Clint's posse is in itself unremarkable. Even more than in the plays, the emphasis of Kureishi's films is on the agency and empowerment of such 'marginal' characters. Far from being passive or defeated victims of prejudice, Omar is the dominant figure in *Laundrette* and, in *Sammy and Rosie*, Rani and Vivia are instrumental in exposing Rafi's crimes against humanity. The utopian implication of Kureishi's films is that contemporary Britain has within its grasp the possibility of expanding traditional conceptions of national identity to create for the first time a genuine and revolutionary, though always *contradictory* rather than blandly harmonious, unity-in-diversity. If they attest to the final collapse of the post-war consensus, they also point to the possibility of a new sense of national community built on the idea of pluralism and of non-hierarchical conceptions of difference.

Form and genre in Kureishi's films

Mixing and diversity are also a marked feature of Kureishi's films at the level of form and genre. As was suggested earlier, the agitprop tradition is a strong influence on the style of his films, as was the older TV tradition of social realist investigation represented by the BBC's *Play for Today*. At the same time, Kureishi also clearly wanted to align his work with 'art' cinema, an ambition signalled on one level by the intertextual allusions in his work, which go well beyond their engagement with 'Heritage' cinema and the 'Raj Revival'. *London Kills Me* seems at one level to want to do for London what Fellini's *La Dolce Vita* (1960) did for Rome (in the script, the latter film is playing at the Electric Cinema in Notting Hill, when Clint is *en route* to Headley). It also draws unmistakably on de Sica's *Bicycle Thieves* (1948), a classic of the post-war Italian realist 'new wave' which also revolves round a tortuous search for employment (for de Sica's protagonist, a bicycle rather than shoes is the crucial requirement). In the bath scene, moreover, it clearly gestures towards Nic Roeg and Donald Cammell's avant-garde treatment of the 'teen-film', *Performance* (1970). The homage Sammy pays to London in *Sammy and Rosie* explicitly invokes the tribute to New York in Woody Allen's *Annie Hall* and, as was suggested in Chapter 1, there are echoes in this film of Ozu's *Tokyo Story*. Rafi's trip to London recalls the disillusioning journey of the parents in Ozu's film to visit children from whom they have become alienated, and both pieces explore rapidly-changing capital cities, which are major 'protagonists' in themselves. In all three works, moreover, there are many moments which employ the conventions of *film noir*, notably the lighting of the riot scenes in *Sammy and Rosie*.

The 'writerly' ambitions of the films are further emphasised by their references to literary classics. In *London Kills Me*, for example, the camera at one point pans slowly over Sylvie's collection of feminist texts. *Sammy and Rosie*, however, provides the most extensive structure of reference to literary sources. Rafi's suicide gestures towards Trepliov's in Chekhov's

The Seagull and, at one point, the script lingers on the Jane Austen novels by Alice's bed, as if to suggest the influence of Austen on Alice's initial vision of both gender roles and 'Englishness'. As the prominent place given to the poster of Virginia Woolf (a feminist and lesbian icon) in Sammy's flat implies, however, the film also challenges the form of traditional realism espoused by Austen (Woolf's *Mrs Dalloway*, 1925, is one of the key works of Modernism as well as a great 'London novel'. There is a clear parallel between Clarissa's privileged daughter's journey of discovery through the less affluent areas of the capital and Rafi's.) As Colette Lindroth points out,[29] T. S. Eliot's *The Waste Land* is the major literary intertext of *Sammy and Rosie* (fragments of Eliot's poem are inscribed on a bus on the site where Danny lives). Lindroth points to extensive parallels between the two works. For example, the film opens with a vista of waste land, to the condition of which, Kureishi implies, Britain is being reduced by Thatcherism. If Rafi takes the role of the 'The Hanged God', Danny/Victoria is the Tiresias figure; not only is his conjunction of names suggestive of hermaphroditism, but he is consistently associated with the Underground (which he rides all day), reworking Tiresias's identification with the underworld. To some extent, Lindroth argues, Kureishi's London invokes Eliot's apocalyptic vision of the 'unreal city' (the fires of the riots recall the motif of 'burning' in *The Waste Land*) and both works end on a note of ambivalent affirmation. Finally, Lindroth suggests, Eliot's poem explores conjunctions between East and West – most obviously in the poet's exploration of elements of eastern religion – which Kureishi's film takes up in more immediate ways, notably in Sammy and Rosie's mixed-race marriage. (The conjunction is present in *Mrs Dalloway*, too, insofar as Clarissa's former lover expounds on his career in India.)

As might be inferred from the multiplicity of such connections, it may be the case that the style of *Sammy and Rosie* reflects a desire to find visual equivalents for modernist literary technique as much as it looks back to the conventions of agitprop. Most notably, Kureishi's film is (de)composed into a collage, recalling Eliot's (de)construction of London in terms of 'a heap of broken images'. As this suggests, *Sammy and Rosie* generates its meanings primarily by (often highly incongruous) juxtaposition, characteristically effected by sudden, unfaded, camera cross-cuts. Instead of relying on traditional narrative unities, such as plot, both artists bind their works together by more indirect means. Thus, like Tiresias's role in Eliot's poem, Danny functions as a unifying structural feature in Kureishi's film, linking disparate characters and situations by his floating presence. Unity is also provided by thematic repetition. In both works, the nature of modern love, explored from different perspectives and in different contexts, is a recurrent preoccupation. Like Eliot, Kureishi sometimes relies on the suggestiveness of symbol, rather than explicit elaboration of themes. Perhaps the most notable example is Rosie herself, who in her role as downwardly mobile social worker represents an increasingly out-of-touch and declining Welfare State (compare the sickly socialist Hussein). Other important symbols include the cabbie/ghost and the finger which Rafi finds on his plate in the restaurant. Equally revealing of Kureishi's desire to work by implication are the quotations of other films noted earlier, which have their equivalent in Eliot's penchant for allusion to the literary canon. Finally, both works eschew an omniscient narrative voice/eye. The most striking evidence of this in *Sammy and Rosie* is the triple 'fuck' scene; this replaces the singular, all-seeing gaze characteristic of mainstream cinema narrative with a multi-perspectival point of view which stresses simultaneity of perception rather than a linear reading of the objects presented. Some critics have followed Spivak's lead in ascribing this emphasis to Kureishi's desire, especially in *Sammy and Rosie*, to produce a more 'collective' mode of representation, in which a polyphony of narrative points of view reflects the film's pluralistic and democratic social vision.[30]

These 'writerly' intertexts are, however, offset by extensive reference in all of Kureishi's films to more populist genres. Both *Laundrette* and *London Kills Me* have what Kureishi describes as 'gangster and thriller' elements (MBL, 5), not least in that the plot of each is bound up with struggles over the supply of drugs. One obvious model which both of these texts pastiche is Coppola's *The Godfather*. Each relies on a number of other popular cinematic form(ula)s. The former is in essence a 'buddy' movie (though Kureishi complicates the genre through his attention to ethnicity and 'perverse' sexuality as central issues), but he is certainly right to suggest that in America, at least, the film's popularity owed much to the ease with which it could be slotted into the archive exemplified by *Butch Cassidy and the Sundance Kid* (1969), with which it shares a focus on a limited transgression of the *status quo*, enacted by lovable (semi-)outlaw 'blood brothers'. The scene in which Johnny and Tania have their cycling mishap is perhaps the most direct allusion to George Roy Hill's film. Meanwhile, Clint's name, boots and his 'posse' link *London Kills Me* to the cowboy genre which, unlikely as it may seem, also influenced the conception of *Sammy and Rosie*. According to Kureishi, the end of the film, with 'the straggly kids waving flags and playing music as the police and heavies invade and evict them … is like a western!' (SR, 99). Like *London Kills Me* (through the citation of *Performance*, albeit a problematic example of the genre), *Sammy and Rosie* also gestures towards the 'teen-movie', not only in its sound-track and the choice of Roland Gift for the male lead, but in the scene in the Underground where the directions state that the whole platform dances 'like in a Cliff Richard film' (SR, 19). The very English genre of Ealing comedy is invoked in Kureishi's predeliction for farce, which is the saving grace of *London Kills Me*. Muffdiver's mistaking the German tourist for Mr G, the local drugs supremo, is hilarious, as are the consequences when the real mobster finally arrives. Finally, all of Kureishi's films are partly plotted as love stories – albeit of unconventional kinds – in which the usual generic obstacles are encountered and overcome (the hostility of parents, peers, cultures of origins). Thus a pastiche of Robert Wise's *West Side Story* (1961) seems to be intended in *Laundrette*.[31]

'Style' in Kureishi's films has important cultural/political significance. Insofar as the vision of England in 'Heritage' cinema (or Jane Austen, for that matter) invokes a hierarchical, orderly and knowable nation, there is a homology between form and political ideology. *Chariots of Fire*, for example, has a clear beginning, middle and end, a definite hierarchy of narrative voices and an all-seeing eye which can resolve the most disparate elements of the film into a final, transparent whole. By contrast, Kureishi's rejection of many of the conventions of narrative realism and his iconoclastic mixture of different genres and cinematic influences complements his thematic interest in 'anarchist' ideas. While in other ways a predictable assault on Kureishi's films (and comparable examples of British cinema in the 1980s), the commentary by the Oxford historian Norman Stone, a leading Thatcherite intellectual, has the virtue of recognising some of these connections between form and meaning. Writing in the right-wing *The Sunday Times*, Stone complained that Kureishi's films were, like the rest of their kind, '[w]orthless and insulting' and 'might have come straight from the agitprop department of the late GLC' (which the Tories had recently suppressed). By contrast, Stone praised the Britain of Ealing comedy and the Boulting brothers as an inspiritingly 'decent place'. Interestingly, however, he attached as much importance to the style as the substance of his favourite kinds of cinema. Unlike the work of Kureishi and some of his contemporaries, such 'well-made films' in part advanced the cause of 'decency' by observing 'the old rules … that there should be a beginning, a middle and an end, that you should want to know what happens next, and that the characters are interesting'.[32] In this light, the ideological import and effects of Kureishi's film styles become much clearer.

Conclusion

Despite the accolade of an Oscar nomination for Best Screenplay for *Laundrette*, an undoubtedly impressive achievement for a first script by a relatively unknown British writer who was at the time barely into his thirties – and despite the incontrovertible effectiveness of their contestation of many aspects of the the 'Raj Revival' and 'Heritage' genres – the achievement of Kureishi's first three films is uneven, as he himself has been the first to admit. The criticism of Kureishi's second and third works, more particularly, is highly polarised.[33] Thus, Colin MacCabe lauded *London Kills Me* as 'a very acute description of London in the early nineties',[34] whereas many critics ridiculed it. Minoritarian critics have been equally divided. Whereas Ranita Chatterjee argues of *Sammy and Rosie* that 'Kureishi's refusal to provide positive representations of South Asians in Britain should be applauded, not condemned', Sandeep Naidoo was scathing about the film: 'There was no dramatic focus, too much was thrown in and one couldn't get the feeling that these were believable characters ... Sammy and Rosie got laid alright – by a giant turkey.'[35]

The films' unevenness can be attributed to several causes. In the first place, cinema represented a new craft (in which, as with writing plays, Kureishi made a highly promising start, before abandoning it seemingly as precipitately as he had drama). Some of the weaknesses of the scripts must be attributed to inexperience, with Kureishi trying to work out what would, and would not, work on screen as he went along. However, while a 'fringe' drama might evolve gradually out of ensemble improvi- sation and, if necessary, could be adapted night-by-night, film allows no such second thoughts. Moreover, while the limited resources of much British cinema in the 1980s offered some advantages, in the same way as 'poor theatre' did *vis-à-vis* the commercial stage, more generous funding might have helped Kureishi's films to achieve more. All three were produced to a very tight budget and schedule; *Laundrette* was shot in six weeks and *Sammy and Rosie* took not much longer. In addition, the shooting of the latter film was suddenly brought forward by six months, owing to a change in Frears's schedule, leaving Kureishi less time to develop the script than he had anticipated.

Perhaps the main reason for the uneven achievement of *Sammy and Rosie* and *London Kills Me*, in particular, is Kureishi's promiscuous mingling of different genres and stylistic influences. To mix realism and anti-realism – or other, similarly opposed modes – implies a desire in part to have each interrogate the other's possibilities and limits, but the effects of this hybridising strategy in Kureishi's films are not always happy in practice. For example, seen from the perspective of the investigative British TV of the 1960s, which Kureishi claims as an influence on his work, each of his films is beset by fundamental improbabilities at the level of plot which compromise their effectiveness as examples of critical social realism. Thus, *Laundrette* is predicated on the intrinsically unlikely scenario of a young British-Asian man falling in love with a member of a vicious racist gang (and vice versa.) From the same perspective, the premise of *Sammy and Rosie* is equally shaky; it is barely credible that an aristocratic former Third World despot, who has practised all manner of barbarities on his own people, could undergo a Pauline conversion on his trip to London and throw in his lot with a group of 'straggly kids' trying to prevent their caravan site from being redeveloped. *London Kills Me*, by contrast, depends on the presumption that Clint cannot lay his hands on the pair of shoes he needs to get a job; yet he is able to borrow other articles of clothing, like Bumble Bee's jersey, or buy them (after double-crossing Muffdiver, he has the money to do so), or even steal them, as he does the cap from the market stall. Such evidence corroborates Kureishi's rueful confession that: 'I'm no good at plots, at working out precisely what the story is' (SR, 121).

While the utopian plot-lines of Kureishi's films are consonant with some of the populist genres which he exploits, other elements jar when placed in that context. Considered as romances they are (productively) complicated by the heavy emphasis he places on the shaping of the 'private sphere', usually sacrosanct in popular romance, by the 'public sphere'. Kureishi has argued that: 'Human relations are meeting points for a whole complex of social arrangements, and that's why I like to write about them.'[36] By contrast, while Kureishi was well aware from his involvement in 'fringe' of the need to avoid 'dourness and didacticism' (MBL, 5), the films do not always avoid the trap, notably *Sammy and Rosie*. Some of the set-piece speeches, particularly Danny's one on 'domestic colonialism', are in fact the essence of didacticism. The at times creaky dialogue of *Sammy and Rosie* (and, to a lesser extent, of *London Kills Me*) also betrays Kureishi's anxiety to get explicit political messages across. On viewing the first cut, he confessed: 'I cringe throughout at the ridiculousness of the dialogue, which seems nothing like the way people actually talk ... though I am attached to some of the ideas contained in the more strident speeches' (SR, 118). To this extent, the agitprop leanings of the film also conflict directly with the intention of creating a quasi-modernist 'art' film.

Seen in the light of both critical social realism and 'art' cinema, characterisation in Kureishi's films is also sometimes unconvincing, particularly in *Sammy and Rosie*, where few of the roles are sufficiently thought through. For example, Kureishi acknowledges early in his diary: 'I lack grip on [Anna's] character' (SR, 67). Yet despite many subsequent drafts, Anna never comes into focus. Kureishi confessed to Roland Gift that the role of Danny was underwritten; given Gift's inexperience (it was his first film part) it seems naive to have expected him to generate from the limited hints which the script provides 'a strong sense of what the character is' (SR, 89). The same problem is evident in Sammy, played by another unknown, Ayub Khan-Din, who also struggled to make sense of his part (as did even such seasoned professionals as Claire Bloom, who played Alice). For example, if Rafi has so cruelly abandoned Sammy, why is his son so loyal and loving towards him? Such lack of clarity is apparent even in the better-drawn role of Rosie. No explanation is given for why the obviously sensitive, feminist social worker has married a ghastly yuppie accountant and, given that Rosie has only just met Rafi, why is this self-confessed radical so eager to forgive the fact that he is a torturer and murderer?

Whether placed once more in the context of critical social realism or of the populist genres on which he draws, Kureishi's latter two films, in particular, are structurally suspect. *Sammy and Rosie* has the greatest problems in this respect. The film contains too many competing interests, none of which are in themselves sufficiently developed, let alone integrated as an ensemble. By turns a film about London, a psychological investigation of the mind of a torturer, an analysis of contemporary gender relations, and a series of thinly-sketched love stories, *Sammy and Rosie* is a disjointed affair, as Kureishi himself nonchalantly noted: 'All the bits and pieces will just have to get along with each other, like people at a party' (SR, 80). If the point of this collage is that the contradictions of contemporary life cannot be resolved by narrative means, Kureishi never acknowledges such an intention in his own commentaries on the film. (This makes some of the more enthusiastic accounts of its style somewhat questionable.)[37] At different stages of the script's development, both the restaurant and 'fuck' scenes were intended as the climax of the film, yet neither could function as such, because too little has happened by the time either arrives. Unable for some time to think of a way of continuing the film beyond the 'fuck' scene, Kureishi almost abandoned it. This perhaps explains the tacked-on feel of the remainder of the film, with its adventitious meetings and often arbitrary developments within, and between, characters.

Conversely, from the perspective of the agitprop tradition, the ideological meanings of the films lack clarity in important respects. One can agree with Kureishi up to a certain point in his argument in 1985 that 'satire and irony are probably the only ways we can approach the complex problems of our time. At the moment, everything is so horrific that if you wrote straight social realism people wouldn't be able to bear to watch it',[38] but objects bell hooks, 'the issue [is] whether irony alone can be used to promote critical consciousness.'[39] Kureishi's articulation of Thatcherism is especially ambiguous. Thus, in *Laundrette* New Right views are certainly sometimes presented ironically. For example, the scene where Nasser voices his credo that '[t]here's no race question in the new enterprise culture' (MBL, 41) immediately succeeds one in which he oversees the forced removal of the tenants from his property, including a fellow-countryman).

Kureishi's representations of figures like Nasser admirably resist the twin temptations to show British-Asians as either simply victims or in an unrealistically positive light. The complexity of Nasser, who is personally attractive yet politically dubious, simultaneously part of the dominant class and of a subordinate ethnicity, prevents the viewer from placing him in any easy or stable role as the 'Other' and thus as a spectacle of ethnicity to be passively or voyeuristically consumed. However, if such characters very effectively embody Kureishi's perception of the contradictory and multiply-determined nature of social identity, they also make clear and instrumentally-orientated moral/political judgements of the kind associated with agitprop almost impossible. Thus, while Rafi often repeats phrases from Thatcher's own speeches, as Una Chaudhuri points out,[40] his personal charm deflects the critical response this might otherwise invite.

Indeed, while films like *Laundrette* rightly celebrate a social mobility notably lacking in the fixed hierarchical world of *Chariots of Fire*, it is sometimes hard to distinguish Omar's values from those of the New Right, in that he can so easily be mapped onto that quintessentially 1980s folk hero, the small businessman who succeeds by hard work and taking risks. (This is one reason why the Academy of Motion Pictures, a body not noted for its radical inclinations, may have nominated the film for an Oscar.) His success in fact reaffirms Nasser's utopian vision that Thatcher's Britain is a place where 'you can get anything you want' (MBL, 17). While one would expect such views from a ruthless entrepreneur like Nasser, the film itself seems unwittingly to corroborate one of the more ambitious elements of the Thatcherite narrative, that business enterprise could be relied upon to effect the regeneration of economically and socially deprived areas of Britain and the communities which inhabit them. (At a strategic level, Thatcher's main response to the inner-city riots of the 1980s was to promote 'business in the community'.) The previously alienated and antisocial Johnny comes to belong to society primarily through Omar's creation of a job for him. As the refurbishment of the laundrette, a fitting symbol of Thatcher's beloved 'service'

industries, gathers momentum, a revealing exchange takes place
between the business's 'godfather' and employee:

> NASSER: 'And we'll drink to Thatcher and your beautiful
> laundrette'.
> JOHNNY: 'Do they go together?'
> NASSER: 'Like dall and chipatis [sic].' (MBL, 37)

Neither Johnny nor the film itself offers any persuasive
alternative to Nasser's faith that social justice is something best
achieved by the workings of the free market. Equally, *Laundrette*
fails to challenge the New Right's ethos of possessive individualism. Omar increasingly resembles that peculiarly 1980s
figure, the self-centred and consumption-driven yuppie. Indeed
Tania's increasing disaffection with him stems from her perception that Omar is getting as greedy as her father (though her
attitude of course represents a critical perspective on his
behaviour). But if Salim is represented unsympathetically as a
caricature Thatcherite for whom ethics are identical with 'the
laws of business' and other people are 'shit' (MBL, 60), it is
troubling that Omar and Johnny so readily become his accom-
plices. It may be poetic justice that money from Salim's heroin
dealings is 'laundered' to start the business, but Omar later asks
Salim to become his partner in his planned expansion. Meanwhile
Johnny, despite his own experience of exploitative landlords,
happily acts as enforcer in Nasser's slum-landlord business.

London Kills Me is similarly ambiguous. The posse declares
war on a 'straight' world which Clint describes as driven by
'power and cruelty' (LKM, 51). Yet the critique offered by the
deeply unpleasant small businessman Stone once more elicits no
persuasive response:

> You only desire to be … what you are now. This. The lazy
> dregs of society. (*Glancing at Muffdiver.*) And superior.
> But none of you know fuck-all. That boy for instance. (*He
> indicates Clint.*) I know him. Absolutely useless. He knows
> nothing about nothing. He can't do fuck-all … You're
> slaves of sensation, just slaves … I pity you. I pity people
> who don't know the purpose that real work gives you.
> (LKM, 58–9)

Indeed, Clint's renewed determination after his encounter with Stone to get a job in the restaurant seems to endorse the substance of the latter's attack. The confusions multiply when one considers that Muffdiver not only at times shows the same sort of ruthlessness as Salim in his dealings with 'friends', but plans to base his drug dealing on sound business methods (he aims at a delivery system based on the rapid and efficient service provided by pizza franchises). *London Kills Me*, too, fails in its stated aim of providing a (clear) 'challenge [to] a Conservatism that had, at last, admitted to being an ideology' (LKM, viii).

Moreover, insofar as the film demonstrates how easily 'alternative life-styles' are co-opted into the dominant,[41] it invites considerable scepticism about the effectiveness of the new modes of oppositional politics which are explored in the films. In *Sammy and Rosie* the commune of 'straggly kids' is driven away with little difficulty, with pessimistic implications for the claims made for the idea of a 'rainbow coalition' of 'new social movements'. Neither Sammy or Rosie is allied in any serious or structural way to the deprived constituencies rioting outside their windows or to the travellers' commune. While Rosie is largely insouciant towards the violence, Sammy retreats into conspicuous consumption. Indeed, it has been argued that the police shooting at the beginning of *Sammy and Rosie* is intended precisely to reveal how trivial and self-indulgent the protagonists' lifestyles are.[42] Moreover, in the light of the film's engagement with Eliot, the implications of Kureishi's representation of the politics of sexuality becomes blurred. If, as Lindroth suggests, the film's references to *The Waste Land* encourage an interpretation of the various couplings in terms of 'the sterile sexuality of "The Lady of the Rocks/The Lady of situations"', Kureishi's ostensible aim of celebrating the anarchic, anti-bourgeois energies of his characters' sexuality is short-circuited.[43]

At the root of his films' conflicting meanings, perhaps, was Kureishi's confusion about what he wanted to do with the medium. For example, when the shooting of *Sammy and Rosie* began, Kureishi's uncertainty was clear: 'I haven't worked out exactly what is going on, what I want to say' (SR, 73). These matters are not entirely clarified by the final cut and, despite being both writer and director of *London Kills Me*, Kureishi disarmingly admits that he arrived at the end of shooting still not knowing 'what sort of movie I was supposed to be making' (LKM, xi).[44] Confusion is also evident in Kureishi's conception of his audience. 'Some Time With Stephen' describes the intended viewers of *Sammy and Rosie* as 'between eighteen and forty, mostly middle class and well-educated, film- and theatre-literate, liberal progressive or leftish [which] doesn't want to be patronized by teen films' (SR, 71). This constituency seems to coincide exactly with that for 'fringe', the limited extent of which in part drove Kureishi to film in the first place. However, the populist generic intertexts (which, as noted, include teen films) suggest that Kureishi in fact hoped that his films would be accepted as mass entertainments. Of *Laundrette*, for example, he comments that, despite its engagement with serious social issues, it was also conceived as 'an amusement' (MBL, 5).

One painful lesson that Kureishi learned in his career as a film maker was that, given the material circumstances by which even subsidised British cinema is constrained, pressure to emphasize the 'popular' was almost inevitable. His desire to incorporate elements of 'art' cinema and political analysis conflicted with the industry's insistence that 'private emotions … have primacy over public acts or moral positions' (SR, 120). Thus, the commercial success of films like *Laundrette*, he admits, is related to the 'harmless threat of disorder' which they embody:

> The pattern is one of there being a fairly rigid social order which is set up in detail in the film. Set against this order there is an individual or two, preferably in love, who violate this conventional structure … Usually there's some kind of individual reconciliation at the end of the film; or the individual is destroyed. But there is rarely any sense that the society could or should be changed. The pattern is, of course, a seductive one because we can see ourselves in the alienated, but authentic, individual standing up against stuffiness, ignorance and hatred of love. In all this we are

not helped to think in any wider sense of the way societies repress legitimate ideals, groups of people, and possible forms of life. (SR, 111)

Even *Sammy and Rosie*, the most partisan and hard-hitting of the films, Kureishi acknowledges, was in the end 'just a commercial product' (SR, 103).[45]

As all this suggests, cinema proved a more difficult medium to adapt to his varied, even conflicting, interests than Kureishi had anticipated, but this is not by any means to suggest that his first three films, completed by the time he was thirty-seven, are failures. *Laundrette* fully deserves its reputation as one of the most distinctive British films of the 1980s, and *Sammy and Rosie* is far more interesting than Kureishi's comment that 'it isn't completely terrible' (SR, 110) might indicate. In many ways it is a much more daring, challenging and innovative film than *Laundrette*. Kureishi's reflections on his films, especially 'Some Time With Stephen', with its disarmingly honest acknowledgements of their shortcomings, indicate that he was learning lessons which would be put to good use in the next stage of his career as a novelist and when he returned to film with *My Son the Fanatic* in 1997. Moreover, while the films enjoyed a mixed critical reception, they certainly reached a much larger audience than his plays had done - most obviously *Laundrette*, which was seen around the world. Its success not only provided the money which enabled Kureishi to focus without other distractions on his first novel, but helped to create the mass readership which *The Buddha of Suburbia* was to enjoy.[46]

The novels

Introduction: from film to fiction

The new direction in Kureishi's career represented by *The Buddha of Suburbia* (1990) was largely prompted by disillusion with his career in film. While he was disappointed with aspects of his own performance as a scriptwriter, and increasingly convinced that cinema could not become 'the precise and serious medium of the age while it is still too intent on charming its audience' (SR, 95), there was another important factor in Kureishi's disenchantment with the medium. Despite his good relationship with Frears, Kureishi had come to realise that 'the film-writer always has to give way to the director, who is the controlling intelligence of the film, the invisible tyrant behind everything' (SR, 95). The changes of emphasis demanded by Frears in *Sammy and Rosie Get Laid* caused Kureishi particular soul-searching.[1] The subordinate role of the scriptwriter, he concluded, explained why 'serious' writers rarely got involved in cinema.

While continuing to think about possible film projects (*London Kills Me*[2] was completed after *The Buddha* and the latter was made into a BBC series two years before *The Black Album* appeared),[3] Kureishi began to reconsider his attitudes towards fiction. As Chapter 2 suggested, the aspiring teenage writer of several novels had been disheartened by his initial contacts with the fiction-publishing world and was unconcerned by the apparently imminent 'death of the novel' which, in Britain at least, he felt had become an antiquated form.

However, the 'situation of the novel' had changed considerably since the late 1960s. *Granta* magazine, launched in late 1979 and quickly established as a major literary forum (it first published Kureishi himself in 1985), identified a new vitality in British fiction as the 1980s dawned. The tone of Bill Buford's editorial in the third issue, for example, contrasted sharply with the often downbeat, even apocalyptic, estimations of the British novel in the previous decade: 'There are arguably more gifted writers [now] than in any other time in the twentieth century.'[4] Most pertinent to Kureishi's predicament was Buford's argument that

> the imagination [now] resides along the peripheries; it is spoken through a minority discourse, with a dominant tongue re-appropriated, re-commanded, and importantly re-invigorated. It is at last, the end of the English novel and the beginning of the British one.[5]

With the emergence of a plethora of new postcolonial and diasporic fiction in the early 1980s, spearheaded by Salman Rushdie, there was no longer any reason for someone with Kureishi's background to feel excluded from the novel as a cultural form. Equally, if publishing had not been ready for Kureishi's teenage novels (he has described them as early versions of *The Buddha*),[6] by the late 1980s the 'Great Immigrant Novel' was one of the industry's grails. Given a two-year window of opportunity by his income from *My Beautiful Laundrette*, Kureishi was ready to accept Rushdie's challenge to prove himself as a 'serious' writer in the medium of fiction.

In contrast to many of these new voices, however, Kureishi's provenance as a novelist – as in his films – is overwhelmingly from within western traditions. While certainly influenced by Rushdie in certain respects, as was argued in Chapter 1, Kureishi's novels eschew not just the linguistic, epistemological and formal play of works like *Midnight's Children*, but also their recourse to non-western narrative resources. The one possible exception to this pattern concerns the orality of *The Buddha*. Throughout the text there are clear markers of orality, notably in Karim's interpellative interjections such as 'I didn't say that' or 'can you believe' (BS, 87, 95) and he amuses Jamila with 'stories of embarrassment and humiliation and failure' (BS, 54). Changez later takes on the role of Jamila's entertainer, with 'a wild soap opera' of interwoven stories about his native India (BS, 98). Indeed Changez takes on the role of a male Scheherazade in his attempts to retain the approving attention of his tyrannical spouse. (Compare the increasingly desperate Saleem's relationship with Padma in *Midnight's Children*.) Equally, his mode of delivery recalls Rushdie's descriptions of the techniques of professional Indian oral story-tellers.[7] There are, moreover, some intriguing correspondences between the spiral form of Changez's story-telling and the structure of Kureishi's own highly episodic text, in which characters like Haroon and Charlie disappear and resurface at regular intervals.

However, these markers of orality also characterise certain kinds of western confessional writing, for example Mark Twain's *Tom Sawyer* (1876) and J. D. Salinger's *The Catcher in the Rye* (1951), both of which are alluded to in Kureishi's fiction. Also, the episodic nature of both novels can be explained in other ways, as Karim's reference to soap opera suggests. Each also draws on the conventions of the picaresque;[8] Karim, especially, can be read as an example of the flawed but lovable rogue who is the genre's characteristic protagonist. That Kureishi was not looking to Rushdie for his narrative technique is indicated during a self-reflexive discussion in *The Black Album*. While expressing admiration for Rushdie (and other postmodernist writers with whom he is often grouped, like Márquez and Kundera), the aspiring writer comments of *Midnight's Children* that it is 'difficult': 'It's [sic] rhythms aren't Western. It dashes all over the place' (BA, 8; only one such writer, Calvino, is mentioned in *The Buddha*; significantly, he is the favourite author of Karim's deadly foe Heater). While highly episodic, moreover, Kureishi's narratives are also strongly linear. Indeed, prolepsis and analepsis are extremely rare in comparison with Rushdie's work.

Instead, Kureishi's primary generic affiliations are to traditional social realism. At the time that he began to think about *The Buddha*, he was advocating 'popular Thackeray and Dickens [the novel alludes to both], say, as opposed to some recent American writing, loaded with experiment, innovation and pretty sentences which is published by minor magazines for an audience of acolytes, friends and university libraries' (SR, 95). Kureishi's novels invoke comparable European writers such as Stendhal and Balzac. Shahid models his work on close observation of life, filling notebooks with raw material for his writing in the manner of naturalists like Zola and Maupassant, an author much admired by Karim, too, who bases his role in Pyke's play directly on Changez. Each novel's status as *reportage* is foregrounded by inclusion of actual historical figures like the musician Kevin Ayers (in *The Buddha*) and by reference to documentarists like Hunter S. Thompson (the sub-plot of *The Black Album* is a kind of 'Fear and Loathing in London'), Truman Capote and Norman Mailer.

Kureishi's novels can be located more particularly within 'the condition of England' genre, which has its roots in the early nineteenth century and continued to flourish in a range of twentieth-century writers with whom Kureishi's novels engage.[9] H. G. Wells – like Kureishi, Bromley-born and equally interested in the place of the suburbs in English national culture – is cited in *The Buddha*;[10] Priestley and Orwell – on whom Kureishi had already commented in some detail in connection with his cinematic visions of the 'state of the nation' – are invoked in *The Black Album*. In *The Buddha*, the 'condition of England' is regularly discussed in Jamila's commune; unsurprisingly, in the light of Kureishi's own plays, it also provides the subject of Pyke's drama. As Eva comments: 'It was about this country ... It blew away the self-myth of tolerant, decent England' (BS, 228). This summarises equally well both of Kureishi's novels, which repeat the films' analysis of the changing nature of England and 'Englishness' in the 1970s and 1980s respectively.

Each text belongs in part to more specific sub-sets of British social realism. *The Buddha* owes something to writers like John Braine, Alan Sillitoe, David Storey and Keith Waterhouse who emerged in the 1950s to explore the shifting contours of class identity within a society which was being reconfigured radically in the aftermath of World War Two (many of their novels had been filmed by the mid-1960s, playing a central role in an earlier 'new wave' of British cinema which Kureishi much admired). 'Bradford' (MBL) demonstrates Kureishi's awareness of Braine and Sillitoe and acknowledges Waterhouse's *Billy Liar* as 'one of [his] favourite films' (MBL, 125).[11] Like many such works, *The Buddha* celebrates the determination of protagonists from various kinds of margin to better themselves socially. Thus, like Eva and Charlie, Karim talks ambitiously of 'going somewhere' (BS, 3) and later celebrates his 'social rise' (BS, 174). The ambivalence which he sometimes feels, both about the world he is leaving and the one he is entering, recalls similar conflicts in characters like Joe Lampton in Braine's *Room at the Top* (1957). Both characters rely substantially on the mentoring of older women in achieving their 'social translation', which is in part represented for each by the capture of upper-class girlfriends. As with Joe, Karim's accumulation of what he describes as 'irreplaceable [social] capital' (BS, 177) begins in the world of theatre. Joe's alternating affirmation of and rebellion against the *status quo* and his emphasis on physical gratification have their analogues in Karim's behaviour, and London acts as a magnet for him as much as it does for some of Waterhouse and Storey's protagonists.

By contrast, *The Black Album* is partly affiliated to the 'condition of England' sub-genre of 'the university novel', which has attempted to calibrate developments in post-war national life and self-image by anatomising the changing nature and function of higher education. Like Malcolm Bradbury's *Eating People is Wrong* (1959) or David Lodge's *Nice Work* (1988),[12] *The Black Album* explores the imbrication of English studies as a social institution within discourses of 'Englishness'.[13] It also follows precedent in two other ways. First it, too, analyses the challenges posed to liberal humanism by more explicitly ideological commitments such as the 'fundamentalism' of Riaz's Muslim group or 'the Party' to which Brownlow belongs; secondly it explores the implications for traditional 'high' culture of the increasing authority of the 'mass' media and other new forms of popular culture. Like *Nice Work*, more specifically, it addresses the effects of Thatcherite programmes of educational 'reform' in the 1980s. Its dispiriting portrait of an under-resourced, over-managerialised, tertiary college complements the scathing critique of New Right educational policy in the short story 'Esther'[14] and essays like 'Bradford' and 'Eight Arms to Hold You' (MBL), particularly its hostility to 'multi-culturalism'.

However, Kureishi gives each of these strands of the post-war British novel a marked inflection by his unrelenting attention to issues of race and ethnicity. Thus, while there are clear parallels between *The Buddha* and the work of writers like Braine in charting the emergence of a new social subject which challenges traditional conceptions of class identity, its primary concern is with the elaboration of new models of English/British ethnicity and identity (writers like Braine barely register the arrival of 'New Commonwealth' immigrants in the 1950s and the social friction which this had begun to generate by the end of the decade). Onto the trajectory of Karim's escape from his class origins, then, Kureishi grafts an archetypally postcolonial imagery of 'translation'. For example, Karim describes the acquisition of the social skills that Eleanor enjoys as akin to mastering 'a second language' (BS, 178) and he is initially overwhelmed by the cultural difference of the capital: 'We could have been from Bombay' (BS, 128). Equally, Bradbury and Lodge's conception of the relationship between English studies, 'Englishness' and the state of the nation is reconfigured by the central role given to Shahid and the Muslim students in *The Black Album*, whose institution is 'sixty per cent black and Asian' (BA, 20). Bradbury and Lodge both certainly touch on the challenge posed to the presumed social inclusiveness of English studies – and the model of national belonging which the discipline symbolises – by non-white immigration in post-war Britain. However, their treatment of the racial 'Other' is limited, both in terms of the space given to the issue and their (unconscious?) repetition of discriminatory attitudes which they ostensibly deplore.[15]

Such issues are by no means the only continuity between Kureishi's novels and his earlier work. As in the films, gender-role and sexual experimentation remain important avenues of liberation from the often coercive effects of traditional discourses of gender and sexuality. In *The Buddha*, for example, Haroon and Allie are at times disorientingly feminised and Changez actually develops breasts after the birth of Jamila's child. Conversely, his wife is strongly 'masculinised'; not only does her adolescent moustache put Karim's in the shade, but she beats her husband. Indeed, hybridity is as much figured through Karim's bisexuality (compare Shahid's gender-role play in Deedee's flat) as through his mixed-race origins. The trajectory of his career draws on Kureishi's own experiences as a dramatist and *The Buddha* offers further insights into his decision to move on into cinema. In both novels, London again plays a determining role. It is once more simultaneously a site in which new forms of both individual and community identity can be worked out and a space in which the dispiriting realities of 'domestic colonialism', together with the breakdown of traditional notions of national community, are all too manifest. While determinedly anti-Thatcherite, like the plays and films, each novel reveals Kureishi's continuing ambivalence about Left politics.

As in all his earlier work, the focus of Kureishi's novels is primarily on Britain's youth and its sub-cultural styles and forms of expression. To this extent, they can also be aligned with texts like Colin MacInnes's *Absolute Beginners* (1959) and Anthony Burgess's *A Clockwork Orange* (1963), to both of which they allude. For Kureishi, the interest of MacInnes lay in the latter's path-finding exploration of the emergence of new kinds of British youth culture in the 1950s and the way that these were being inflected by contact with London's growing 'New Commonwealth' populations;[16] of Burgess, in his analysis of how larger forces of globalisation were influencing those same youth cultures. Like these texts, Kureishi's novels are examples of *Bildungsroman*, charting their protagonists' often painful growth towards maturity through a range of conflicts and dilemmas, social, sexual and political. Other *Bildungsromane* they allude to include Voltaire's *Candide* (1759), Twain's *Tom Sawyer*, Gosse's *Father and Son* (1907) and Salinger's *The*

Catcher in the Rye. This last, a first-person narrative mediated in a hip, demotic register, of a knowing innocent's escape from the provinces to the metropolis (in this case New York), has the most obvious parallels with *The Buddha*.[17]

In returning to such themes, Kureishi reworks tropes, character types and plot lines from previous work. Like Omar and Johnny in *Laundrette*, Charlie and Karim in *The Buddha* are involved in a cross-race gay relationship and also on the make. Jamila is a more complex version of the rebellious young British-Asian woman who descends from Yasmin in *Borderline* through Tania in *Laundrette*. Jamila's commune, like Danny's in *Sammy and Rosie*, contrasts with the traditional nuclear family, which both novels again subject to a biting critique. In Pyke's play in *The Buddha*, Eleanor plays a colonial-born Englishwoman who, like Alice in *Sammy and Rosie*, cannot adjust to the dispiriting realities of post-imperial Britain. A similar pattern is evident in *The Black Album*, where the relationship between Shahid and Strapper, another former skinhead, also invokes Omar and Johnny's. The choice Shahid has to make recalls Omar's tug of loyalties between his father and uncle. Shahid's businessman father resembles Nasser, Chili and Zulma owe much to those earlier cosmopolitan yuppies, Salim and Cherry, and Shahid's cross-race relationship with Deedee Osgood invites comparison with those between Rosie, Danny and Sammy in Kureishi's second film. Nonetheless, there are some significant developments and differences of emphasis in the novels' approach to issues which are carried over from earlier work as well as the emergence of new preoccupations.

Culture wars

As previous chapters have indicated, Kureishi's interest in popular culture is evident throughout his earlier work, most obviously in the attention given to pop music. A career in pop is Imran's goal in *The Mother Country* and the music of Elvis is the focus of *The King and Me*, recurring as one of Stone's obsessions in *London Kills Me*. Pop sound-tracks make an important contribution to the moods and meanings of all the films, helping to define them generically and in terms of their target audiences. Equally, Kureishi's non-fiction is peppered with references to pop, which is the central concern of essays like 'Eight Arms to Hold You' (MBL) and 'That's How Good It Was', Kureishi's introduction to the co-edited *The Faber Book of Pop*.

The Buddha provides a compendium of references to pop's evolution through the 1960s and 1970s, from the Beatles and the Rolling Stones to hippy music, psychedelia, glam rock and punk; and *The Black Album* performs a similar role *vis-à-vis* the music of the following decade. This web of allusions reinforces each text's status as 'condition of England' novels (Prince's 'Sign O'the Times' is an obviously self-reflexive intertext in the second novel). In *The Faber Book of Pop*, Kureishi argues that pop provides an immediate index of the changing social attitudes and formations with which 'state of the nation' writers are characteristically preoccupied, as well as, in itself, providing 'new areas to explore' (FBP, xix). However, in contrast to leading visual artists like Peter Blake (who designed the covers for both the Beatles' *Sergeant Pepper* and *The Buddha*), Kureishi felt that 'serious' contemporary writers had largely ignored pop culture, an oversight which his own novels seek to remedy. The network of references to pop is also consonant with the two novels' identity as *Bildungsromane* insofar as their respective protagonists' moods, expectations and memories are so often illuminated and inflected by the music they listen to.

For Kureishi pop epitomises the liberating energies of the 'cultural revolution' which began the 1960s. On one level, it is always associated with pleasure in Kureishi's novels, particularly sexual and drug experimentation, and as such is set against the 'straight' world's emphasis on duty and self-denial, particularly in Thatcherite discourse. Conversely, pop is also prized for its involvement in political protest. Kureishi suggests that music as diverse as the Beatles and punk has at times taken on the same role of agitation as some of his own work. Its democratising thrust is evident in various ways. Kureishi argues that the genre speaks of and to 'ordinary experience with far more precision, real knowledge and wit than, say, British fiction of the equivalent period' (MBL, 118). In 'Eight Arms', he emphasises the achievement of the Beatles, a lower-middle-class group from the provinces, in opening up to their audiences unforeseen conceptions of social mobility and opportunity. He has also asserted that pop is the most easily accessible contemporary cultural form, 'both for spectators and, especially, for participants' (*ibid.*) Thus, at his first punk gig Karim is impressed (as well as alarmed) by the the fact that both spectators and band are composed mainly of 'pallid, vicious little council estate kids' (BS, 130).

As indicated in Chapter 1, Kureishi felt that by the 1960s pop music had become a mature cultural form, capable of comparison with much longer-established genres. Indeed, he has described it as 'the richest cultural form of post-war Britain' (MBL, 117). To this extent it had, in Kureishi's view, helpfully accelerated the break-down of the hierarchies which had traditionally informed thinking about culture and the antiquated social attitudes which underpinned them.[18] In 'Eight Arms', Kureishi criticises the snobbery of his schoolteachers towards pop (Mr Hogg is certain that, given their background, the Beatles could never have written such high-quality songs themselves) and in *The Faber Book of Pop*, he takes the renowned educationalist Richard Hoggart to task for similar 'condescension and implicit paternalism' (FBP, xviii).

The fiction also indicates Kureishi's belief that, especially for young people, pop offers the basis of a common culture to a far greater extent that the traditional 'high' cultural canon – as is suggested by Deedee's rhetorical question in *The Black Album*: 'Could literature connect a generation in the same way?' (BA, 111). In *The Buddha* it provides a bridge between the estate kids at the Nashville, the lower-middle-class Charlie and the privately-educated manager of Charlie's group. (Conversely, it also feeds the more specialised – and sometimes conflictual – micro-communities represented by the various tribes of Teds, Rockers, Punks and Mods which Karim encounters.) As was also indicated in Chapter 1, however, popular music plays a role in building wider kinds of community. *The Buddha* provides the most explicit instance of Kureishi's perception that it was in this medium that a process of cross-cultural exchange first developed which might provide a template for more productive relations between different ethnicities in contemporary society. Haroon and Margaret meet at a music venue in 1950s London, where Glenn Miller is played alongside Louis Armstrong, their music dissolving traditional borderlines between races as well as classes (Haroon is an upper-middle-class law student, his future wife working-class).[19] Moreover, the novel implies that whatever hostility the Asian punk band members may encounter in other contexts, British-Asians are more likely to be accepted in the music world than in other cultural and employment contexts, a perception first evident in *The Mother Country*. (Such evidence has a bearing on the less enthusiastic treatment of 1980s British pop culture in *The Black Album*, which Kureishi represents as fragmenting along the fault-lines of ethnicity. As its name implies, London's 'White Room' club is ethnically homogenous and Shahid stands out at the 'rave' in Kent. This may also partially explain the greater emphasis given to jazz in more recent work like *My Son the Fanatic*.)

The integrative dynamic which Kureishi attributes to certain kinds of pop is best symbolised by the figure of Prince, probably the most important music icon in either novel (the second of which is named after Prince's album of 1988). As Deedee puts it: 'He's half black and half white, half man, half woman, half size, feminine but macho too.' To which Shahid adds that he 'can play soul and funk and rock and rap' (BA, 21). Insofar as Prince's LP gestures critically towards the Beatles' seminal *White Album* (1969), the performer does not simply rewrite the histories of black music but draws on 'white' pop, too. In Prince, famous for his makeovers and aliases,[20] Kureishi most graphically represents pop as the crossroads not only of different cultural influences but as a site in which plurality of identity – whether at the level of ethnicity, class, gender or sexuality – is celebrated. As such Prince's music symbolises those trends in the contemporary world which Kureishi most prizes.[21]

The stylistic influence of pop is most evident in the language of each novel. Kureishi has argued that it 'has enlivened and altered the language, introducing a Jonsonian proliferation of idioms, slang and fresh locutions' (FBP, xix). The vitality of *The Buddha*, in particular, owes much to the variety of Karim's subcultural registers, diction and phrasing. What Kureishi calls pop's characteristic 'lightness of touch' (FBP, xx) is also evident, especially in the first novel (but also in the comedy of *The Black Album*, which is centred on the sub-plots involving Chili, Zulma and Strapper). Though it has darker moments and raises many serious issues, *The Buddha* is characterised by an intense comic imagination and wit. Finally, it may even be the case that the episodic structure of both texts is a fictional analogue to the unified disparity of the LP as a form.

Kureishi's high valuation of pop music must not, however, be confused with a disavowal of traditional 'high' culture, even in *The Buddha*, which of all his texts is the most positive in its treatment of pop. Classical music has a pronounced presence in the text (Verdi, Wagner, Dvorak are all alluded to and Bach is the first music which the future Charlie Hero enthuses about to Karim). Moreover, the novel's treatment of other aspects of popular culture is sometimes ambivalent. There is positive reference to the very English genre of Ealing comedy (and the pronounced farce of *The Buddha*, such as Karim's misadventures with Hairy Back's dog, belong squarely within this tradition). Although Allie is enthusiastic about Karim's graduation to soap operas, Margaret's addiction to TV is a source of heart-ache for her elder son and, whereas the pulp fiction that Changez loves is represented as harmless fun, Karim clearly prefers 'serious' literature, which he reads voraciously and alludes to showily.

The Buddha certainly broaches the crucial question of the relevance of traditional 'high' culture to Britain's ethnic minorities. Jamila is introduced to literary classics by the enthusiastic Miss Cutmore who, significantly, was once an educational missionary in Africa. Jamila, however, soon rejects her mentor, accusing her of a quasi-imperial paternalism, and switches her allegiance to African-American literature, which she sees as more relevant to her predicament. This provokes a significant falling-out with Karim, who accuses her of ingratitude. More important, Jamila sees Miss Cutmore's attempted incorporation of her into the dominant culture as coercive in tendency, whereas Karim has a more positive view, considering it to be the source of liberating paths to personal growth and an empowering knowledge of the world.

The more socially and racially polarised context of 1980s Britain in *The Black Album* generates more ambitious treatment of the lovers' debate. Here, the obstacles to achieving the mission of social inclusiveness represented by Miss Cutmore's 'taking up' of Jamila – and associated with a literary education in *Eating People Is Wrong* and *Nice Work* – seem more formidable. For many of Deedee's students 'the great tradition' is an object of suspicion: 'Many of them regarded the white elite culture as self-deceiving and hypocritical ... they didn't want to find the culture that put them down profound' (BA, 112). Shahid has some sympathy for the doubters when he remembers his schooling, 'where books were stuck down their throats like medicinal biscuits, until they spat them out' (BA, 62). His suspicion about the role of literary studies in a secondary education system, which he sees as operating primarily as a means of social control, influences Shahid's conception of higher education, too: 'Could this place be like those youth clubs that merely kept bad kids out of trouble?' (BA, 22).

Deedee makes considerable efforts to adjust the traditional syllabus of English studies to make it more sensitive to the experience of the marginalised constituencies she is addressing (she herself has used a literary education to emancipate herself from a deprived early life). Thus, she introduces more Black and Women's writing, as well as popular genre fiction to the curriculum. To make explicit the historical links between metropolitan 'high' culture and imperialism, moreover, she offers a course on 'colonialism and literature' which leaves Shahid 'in a fog of inchoate anger and illumination' (BA, 25). These initiatives are complemented by her attention to pop, especially Black pop. The fact that Shahid's first assignment is on Prince indicates Deedee's acceptance that such figures, and the medium in which they work, are of something like equivalent importance to what Hat lampoons as 'the whole white doo-dah' (BA, 181).

If such evidence points to a legitimate contestation of the supposedly inclusive model of community traditionally claimed on behalf of English studies as a social insitution, *The Black Album* is much more positive about the value of canonical western literature than might be inferred from Hat's attitudes. Kureishi's largely affirmative treatment of the canon may be explained in part by the fact that, in contrast to the novels of Bradbury and Lodge, *The Black Album* registers anxiety about the vulnerability of *all* forms of traditional culture to con- sumerism and 'mass' mediatisation. Thus, Shahid's school- friends 'knew nothing of their own culture' and he is appalled by the deracination of the white supremacists on the estates surrounding college: 'How could they bear their own ignorance, living without culture, their lives reduced to watching soap operas three-quarters of the day? They were powerless and lost' (BA, 113). To this extext, indeed, Kureishi implies that racism and xenophobia provide a last, shrunken focus of identity for many indigenous Britons, whose traditional culture has been swamped by globalised 'mass' media pap. In this context it is notable that in comparison to *The Buddha*, *The Black Album* barely refers to British pop, as if to suggest that by the late 1980s, 'rave' music aside, this last bastion of popular British cultural identity had fallen.

The decline of 'high' culture, too, is registered in the fact that even Deedee has to steel herself to read texts like *Little Dorrit*; this produces some uncomfortable reflections:

> Serious reading required dedication. Who, now, believed it did them good? And how many people knew a book as they knew *Blonde on Blonde*, *Annie Hall* or Prince, even? Could literature connect a generation in the same way? Some exceptional students would read hard books; most wouldn't, and they weren't fools. (BA, 111)

Shahid, of course, dissents from this pessimistic analysis, a response which can be largely attributed to an apprentice's burning conviction of the superiority of the medium he has chosen: 'Sometimes I see certain people and I want to grab them and say, read this story by Maupassant or Faulkner … it's better than television' (BA, 17). The longer he is associated with Riaz's group, the more Shahid comes to prize the canon as the epitome of independent thought and individual imagination, if not the highest form of human achievement. In successive set-piece debates with his Muslim associates, Shahid becomes ever more determined to defend its local truths against Riaz's Truth, leading to his final departure from the group.

Given his affirmation of the enduring importance of canonical literature and his distaste for 'mass' cultural forms – certain kinds of film and pop music aside – it is little surprise that on more than one occasion, Shahid resists Deedee's attempt to tilt English in the direction of a globalised 'cultural studies':

> She and the other post-modern types encouraged their students to study anything that took their interest, from Madonna's hair to a history of the leather jacket. Was it really learning or only diversion dressed up in the latest words? Were students in better colleges studying stuff to give them the advantage in life? (BA, 22)

Later in the text, Shahid reconsiders this issue in a way which explicitly reconnects to Kureishi's inquiry into the relevance of traditional 'high' culture to modern multiracial Britain:

> He didn't always appreciate being played Madonna or George Clinton in class, or offered a lecture on the history of funk as if it were somehow more 'him' than *Fathers and Sons*. Any art could become 'his', if its value was demonstrated. (BA, 112)

From one perspective, Shahid's response might be taken as an endorsement of a (suspect) humanist 'universalism' which would not be out of place in the staff-rooms in *Eating People is Wrong* or *Nice Work*.[22] Yet it is undoubtedly legitimate for Shahid to wonder whether Deedee's pedagogic strategy does not represent a subtle new form of exclusion, rather than empowerment, of the minorities on whose behalf she seems so interested.

Kureishi and colonial discourse

Kureishi's nuanced treatment of the 'canon wars' is particularly evident in his engagements with colonial discourse, notably with what Said has described as 'Orientalism'. In the novels as in his earlier work, Kureishi is much preoccupied by the continuing purchase in contemporary Britain of negative and dichotomising attitudes towards cultures of non-western origin which were formed in the colonial period. 'Modern' Orientalism is represented in its most extreme form by Zulma's aristocratic lover Jump in *The Black Album*, for whom Islam remains an immediate and direct threat to the West: 'I'm telling you ... they are entering France through Marseilles and Italy through the south. Soon they will be sweeping through the weakened Communist regions, into the heart of civilized Europe' (BA, 159). For Jump, every Muslim is potentially a militant, if not a terrorist, and for him the culture of Islam is both inferior to, and incompatible with, his own.

Said argued in *Orientalism* that such hostile attitudes have their roots in literary as much as non-literary forms of colonial discourse, as Shahid's reactions to Deedee's course on colonial literature seem to confirm. *The Buddha* invokes several major figures within this tradition. Like Dr Bubba in *London Kills Me*, Haroon parodies the eastern spirituality represented by Professor Godbole in Forster's *A Passage to India*, with whom is contrasted the materialism of the West (Haroon's dress is as eclectic as Godbole's, some of his pronouncements equally gnomic and he, too, increasingly disavows all things British). By contrast, the slippage between his identities as Haroon and 'Harry' (as Aunt Jean insists he calls himself) invokes Hari/'Harry' Kumar, a key player in Paul Scott's *Raj Quartet* (1964- 1975), who is a tragic example of intercultural hybridity. (Art Malik, who played Kumar in the Channel 4 series, was first choice for the male lead in *Sammy and Rosie*.) The buggery on which Karim's relationship with Pyke turns may owe something to *The Raj Quartet*, representing a contemporary reinscription of the power relations embodied in Merrick's rape of Kumar.

In both novels, one can detect further instances of Kureishi's direct challenge to the ways that the 'Oriental' is imagined in such examples of metropolitan literature of empire, primarily through the techniques of parody and pastiche. For example, despite his role as a guide to many of his white acquaintances, Haroon's career also functions as a critique of the common equation of the East with spirituality in colonial discourse.[23] In contrast to disciples like Fruitbat, Karim and Jamila both see Haroon as a fake and his teaching as a stratagem for the possession of Eva, domination of Uncle Ted and escape from work and family responsibilities. In the enthusiasm of some of Haroon's white admirers, moreover, Kureishi parodies the narrative of empire as an evangelising project and reverses the power relations embodied in colonial proselytism. Instead of Indian natives compliantly absorbing the religious wisdom of the West, the native British seek deliverance from their ersatz immigrant *guru*.

The appropriation of colonial trope and stereotype is also evident in Kureishi's counter-discursive treatment of 'Oriental' sexuality in his fiction. Thus, Jamila's powerful sexual appetite is another instance of his rebuttal of the Orientalist figure of the silent, passive, native woman whose fate is to be both 'saved' by the colonizer and used as his sexual object.[24] Kureishi also redeploys the homoerotic figure of the 'Oriental groom',[25] the male native who is amenable to polymorphous sexual 'perversities'. In *The Buddha* Kureishi uses the trope not to represent the moral inferiority of the (formerly) colonised, but to further his critique of over-rigid and discriminatory conceptions of gender and sexual identity in contemporary society (on *both* sides of the ethnic divide). The sexuality of the 'Oriental' male in Kureishi's novels also plays ironically (if sometimes uncomfortably) off the figure of the colonized male subject as over-sexed, even a potential rapist of white women, which is an enduring trope in metropolitan literature of empire, from Shakespeare's *The Tempest* to Scott's *Raj Quartet*.[26] Kureishi's novels subvert this trope on the one hand by stressing the active desire of white women for exotic sexual 'Others'; thus Helen and Eleanor take the initiative in their relationships with Karim. He, on the other hand, has sex with them in part to revenge himself against figures like Helen's father, who regards Karim's interest in his daughter as a threat to British racial purity; Karim comments that 'by possessing these prizes ... we stared defiantly into the eye of the Empire and all its self-regard – into the eye of Hairy Back, into the the eye of the Great Fucking Dane' (BS, 227).

It is with Kipling, however, that Kureishi's fiction engages most extensively and explicitly. For example, he is invoked at the beginning of *The Black Album*, when Kureishi repeats the joke in *Birds of Passage* about the immigrant's predicament in modern Britain being 'the brown man's burden' (BA, 5). Kipling is a major presence in *The Buddha*, most obviously because of the space devoted to the stage version of *The Jungle Books*, which provides Karim with his professional breakthrough in the role of Mowgli. The strongly satirical representation of this production, together with the hostile responses of Haroon and Jamila after the opening night, suggest that Kureishi's intention is to discredit Kipling. Jamila, for instance, comments that the play is 'completely neo-fascist' and Haroon objects to it in violent, if not wholly coherent terms: 'That bloody fucker Mr Kipling pretending to whity he knew something about India!' (BS, 157) [*sic*].

Such criticisms might be understood as further evidence of Kureishi's corroboration of Rushdie's arguments about the dangerous phenomenon of 'Raj revivalism'. He may be suggesting that, in reviving Kipling, even Left-liberals like Shadwell are not exempt from the kind of nostalgia for vanished national glories which Kureishi anatomised in his engagement with 'Raj' and 'Heritage' cinema. However, *The Buddha*'s treatment of Kipling is far more complex than might be inferred from the reactions of Jamila or Haroon. In fact, Kureishi seems to want to emphasise that it is Shadwell's production values, and the power relations inscribed in his role as white director of an ethnic-minority actor, which are the real causes for concern. It is Shadwell, not Kipling, who is responsible for Karim's demeaning mock-Indian accent and the director's choice that Karim go onstage looking 'like a Black and White Minstrel' (BS, 157). Karim, certainly, has no objections to Kipling's text in itself. Indeed, early in the novel he describes his pursuit of Jamila without any irony as being like Mowgli hunting Shere Khan – and later cites Kipling again in his description of Changez's assault on his father-in-law: 'Kipling had written "to each his own fear", but this was not Anwar's' (BS, 211). To a significant extent, moreover, Kureishi's novel uses *The Jungle Books* as a template. For example, London is represented as a similarly ambiguous kind of jungle to Kipling's; on the one hand full of dangers, it also offers Karim new kinds of community and ways of living as much as the *rukh* does Mowgli.[27] Just as Mowgli must negotiate between his identities as man and wolf-cub, so Karim is torn between different cultural identifications and, like Mowgli, he is in a process of maturation which involves choices between conformity to moral law and the promptings of nature.

It could be argued that, although it is never explicitly cited, Kipling's masterpiece *Kim* plays an even more important role in *The Buddha*. There are many parallels between Kim himself and K(ar)im, not least in their names. From the outset, both texts are concerned with issues of 'pedigree'. If Kim is, at the start of Kipling's text, 'burned black as any native',[28] Karim is 'creamy' to the point of being almost indistinguishable from whites (he can go to football matches without fear of abuse), thus – from Shadwell's point of view – necessitating the stage make-up which Karim so detests. Both characters are extremely attractive to women from the majority culture (although, unlike Kim, Karim is happy to take advantage of his attractiveness). Karim's relentless renewals of his (eclectically-sourced) wardrobe recall Kim's constant switching between English and various native modes of dress. Like Kim, Karim is a spy – on a number of levels. His nosiness (compare Saleem in *Midnight's*

Children) leads to his teachers recommending a job in Customs and Excise and at home he surreptitiously goes through his parents' papers, commenting: 'No secrets were safe from me' (BS, 20). He is literally sent to spy on Pyke by Terry on behalf of 'the Party', an organisation as shadowy as Creighton's Secret Service in *Kim* (though of course its subversive objectives are the antithesis of Creighton's). The spy motif is adapted in Karim's role as 'voyeur', whether observing Changez to provide material for his role in Pyke's play, or as the spectator of Charlie's sexual adventures in New York. Perhaps most emphatic are the analogies between Kim's role as *chela* to the Lama (his principal father-figure) and Karim's service to his *guru* parent. Like the Lama, Haroon tends increasingly towards helplessness (even at the outset he relies on Karim to navigate him round London, and his disorientation with buses and telephones recalls the Lama's bafflement by train and telegraph). Like the Lama, Haroon is searching for enlightenment, which involves the attempt to educate his son morally (a pastiche of the Lama's instruction of Kim).

As is appropriate to the *Bildungsroman* genre, both Kim and Karim are involved in a process of inner growth and each suffers a series of crises which marks their evolution towards adulthood.[29] These entail bouts of severe depression, notably immediately after what appear to be each character's moments of greatest triumph. For both protagonists, such episodes centre on issues of identity. To some extent they involve the typical confusions of adolescence. More specifically, they concern the conflict between different cultural affiliations. Thus, despite his disavowals of suburbia, it is remarkable how often Karim is drawn back to his roots, particularly after suffering setbacks. As with Kim, Karim's most important dilemma, however, concerns the competing claims of 'Indianness' and 'Englishness'. Whereas Kim is symbolically of mixed race (he is brought up by an Indian foster-mother), Karim is so literally. It could be argued that neither novel fully resolves the issues of cultural belonging which they raise and both end openly and ambiguously, with neither protagonist having either chosen decisively between the respective cultures to which they are affiliated or having found a fully satisfying synthesis of, or compromise between, them.

To this extent, Kureishi's recourse to Kipling does not bespeak a desire simply to disavow colonial discourse in the manner of more obviously cultural nationalist postcolonial writers, like Ngugi. Stephen Slemon has argued that a key feature of 'a specifically anti- or *post*-colonial discursive purchase' is 'the figuration of a reiterative quotation, or intertextual citation, in relation to colonialist "textuality"'.[30] While certainly 'reiterative' in this sense, *The Buddha*'s quotation of Kipling attests rather to a desire to 'hybridise' colonial discourse by adapting it 'catachrestically'[31] to address new cultural problematics. It could be argued that, like Rushdie, Kureishi seeks to recuperate and develop Kipling's interest in cross-cultural transactions, seeing in this aspect of his work a precedent for explorations of the contemporary predicament of cultural 'in-betweenness'. Throughout Rushdie's work there is clear evidence of the enabling precedent of Kipling's work, especially *Kim*, in his own rethinking of issues of national identity and cultural belonging, both within Britain and in the subcontinent.[32] Thus, in *The Moor's Last Sigh* there is a sympathetic discussion of 'Kipling's almost schizophrenic early stories of the Indiannesses and Englishnesses that struggled within him'.[33] (This, then, is a further area in which Rushdie's influence on Kureishi can be detected.)

Kureishi's choice of *Bildungsroman* as a genre is particularly significant, given that it is one which insistently presents identity as a developmental, unstable and shifting *process*, rather than a given and stable *product*. *The Buddha* is, of course, largely bound up with the theatre world and Kureishi repeatedly draws analogies between the way that roles are learned, adapted and worked out through collaboration and negotiation (while also being subject to external constraints symbolised by directorial intervention) in that context and within the wider social milieu of which the theatre forms part. Pyke presents interpersonal relations as a 'performance' (BS, 199), indicating that identity is in part the effect of dialogical interaction which always leaves the imprint of the interlocuted individual on the interlocutor. Karim and Charlie often act as a 'mirror' to each other (BS 16 and 250–1), which suggests their individual onto-logical incompleteness. Nor can identity ever reach closure through (solipsistic) self-reflection. Karim's self-narration splits him into observer and observed, a fracture which is also figured in his habit of looking into reflective surfaces, whether mirrors, shop-windows or the glass in underground trains.[34]

As might be inferred from this, the more flexible a character's conception of self is in Kureishi's novels, the more sympathetic they are to both the central protagonists and the reader. Thus, in *The Buddha*, once his feeble attempt to assert himself as a traditional Muslim husband has failed, Changez evolves into perhaps the most immediately appealing character in the text. As his name implies, Changez becomes increasingly open to the new roles and identities which are thrust upon him, culminating in that of surrogate parent to Jamila's child by Stephen. Eva, too, goes through several transformations, from oppressed Orpington housewife to self-empowered London socialite and country-house designer, as her relationship with Haroon develops. Even more striking is the example of Uncle Ted, who by the end of the novel has turned into a far more tolerant being than the timidly conventional and prejudiced figure he is at the outset. By contrast, the less sympathetic figures, such as Uncle Anwar, Aunt Jean and, for much of the novel, Margaret, are antipathetic precisely because of the rigid social roles and identities within which they confine themselves and to which they expect others to conform (relatively late in the novel, Margaret still insists on her son's singular identity as an Englishman, refusing to accept the reality of his hybridity).

Like *Kim* and much of Rushdie's fiction, furthermore, Kureishi's novels present 'public' forms of identity like nation-ality and ethnicity not as 'found' or, indeed, foundational, but as socially constructed and therefore always already provisional. Thus, Shahid's temporary adoption of 'national dress' in *The Black Album* suggests that 'nationality' is primarily an effect of what are in the end semiotic systems rather than independent of, or prior to, them. The constructed nature of ethnicity is brilliantly figured in *The Buddha* in Karim's recourse to the jar of 'shit-brown cream' (BS, 146) in order (in Shadwell's view) to adequately figure his 'Indianness'. At Anwar's funeral, the young actor realises that he has perhaps become too assimilated (for example, he has a habit of mocking Jeeta's accent), so 'colluding with [his] enemies, those whites who wanted Indians to be like them' (BS, 212). However, he also understands that, like his father, whom he has seen self-consciously composing an 'Oriental' identity from an eclectic mixture of eastern sources, 'if I wanted the additional personality bonus of an Indian past, I would have to *create* it' (BA, 213) (my emphasis).

In Kureishi's novels 'Englishness', too, is simply one more constructed and multiply-determined ethnicity, as Karim's encounter with his old schoolfriend in New York makes clear: 'Charlie had acquired this cockney accent when my first memory of him at school was that he'd cried after being mocked by the stinking gypsy kids for talking so posh ... He was selling Englishness, and getting a lot of money for it' (BS, 247). Moreover, as the place of 'ethnic' objects in the domestic iconography of both novels indicates, 'Englishness' is in fact already inflected by elements of what its more extreme apologists are keen to exclude.[35] This is suggested in the description of Eva's new home: '"As you can see, it's very feminine in the English manner," she said to the journalist as we looked over the cream carpets, gardenia paintwork, wooden shutters, English country-house armchairs and cane tables. There were baskets of dried flowers in the kitchen and coconut matting on the floor' (BS, 261). The cane tables, coconut matting and shutters all reflect the incorporation of foreign, more specifically eastern, items within 'English' decor. (Equally, when Karim and Charlie act as mirrors to each other, Kureishi symbolises the mutual imbrication and relativity of 'Asian' and 'white' as ethnicities.) If, as Said argues, such evidence suggests that the East exists as an underground presence *within* western identity,[36] the converse is also true in Kureishi's eyes. When Karim constructs the role for Pyke's play of 'an immigrant fresh from a small Indian town', he selects a wardrobe consisting of 'high white platform boots, wide cherry flares ... and a spotted shirt with a wide "Concorde" collar' (BS, 220). This further indicates how an increasingly globalised economy is binding together the most distant parts of the world in ways which are accelerating the breakdown of dichotomies between them.[37]

Kureishi's conviction of the ultimately provisional and decentred nature of both personal and public modes of identity points to his most interesting departure from the conventions of *Bildungsroman*. Whereas the genre usually charts the protagonist's *eventual* attainment of a stable personal and public identity, the lesson learned by Kureishi's major characters (like Kipling's Kim) is quite different in emphasis. For them, maturity consists in accepting as an ethical principle the terminally polymorphous and unstable nature of selfhood.[38] As Shahid puts it in *The Black Album*: 'How many warring selves were there within him? Which was his real, natural self? Was there such a thing? How would he know it when he saw it? Would it have a guarantee attached to it?' (BA, 122). If such questions cause Shahid extreme anxiety to begin with, by the end of the novel he is more at ease: 'There was no fixed self; surely our several selves melted and mutated daily? There had to be innumerable ways of being in the world' (BA, 228). Such perceptions have crucial implications for Kureishi's reconsideration of the politics of race in his fiction.

Identity politics and cultural nationalism

Kureishi's novels provide a persistent critique of a variety of perspectives and positions which are hostile to this plural and mobile conception of identity. As in the films, the most important of these are discourses of cultural nationalism, the dominant and most dangerous forms of which are autochthonous British ones. These are characteristically organised around a singular, racialised conception of national identity, which is taken to be superior to other kinds of self-identification. As Chapter 3 suggested, the more that national belonging is associated with ethnic homogeneity, the more pernicious domestic cultural nationalism tends to be in Kureishi's fiction. At one extreme is Helen's father in *The Buddha*, who implies that 'Englishness' can only be compromised or tainted by contact with other, particularly non-western, cultures. Immigrants from such backgrounds, according to Hairy Back, consequently have no permanent place in Britain.[39]

The most destructive effects of such ideas are registered in extreme Right political activity. In *The Black Album*, Sadiq's brother has had 'his skull crushed by a dozen youths' (BA, 83) and, in *The Buddha*, Changez has the initials of the National Front carved into his stomach. Jamila, meanwhile, has sufficient raw material relating to racial attacks on immigrant women for a research project on the issue. More dilute expressions of domestic cultural nationalism are also evident in both novels. Whereas the far Right seeks the expulsion of 'aliens', 'cultural assimilationism' advances the ostensibly more moderate position that immigrants can, indeed, belong to British society – provided that they surrender the cultural identities which they have brought with them and adopt the norms, values and social practices of the host society. Discourses of 'assimilationism' further reveal contemporary Britain's inability to shake off its colonial past. The production of acculturated 'brown-skinned Englishmen' amongst certain sections of the native populace was a goal of imperial policy in India, most famously articulated in T. B. (later Lord) Macaulay's 1835 'Minute on Education'.[40] Vulgar echoes of Macaulay's thinking can be detected in many of Kureishi's white British characters. In *The Buddha*, for example, Aunt Jean demands that Haroon reconstitute himself as 'Harry': 'It was bad enough his being an Indian in the first place, without having an awkward name' (BS, 33). Initially, at least, Uncle Ted has similar attitudes, as is suggested by his outrage at Haroon's turn to eastern philosophy: 'Buddhism isn't the kind of thing she's [Margaret] used to. It's got to stop!' (BS, 48). Fearful of compromising their success in artistic London, even Eva eventually turns against Haroon's mysticism.

As with his earlier work, Kureishi's novels unrelentingly

attack these different forms of British cultural nationalism and express considerable sympathy for various modes of opposition to them. Thus, although there is some satire of Haroon's vocation as a *guru* in *The Buddha*, it is also represented as a contestation of the coercive expectations of characters like Aunt Jean. At the beginning of the novel, Haroon in many ways seems to represent 'the brown-skinned Englishman'. He is a civil servant, commuting from the leafy suburbs into London, with conventional ambitions for his son, and conforms in all outward appearances to the norms of the English middle classes (he disdains the 'chaos' of India and even warns Karim off Asian girls). However, as is suggested by his dietary preferences, love of yoga and propensity to mock the British, Haroon has never entirely effaced his origins. This suggests that the 'Englishness' he has espoused in public life is to some degree tactical, a form of mimicry which, like Amar's preference to be identified as Allie, is a means of deflecting the racist gaze of the dominant culture by being 'less risibly conspicuous' (BS, 21).[41] As Haroon's discontent with the conformity of suburban life grows, however, he increasingly affirms his non-western roots. Towards the end of the text, indeed, Haroon disavows his 'Englishness' whole-sale: 'I have lived in the West for most of my life, and I will die here, yet I remain to all intents and purposes an Indian man. I will never be anything but an Indian' (BS, 263).

If Haroon's trajectory represents an individualistic mode of refusal of the centre's norms, Jamila's rebellion is more obviously political in nature. While her wholesale rejection of Miss Cutmore is certainly viewed ironically by Karim, her commit-ment to organised anti-racism is represented sympathetically throughout the novel. Her espousal of Black Liberation ideology is used to show up Karim's wavering loyalties to the social formation to which he at least partly belongs, his failure to attend the anti-Nazi march which she has helped to organise being particularly conspicuous. (Of course, Jamila's radicalism once again reflects Kureishi's desire to challenge the perception that British Asians – and the community's women, in particular – are simply hapless victims.)

Nevertheless, in representing Jamila's reactions as a legitimate response to the more extreme forms of domestic cultural nationalism, Kureishi stresses a number of factors which explain his quite different treatment of other kinds of minoritarian cultural/political mobilisation. First of all, Jamila's politics are secular, modern and democratic in orientation. Secondly, she sees herself as engaged in a struggle for social justice which necessitates the nurturing of broad solidarities, rather than following a particularist path which reflects the interests or predicament of a single constituency. Thus, like the coalition based round Sammy and Rosie's flat, her commune brings together a 'rainbow coalition' of different interest groups, including socialists, ecological warriors and lesbians. Thirdly, Jamila's politics can be understood as exemplifying what Spivak has termed 'strategic essentialism' in the pursuit of 'a scrupulously visible political interest'.[42] Thus, for Jamila ethnicity is not an absolute and indivisible attribute to be defended at all costs, but constitutes the basis of mobilisation towards determinate ends, the achievement of which will, by inference, depoliticise ethnicity altogether.

In these regards Jamila's position competes directly with some other forms of minoritarian self-assertion in Kureishi's novels, as is suggested by Karim's troubled relationship with the black actress Tracey. Whereas Jamila's commune represents a form of alliance which does not repress internal differences, Tracey's politics are more narrowly based around the 'single issue' of race. Although she extends a hand to Karim, her insistence that Karim is, politically speaking, 'Black', indicates a blindness to the heterogeneity of British minority culture and experience which, the novel implies, has its analogue in mainstream society's blanket homogenisation of Asian Britain (as 'Paki', for example).[43] To this extent, the censorship of which Karim complains at Tracey's hands links her to the politics of exclusion espoused by Riaz's group in *The Black Album*.

Equally, Jamila's position conflicts with her father's attitudes. At the root of Kureishi's objections to Anwar's 'nativism' is its reliance on fixed and essentialist conceptions of identity, which replicate precisely the assumptions that the author most deplores in the cultural nationalism of the host culture. Haroon's understanding that his roots are located in an 'imagined India' (BS, 74), with all the provisionality which this implies, distinguishes him sharply from Anwar who, as the novel progresses, increasingly embraces a damagingly rigid and exclusionary conception of his 'original' identity. This generates a number of ironies. For example, Anwar's antipathy towards Hindus in Britain echoes attitudes associated with the terrible inter-communal violence of Partition in 1947, to which *The Buddha* refers early on; and at Jamila's wedding, his relative's abuse of Helen simply invokes the most demeaning stereotypes of the host society: 'Pork, pork, pork, VD, VD, white woman, white woman' (BS, 84–5).

Anwar's views are absolutely guaranteed by a faith which has no place in Jamila's politics. She, of course, is the chief victim of her father's insistence on the sanctity of religiously-sanctioned tradition. Anwar's oppression of his daughter (and wife), which leads to Jamila's forced marriage to Changez, graphically illustrates the subordinate role in which women can remain confined in such forms of 'nativism'. That the issue is not properly one of religion, but of patriarchal rights, is suggested by Anwar's personal hypocrisy. While he takes a hard-line attitude towards Haroon's relationship with Eva, Anwar himself has been involved with 'the prostitutes who hung around Hyde Park' (BS, 25) and, while he deems Haroon's interest in pop music to be a sign of the latter's decadence, he still continues to smoke and drink alcohol long after his readoption of an apparently strict Islamic identity. Nonetheless, Karim, at least, identifies Islam as particularly susceptible to appropriation by certain kinds of 'nativism': 'Like many Muslim men – beginning with the Prophet Mohammed himself, whose absolute statements, served up piping hot from God, inevitably gave rise to absolutism, Anwar thought he was right about everything. No doubt on any subject ever entered his head' (BS, 172).

However, *The Black Album* suggests that some distinction needs to be made between Karim's attitudes to Islam and those of Kureishi himself. Shahid – at least in the beginning – respects Islam as a faith and understands its appeal both in the context of his own existential uncertainties and of the hostile attitudes of the host society. Riaz is initially a relatively complex character, and is by no means unsympathetic, as his avuncular interest in Shahid indicates. Other than the minor vanities of wanting to get his poetry published and to appear on television, he seems unreproachable on a personal level (in contrast to Anwar, the *maulvi* in *My Son the Fanatic*, or, indeed, the French-based *mullah* of Rushdie's *Satanic Verses*). Moreover, Kureishi is at pains to avoid suggesting that Riaz is simply an aged obscurantist. In the mosque he preaches toleration of other religious beliefs and Chad intimates that Riaz's poetry-writing would be deprecated by some associates: 'It's too frivolous, too merry for them. Some of those guys go into a supermarket and if music is playing, they run out again' (BA, 58).

Furthermore, *The Black Album* programmatically counters many stereotypes about 'fundamentalism'. Shahid's visit to the mosque leads to his recognition of the hybrid nature of Islam's adherents, rebutting the widespread conception that the religion is a monolithic (and essentially non-western) formation: 'Men of so many types and nationalities – Tunisians, Indians, Algerians, Scots, French ... gathered there ... Here race and class barriers had been suspended' (BA, 109). The Islamophobia expressed in a variety of registers, from the aristocratic Jump to the working-class racists on the 'sink' estate, is challenged by many aspects of Kureishi's depiction of Riaz's group. Its desire for social justice, its hostility to the unrestrained capitalism of the Thatcher era, the second chance in life which it offers characters as diverse as Chad and Strapper, are all represented positively. Equally, the group is seen favourably in comparison with the extreme assimilationism represented by the 'arch-Thatcherite' (BA, 72) Chili, the dissolute yuppie who is only partially redeemed by his courageous confrontation of Chad at the end of the novel. Finally, the degree of real threat posed by Riaz's group is put into perspective by the novel's references to the violence of the extreme Right and the campaign of urban terror waged by the

IRA, whose disruptions to the life of the capital in the 1980s punctuate the narrative. The arson attack on the bookshop is, by comparison, a relatively minor incident which, as is suggested by the wounds which Chad receives, is primarily *self*-destructive.

Moreover, if Kureishi's novel draws a distinction between Riaz and disciples like Chad, in the end the most unsympathetic character in the text, *The Black Album* nonetheless lays great stress on explaining the latter's extremism in terms of his early life-experience in Britain. Brought up in the country by white foster-parents who are determined to extirpate every trace of his roots, Chad's turn to 'fundamentalism' is presented as an understandable, if overstated, attempt to recover legitimate parts of his cultural identity. From their first meeting, Shahid is struck by the residual hurt from his early life in Chad's eyes, which also generates the 'mad kindness' (BA, 66) the latter initially displays to his new friend. If Chad is a soul 'lost in translation' (BA, 89), the most ironic lesson of his trajectory is that it is precisely the intolerance of the host society towards its 'Others' which generates the physical and ideological resistance that the dominant ethnicity most abhors and fears.

Nonetheless, *The Black Album* in the end clearly disavows the path taken by Chad and his colleagues. Primarily this is because Riaz's group is unable to tolerate difference. For example it is determinedly homophobic, echoing Anwar's (and Haroon's) attitudes in *The Buddha*. It is even more dismayed by the difference represented by British-born, secularised Asians like Shahid, who are comfortable in Britain. If Karim's alias 'Creamy' suggests the problems posed to traditional conceptions of British identity by a character who, in Bhabha's terms, is 'not quite/not white',[44] Shahid – who is 'not quite' Pakistani (BA, 2) – poses a similar challenge to the singular conception of origin around which Riaz's group organises. Its purist conception of identity is sustained only by severe – and, for Kureishi, unnecessary – (self-)repressions. Thus Chad's self-mutilation during the arson attack is prefigured in his struggle against the temptations of Shahid's music collection. Shahid is constantly expected to conform to the cultural attitudes and practices of village life in Pakistan. As in his other writing, however, Kureishi's novels use Pakistan as a point of reference which shows Britain in a relatively positive light. Thus, on his visits to his own family in the subcontinent, Shahid has been dismayed by even his middle-class relatives' antipathy to what is foreign, especially all things Indian. For example, one cousin detests yoga because it is 'Hindu' (while also advocating Gandhism!). The group's attempts to coerce Shahid, intellectually, psychologically and physically, and to enforce the principle of obedience to the leader have quasi-fascist overtones, which the book-burning reinforces. The attempted sacking of Deedee's house, which forces her into hiding, has all too ironic parallels with the far Right's attacks on the home of the Bengali family on the estate. As is the case with Anwar, such 'resistance' replicates the worst aspects of the system which the group is fighting (compare the treatment of the Asian Youth Movement in *Borderline*).

The politics of anti-racism

However, if Kureishi's novels are hostile to cultural nationalism, whether this is expressed from within the majority or minority ethnicities, they are – perhaps more surprisingly, given each text's depiction of the grim realities of racism in contemporary England – also critical of a variety of metropolitan anti-racisms. The detailed attention given in the novels to this issue marks a significant extension of Kureishi's previous treatment of questions of race and ethnicity, though the issue is certainly broached in earlier work, for example – as Chapter 2 suggested – in the context of Susan's attitudes in *Borderline*.

In neither novel is 'liberal' anti-racism ever dismissed out of hand. One mark of Riaz's fanaticism is that he 'pronounced the word "liberal" as if it were the name of a murderer' (BA, 153). The attitudes of characters like Helen and Eva in *The Buddha* are clearly preferable to those of Hairy Back or Aunt Jean. Nonetheless, they are consistently linked to an unhealthy veneration of cultures of non-western origin, which is often expressed in the language of a patronising exoticism. Thus, Eva prizes Karim because he is 'so exotic, so original!' (BS, 9); conversely, she despises Margaret in part because the latter is simply too English. The racial 'Other' in Kureishi's novels is often repre-sented as one more niche object of consumption by the liberal centre, whether in regard to his/her exotic ways of thinking (Haroon's teachings), in terms of novel kinds of sexual experience (the basis of Helen's attraction to Karim), or in the more material form of tourism or 'ethnic' products such as the 'lacquered boxes on the dresser, the silk cushion from Thailand' in Eleanor's home (BS, 186). If all this points to what Karim complains of as liberalism's habit of 'fetishizing' the non-western 'Other' (BS, 213), such exoticising attitudes are, ironic-ally, often accompanied by ignorance, or even plain ethno-centrism. Thus, Helen's eager approval of Haroon is offset by her refusal to touch the baggage of the recently-arrived Changez, through a ludicrous fear of contracting malaria, and she turns away from him in disgust at Jamila's wedding party when she sees him eating with his fingers.

Implicit in Helen's attitudes is a conception of multi-culturalism which accepts difference only *in relation to* a centre, the normative cultural authority of which remains essentially undisturbed. As she comments to Haroon: 'We like you being here. You benefit our country with your traditions' (BS, 74). At times, such exoticism has a more obviously coercive quality, becoming a mirror image of Anwar's insistence that minorities remain true to their roots. While emphasising the crucial value of Karim's 'colour' and cultural background to the role of Mowgli, Shadwell sneers at his protégé's inability to speak an Indian language and the fact that he has never visited the subcontinent. Such demands for authenticity are evident in *The Black Album* too, for example in Strapper's increasing disgust with Shahid, whom he sees as betraying his supposed culture of origin:

> 'I thought you loved the Asian people'.
> 'Not when they get too fucking Westernized. You all wanna be just like us now. It's the wrong turnin'.' (BA, 162)

The absurd double bind in which characters like Shahid and Karim are placed by such attitudes has a deeply ironic resonance when placed in the context of the metropolitan literature of empire. A streak of primitivism runs through such work which privileges the unspoiled pastoralist over the (semi-)educated, urban-dwelling native (variously figured through the trope of the 'babu' or 'mission boy'), who is the product of (partial) assimilation to western norms. This attitude, of course, conflicts radically with the colonial project of 'redeeming' the colonised subject by imposing western civilisation on him/her (as in Macaulay's 'Minute on Education'). If, as Bhabha suggests, this divided vision of the colonised reveals the conflictual nature of colonial discourse, it can also place the (formerly) colonised in a disempoweringly contradictory subject-position (rather than, as Bhabha implies, simply providing a space for resistance).[45] Thus, in Dr. Bob's apartment in New York, Karim and Tracey are given the best seats at the performance by the Haitian troupe precisely because of their minority status. Simultaneously feted and marginalised by this arrangement, the disturbed Karim comments knowingly: 'It made me feel like a colonial watching the natives perform' (BS, 244).

Kureishi is harsher still about seemingly more self-aware and sophisticated radical-Left anti-racist politics. Again, neither novel represents the Left entirely unsympathetically (after all Haroon is a former socialist – compare Hussein in *Laundrette* – and Jamila admires Gramsci). In *The Black Album*, Brownlow's solidarity with Riaz puts his career on the line and he acts throughout with a kind of 'mad honesty' (BA, 203) which Shahid finds beguiling; but, like Pyke in *The Buddha*, Brownlow is personally compromised in a number of obvious ways. The descent of this representative of the 'upper-middle-classes' (BA, 26) on the oppressed Bangladeshi family smacks of the 'political tourism' associated with his visit to Soweto. His attitude of 'unmistakable lewdness' (BA, 78) towards Tahira aligns with him the male Orientalist gaze anatomised by Said and his consistent misrecognition of Shahid (whom he believes to be Tariq) implies that even to Brownlow all British Asians 'look the same'.

While both novels consistently identify the radical Left with the same kind of personal hypocrisy associated with religious 'nativists' like Anwar, it is, nevertheless, the shortcomings of its politics which are Kureishi's primary interest. In *The Black Album*, for example, the Labour politician George Rugman Rudder's professed solidarity with Riaz's group is clearly an opportunistic means to winning votes. Kureishi wickedly deflates his anti-racist credentials by giving the hungry activist the line 'I could murder an Indian' (BA, 149), a (comically) grotesque solecism in the context of the text's engagement with the Rushdie affair. In *The Buddha* Eleanor detests Labour and refuses to donate to 'the Party' on the grounds that both are racist institutions. Like Terry and Pyke in *The Buddha*, Brownlow sees racism in the last analysis as an expression of economic disadvantage amongst both those who articulate it and those who have to deal with it, implicitly reducing race to a secondary category in the more important dialectic of class struggle.[46] Brownlow's advocacy of 'Reason' – which Riaz contextualises as the reason of 'a minority who live in northern Europe' (BA, 82) – even leads him at one point to describe his ally as 'the slave of superstition' (BA, 80). This suggests that Brownlow, no less than Helen, approaches questions of cultural difference from a supposedly 'universalist' perspective which in practice orders and assigns value to cultural beliefs and practices in a way which reinforces the West as normative. His master-narratives thus amount to little more than a different kind of regulation, even subordination, of the 'Other' in the contemporary metropolis.

The Black Album extends Kureishi's critique of radical forms of metropolitan anti-racism by a more specific focus on the relationship between western feminism and the struggles of the racially oppressed, a topic which is by comparison less explicit in *Sammy and Rosie*. Deedee clearly identifies herself as a feminist (she has been awakened by Gloria Steinem and *Spare Rib*), a commitment she shares with fictional predecessors in the sub-genre of 'the university novel' like Robyn Penrose in Lodge's *Nice Work*, of whom she is a more radicalised version, both in her pedagogical politics and in the conduct of her private life. As with Robyn (and Miss Cutmore in *The Buddha*), there is an unmistakable whiff of the female colonial missionary about Deedee. For instance, amongst the three college students who are lodgers in her home are two young British-Asian women whom Deedee sees herself as having 'liberated' from an oppressive and obscurantist home environment. In this context Deedee's feminism is clearly vulnerable to the charge of ethnocentrism brought by Chad: 'Would I dare to hide a member of Osgood's family in my house and fill her with propaganda? If I did, what accusations? Terrorist! Fanatic! Lunatic! We can never win. The imperialist idea hasn't died' (BA, 191).[47]

The problem is again apparent in Deedee's conduct as a teacher. At one point, Shahid passes 'the hut in which she was teaching "her" girls, a class of black women fashion students. One of them was, somewhat embarrassedly, standing on a chair. The others were giggling and clapping. Deedee was also laughing and pointing at the woman's shoes' (BA, 184). The location (a 'hut'), the 'spectacle' which the black student is making of herself at her teacher's behest, the emphatic use of the possessive adjective – all contribute to making this scene a parodic reinscription of a common trope in colonial discourse, the gaze of the coloniser on the 'manners and customs' of the subject peoples.[48]

Deedee's relationship with Shahid raises similar issues. Kureishi performs a bold stroke in revising a common theme in post-war academic fiction, the desire of male lecturers for female students. From Amis's *Lucky Jim* (1954), through Bradbury's *Eating People is Wrong* and *The History Man* (1975), to Howard Jacobson's *Coming from Behind* (1983) and Lodge's *Small World* (1984), this is a consistent trope. *The Black Album* is perhaps the first novel of its kind to admit the possibility not just of a cross-race, staff–student liaison but that women lecturers, characteristically represented by these earlier male writers as 'neurotic', isolated and unlovable – especially if they have feminist inclinations – can be both attractive and capable of desire, which might even extend to their male students (though it has to be said that Deedee remains in some respects stereotypically 'neurotic').

However, while Shahid is by no means an innocent – he has hastily abandoned a girlfriend after a late abortion and at moments glories in his 'possession' of Deedee – and while the affair conforms in some respects to the conventions of an *éducation sentimentale* (Flaubert's text is part of Shahid's syllabus) – Deedee's attitude to her lover nonetheless reinscribes certain elements of Orientalist discourse. Thus, although Shahid is never simply the silent and passive object of her attention, Deedee instigates the liaison and there is an inescapable sense that she is abusing her position of power, as she herself seems to acknowledge implicitly in her anxiety that the relationship should not be discovered at college. The unequal power relations are particularly evident early in their affair, when Shahid often feels coerced by a mentor who behaves towards him in a manner reminiscent of Riaz (and of Shadwell and Pyke's treatment of Karim in *The Buddha*): 'But he didn't like being slotted into her plans, as if he were being hired for a job, the specifications of which she had prepared already' (BA, 102). Sadiq's comment that 'she is having it away with two Rastamen' (BA, 190) may be simply a slur to alienate Shahid from Deedee, but there is no evidence to contradict the supposition that Shahid's ethnicity is a crucial factor in Deedee's choice of him as a sexual partner, especially when she waxes lyrical about his 'cafe-au-lait' skin. As Tahira complains: 'Our people have always been sexual objects for the whites' (BA, 190).

Deedee increasingly sees it as her mission to save Shahid from the fate that his attraction to Riaz's community represents in her eyes. To this extent, *The Black Album* can be approached in terms of Spivak's analysis of the discourse surrounding the prohibition of *sati* in nineteenth-century India which was organised, she suggests, around the trope of '[w]hite men saving brown women from brown men'.[49] By contrast, Deedee can be understood as the 'benevolent' white woman who intervenes to save the brown man from his fellows. This rearranges the terms of the colonial trope without disturbing the racialised power relations which underpin it. Moreover, Kureishi stresses that it is only by placing Shahid in the subject-position of oppressed victim (which he strenuously resists) that the 'benevolence' of figures like Deedee, no less than that of Pyke and Terry in *The Buddha*, can operate. The coercive nature of her 'benevolence' is particularly evident in Deedee's insistence on Shahid's unequivocal rejection of Riaz, which entails the rejection of potentially crucial parts of his identity. Damagingly for Deedee, this links her to much more obviously racist figures like Chad's foster-mother.

Kureishi's anxieties about Deedee's politics reach a climax with her attempt to disrupt Riaz's book-burning protest by calling in the police. Certain kinds of western feminism, it seems, may be no less absolutist – and no less unwilling to resort to force and censorship, in support of supposedly 'universal' values (from the effects of which, ironically, feminists have complained that they have suffered historically quite as much as any other 'minority' formation), than the 'fundamentalism' she opposes. As Sadiq complains: 'Our voices suppressed by Osgood types with the colonial mentality. To her we coolies not cool' (BA, 181). As such responses suggest, as much as other kinds of western radicalism, metropolitan feminism's desire to help give voice to or liberate the oppressed may reinscribe power relations which preserve the authority of the ethnic centre.

Conclusion

The Buddha is, by common consent, the more accomplished of Kureishi's novels. Indeed, it is often regarded as his single best work.[50] *The Black Album*, by comparison, has been seen as an altogether inferior achievement, both by reviewers and in the academic world. To some extent, the differences between the novels are comparable to those between *Laundrette* and *Sammy and Rosie*, as one might infer from one of the most perceptive initial responses to Kureishi's second novel, Anthony Appiah's review in *The New York Times*:

> Unfortunately, what is arresting in 'The Black Album' is overwhelmed by its longueurs. Mr Kureishi, though best known as a screen-writer, is essentially a comic novelist.

'The Buddha of Suburbia' was extremely funny; its characters managed to be both flawed and appealing: and, if it dragged just a little at the end, one forgave it after its brilliant beginning. But the humour in 'The Black Album' largely fails; though Mr Kureishi has not lost his ear for the many dialects of modern British speech, his characters are schematic and, one feels, unloved even by their author. The raunchiness that some, at least, admired in the earlier book has been replaced by routinized descriptions of the hydraulics of moderately unroutine sex. All of which is especially disappointing, since in the passages that impinge on the Rushdie affair, where Mr Kureishi explores the path that has led some young British Pakistanis to a form of Islamic fundamentalism, the book is both compassionate and illuminating.[51]

Formally, the second novel is certainly less assured than the first. Although highly episodic, *The Buddha* is successfully shaped and held together by its focalisation through Karim's first-person vision of his emergence into adulthood. The social issues tackled in the text emerge more organically as part of Karim's developing vision of the world. As Appiah suggests, *The Black Album* is more 'objective', largely because of its third-person narrative mode, and more schematic. It is structured by the binary opposition, established at the outset, between the values represented by Riaz and Deedee respectively. Episodes and scenes are arranged symmetrically across this fault line. Thus Shahid goes first to the rave, then to the mosque, contrasting the different kinds of community and (comparably 'ecstatic'?) human experience they are respectively capable of creating; and the white extremists' attack on the Bengali family goes in tandem with the brown extremists' attack on Deedee's house. The main plot is not so much a plot in the traditional sense as the repetition of the dilemma that one knows from the beginning that Shahid will sooner or later have to resolve. In contrast to the open-ended *Buddha*, Shahid does apparently resolve his dilemma (though – as will be seen – the significance of his choice is deeply ambiguous).

As is the case with *Sammy and Rosie*, some of the problems

of *The Black Album* can be attributed to an insufficiently integrated mixture of styles and aims. Insofar as he tries to provide
a more 'collective' vision than in *The Buddha* (compare the
differences Spivak identifies between the 'lyrical' *Laundrette*
and *Sammy and Rosie*), Kureishi attempts to give Shahid, Deedee
– and even Riaz up to a point – the distinctness, *gravitas* and
complexity traditionally associated with the three-dimensional
characters of social realism. In fact, however, each of them
remains fundamentally static throughout the text, representing
the various cultural/political choices and perspectives in which
Kureishi is interested in a way which is more consonant with a
roman à thèse. (Kureishi's 'fringe' background is an influence in
this respect.) Even Shahid develops relatively little and, insofar
as he does so, the process is presented primarily in terms of
intellectual rather than affective choices. (In any case, it is never
made clear why a figure who is so obviously comfortable in
secular Britain should turn to 'fundamentalism' in the first place.)
Indeed, none of the major characters has real vitality of inner
life. Consequently, as Appiah suggests, one feels little empathy
for them. Certainly, none have the appeal of a character like
Changez in *The Buddha*. (In this regard, the subjective mode of
The Buddha generates a much more intimate engagement with
Karim's emotional life.)

As Appiah also notes, some of the writing in *The Black
Album* is laboured, particularly in the scenes depicting Shahid's
relationship with Deedee. Not only is the lovers' dialogue often
wooden but the sex scenes are perhaps primarily responsible for
the longueurs of which Appiah complains. Both texts refer to
the work of Henry Miller and one suspects that Kureishi has
either the ambition to emulate the American author's innovative, if politically problematic, writing about sexuality – or to
parody it as part of the critique of counter-cultural hedonism
which becomes much more explicit in Kureishi's subsequent
writing. Neither of these putative aims is fulfilled. The sex
scenes in fact read like the tired 'eroticism' of men's magazines
(for which Kureishi occasionally wrote in his apprentice years).[52]
In fact, as Appiah suggests, *The Black Album* only really comes

to novelistic life in the subplot involving the comic caricatures Chili, Strapper and Zulma.

However, not only do such caricatures clash formally with the more developed characters, but the subplot poses problems for the novel as a whole which are never resolved. In the first place, it bears only a somewhat adventitious relation to Shahid's problem of choosing between the values represented by Deedee and Riaz respectively. As in *Laundrette*, this subplot involves a pastiche of the conventions of the gangster genre, with drugs once again the focus of interest. However, while it perhaps constitutes a response to Kureishi's complaint that 'religion [can't] admit the comic' (BA, 124), it also runs the danger of trivialising the central issues addressed by the book. In any case, *The Black Album* rarely reaches the level of comedy achieved in *The Buddha*. There are moments of the latter text's wit, as when the would-be gangster Chili complains of England that 'real glory was impossible in a country where the policemen wore helmets shaped like sawn-off marrows' (BA, 44), but the wit and jokes are as often leaden as successful.

However, if *The Black Album* is less impressive *as a novel* than *The Buddha*, its shortcomings are partly offset by what one might infer from Appiah's review to be its greater ambition as a 'condition of England' text. It confronts much more explicitly than the first novel the *political* challenges of 'multiculturalism', unerringly jarring the raw nerve of what is perhaps the central dilemma of contemporary Left-liberal thinking about issues of race and ethnicity. In Amy Gutmann's view, this pulls in contradictory, potentially incommensurable, directions, 'both to the protection of the basic rights of individuals as human beings and to the acknowledgement of the particular needs of individuals as members of specific groups'.[53] What she calls 'the demand for recognition' by such groups constitutes a crucial problem for strategies aimed at the achievement of social justice:

> Do most people need a secure cultural context to give meaning and guidance to their choices in life? If so, then a secure cultural context also ranks among the primary

goods, basic to most people's prospects for living what they
can identify as a good life. And liberal democratic states
are obligated to help disadvantaged groups preserve their
culture against intrusions by majoritarian or 'mass'
cultures.[54]

The conflict which Shahid experiences between the values
espoused by Deedee and Riaz involves this contest between the
rights of the individual and the rights of minorities *as communities*.
As Tahira objects about Deedee: 'She believes in equality,
all right, but only if we forget that we are different' (BA, 191).
Tahira's comments suggest Kureishi's troubled recognition that
the question of intercultural conflict in the contemporary West
cannot be resolved within a legal and cultural framework which
is exclusively concerned with the rights of the individual. At the
same time, however, *The Black Album* clearly endorses the right
of the individual, especially the artist, to liberty of thought and
expression. Seen in this light, the meaning of the novel's ending
is hard to unravel. Kureishi's decision to conclude it with Shahid
fleeing London in Deedee's company might be understood as a
final endorsement of her perspective, flawed as it undoubtedly
seems. Equally, it could be seen as an evasion of the issues which
have been raised. There is possibly a 'third way' of interpreting
the ending, however. If Shahid finally disavows Riaz's
conviction of a given community's right to determine the social
function of 'its' art and the work of the individual artist who
supposedly belongs to that community, his reconciliation with
Deedee at the end of the text may represent no more than a
partial, temporary and 'strategic' alignment with her.

Kureishi's novel could be claimed as a courageous example
of a minority artist's refusal to pass over the shortcomings of the
politics of certain minority formations with which he might be
deemed to be (however loosely) connected.[55] However, *The
Black Album* also lends itself in certain respects to being
interpreted as an example of the 'Orientalist' thinking which it
is ostensibly so keen to challenge. Two of the oldest 'Orientalist'
stereotypes, 'eastern' despotism and the superstitious nature of
Islam, recur in the treatment of Riaz and the unfortunate

passages relating to the divinely-inscribed aubergine.[56] It is also curious that a novel which is so preoccupied with the evils of censorship should itself be so circumspect about the fact that it is addressing the Rushdie affair. *The Satanic Verses* is never named as the text which Riaz's group burns. This has serious implications for the text's representation of Islam. Whereas the *Satanic Verses* affair was a one-off, one might infer from *The Black Album* that Muslims would be likely to react in a similar way to any kind of artistic representation which was felt to be against the spirit of Islam. The problem is compounded by the absence of any other kind of Muslim than those associated with Riaz. The inference might be drawn that there is no such thing as a moderate Muslim.[57] To this extent, *The Black Album* reiterates the association of Islam with extremism in 'university novels' like *Eating People is Wrong* or D. J. Enright's *Academic Year* (1955). The other aspects of Riaz's resistance – against police harassment of minorities, for example – get forgotten in the rush to condemn his hostility to certain kinds of art.[58] To this extent, Kureishi's own liberalism proves no less absolutist that Deedee's, whatever the force of his critique of her perspectives. If *The Black Album* manifests a similar degree of ideological confusion to *Sammy and Rosie,* it might also be argued that Kureishi's recognition of the 'incommensurability' of the competing claims involved in 'the politics of recognition' hastened his decision to turn away in his more recent work from his hitherto characteristic focus on issues of race and ethnicity (although *My Son the Fanatic* represents one final attempt to grapple with some of the most vexing but pressing issues in contemporary cultural/political life which are raised in *The Black Album*).

Recent work

The short stories

Since *The Black Album*, Kureishi has so far produced two volumes of short stories, a screenplay, a novella and his first original play since *Birds of Passage* (1983). Although these are discrete pieces, and encompass a wide variety of genres, there is good reason for considering the five works as a group. In his recent writing, as earlier in his career, Kureishi works incrementally, continuously revising and elaborating key themes, attitudes and ideas. Thus, the film of *My Son the Fanatic* (1997) develops out of a tale in *Love in a Blue Time* (1997) and *Sleep With Me* (1999) reworks aspects of *Intimacy* (1998) in dramatic form. Indeed, certain lines in *Love in a Blue Time* are repeated verbatim in *Intimacy* and from there to *Sleep With Me*. For this reason, while focusing on the two volumes of stories which as I write (*Gabriel's Gift*, published in February 2001, has appeared too late for consideration in this volume) stand either side of Kureishi's output since 1995, the first section of this chapter will offer some frameworks for understanding the recent work as a whole.

Despite what was intimated in the conclusion to the last chapter, Kureishi's recent writing does not mark a complete break from his previous work. Themes, character types and tropes from the novels (and before) are all reshuffled and reconsidered. 'My Son the Fanatic' (and the film which it inspired), 'We're Not Jews' and 'With Your Tongue Down My Throat' (all LBT) provide further examinations of race and ethnicity. Dysfunctional families are as common as ever, as is the breakdown of long-term relationships. As Bill puts it in 'D'Accord, Baby': 'These days every man and woman was a cuckold. And why not, when marriage was insufficient to satisfy most human need?' (LBT, 54). Parvez in *My Son the Fanatic* has many points in common with Haroon in *The Buddha*, from a commitment to liberalism to a love of jazz. Meanwhile his son shares much with Farhat ('Hat') in *The Black Album*; both are accountancy students who, disgusted with secular Britain, turn to religion. Parvez's relationship with Bettina is another in the series of cross-racial liaisons and his increasingly problematic friendship with the small businessman Fizzy echoes Haroon's with Anwar. Tropes which are reworked include those of escape and roots. However, these are now often presented in more abstract terms, with philosophers like Kierkegaard, Sartre and Camus being important points of reference. The absence of secure anchors leaves many of Kureishi's characters adrift on a storm-filled existential sea from which no harbours are visible: 'But what were lives for? Who could say?' (LBT, 158).

Moreover, although the short story ostensibly marks a new departure in Kureishi's restless journey through successive genres, he had in fact been working intermittently in the form for some ten years. Indeed, *Laundrette* and *The Buddha* were initially conceived as short stories. What became the first chapter of the latter began life in rather different form in *Harper's* magazine in 1987, the same year as 'With Your Tongue Down My Throat' (LBT) was published in *Granta*; two years later, 'Esther' appeared in *Atlantic Monthly*. *Love in a Blue Time* and *Midnight All Day* thus represent a decision to concentrate on a genre which had long fascinated Kureishi. At the launch of the former volume, he stated that he had for many years been in the habit of reading short stories before going to sleep and mentioned Isaac Bashevis Singer, Raymond Carver and John Cheever as favourites.[1] Kureishi's novels indicate a great admiration for classical exponents of the genre; *The Buddha* refers to Chekhov and *The Black Album* to Maupassant as figures of whom Karim and Shahid (himself an aspiring short-story writer) are particularly fond. (Indeed, Kureishi's short stories seem a logical development from the often highly episodic novels.)

Furthermore, Kureishi's recent work is still, in the main, resolutely realist in mode, favouring what the photographer Eshan in 'Blue, Blue Pictures of You' describes as 'minimal props and hard, direct lighting' (LBT, 108). Very few of the short stories are experimental to any degree. 'The Penis' (MAD) is a surrealistic (cod)piece along the lines of a beast fable and there is some evidence of what one might call 'postmodern rewriting'; examples of such pastiche include 'Flies' (LBT), which draws heavily on Calvino's 'The Argentine Ant', 'Lately' (LBT), based on Chekhov's 'The Duel' and 'That Was Then' (MAD), which reworks Carver's 'Intimacy'.[2] However, it is notable that the models on which Kureishi bases his pastiches are not in any way avant-garde. Even 'The Argentine Ant', like Camus's *The Plague* (1947), to which Kureishi's tale also apparently alludes (LBT, 209), is primarily a realist allegory of the effects of moral bad faith on a whole community.

In terms of technique there is, nonetheless, a difference of emphasis between the two collections of short stories. *Love in a Blue Time* belongs more to the tradition represented by Maupassant, the early Kipling and Saki, in which there is an emphasis on suspense and dramatic revelation, often achieved by surprising reversals, as in the denouements of 'In a Blue Time' or 'My Son the Fanatic'. Perhaps the best example, however, is 'With Your Tongue Down My Throat', which turns on the startling revelation that Howard Coleman has in fact been ventriloquising Nina's voice throughout. As well as providing an effective narrative climax, the reversal enforces a thorough revaluation of the tale's ostensible cultural/political meanings.[3] In *Midnight All Day*, by contrast, the predominant influences are Chekhov and the Joyce of *Dubliners*, whom the protagonist of 'Midnight All Day' (MAD) regrets not having spent more time reading when he was younger (MAD, 171). The characteristically anti-climactic and naturalistic slices of largely unexceptional lives in this volume emulate these masters' seemingly inconsequential, observational style which achieves its effects by delicacy of perception, moral implication and psychological insight, rather than by manipulation of plot.

Nonetheless, Kureishi's recent work does represent something of a watershed. His turning to the short story form indicates a weariness with the ambitious canvases of the films and novels which address in extensive fashion the massive theme of 'the condition of England' in the 1970s and 1980s. In relation to Kureishi's identity as a 'world writer', the most important development is the diminished importance of issues of race and ethnicity. None of the three stories in which they remain central was written later than 1994 (and 'With Your Tongue Down My Throat' dates back to the time of *Sammy and Rosie*). Of the seven more recent tales in *Love in a Blue Time*, none has a protagonist who is obviously from an ethnic minority. Only one story in *Midnight All Day*, 'Girl', revolves around an Asian-British character, but even here Majid's ethnicity is ostensibly of marginal importance. Similarly, while the narrator of *Intimacy* and his best friend are Asian-British, this has little obvious relevance to the meanings of the novella. Meanwhile in *Sleep With Me*, there is no ethnic minority character, nor is race even mentioned.[4]

The recent writing is also ostensibly more 'personal' than previous work. While it is dangerous to approach any of Kureishi's texts as transparent reflections of his own experience, it is certainly the case that his output since 1995 bears the marks of dramatic changes in his private life. *Love in a Blue Time* prefigures *Intimacy* in its teasing invitations to see his latest texts as autobiographical. For example, the narrator of 'In a Blue Time' (LBT) admires *Armacord* as a film in which 'Fellini's whole life was present' (LBT, 17) and 'Blue, Blue Pictures of You' asserts that to 'represent oneself – a changing being, alive with virtues and idiocies – was, for Eshan, the task that entailed the most honesty and fulfilment' (LBT, 108). Kureishi's troubling of the boundaries between fiction and autobiography (perhaps the most experimental aspect of his recent writing) is also evident in the frame-breaking self-referentiality of stories like 'Strangers When We Meet', in which the narrator refers to a film he has made that closely resembles *London Kills Me* and to a contemporary account of the breakdown of a relationship with clear parallels to *Intimacy*: 'It is relentless, and, probably because it rings true, has been taken exception to' (MAD, 48).

In this context, the most important facts are as follows: in 1993, Kureishi became the father of twins and the following year turned forty. He became increasingly unhappy in his personal life and in 1995 began a relationship with Monique Proudlove, with whom he had a son in 1998. The acrimonious parting from the mother of his twin boys and partner of seven years, Tracey Scoffield, received a lot of unfavourable media coverage which, it could be argued, unfairly influenced the reception of much of his subsequent work, particularly *Intimacy* and *Sleep With Me*.[5] Career factors also played a part in Kureishi's mid-life crisis. By the early 1990s the *enfant terrible* of the 1970s and 1980s had established a considerable reputation, with an Oscar nomination, a Whitbread prize for fiction and a blue- blood publisher; he was in demand as a scriptwriter (*The Buddha* was made into a four-part BBC series in 1993 and projects that Kureishi declined included the Corporation's ultimately aborted adaptation of Rushdie's *Midnight's Children*). Such success did not, however, keep self-doubt at bay, particularly when *London Kills Me* and *The Black Album* signally failed to repeat the success of some of his earlier work.

These developments are reflected in certain distinctly new emphases in Kureishi's recent work. The characteristic social milieu of the short stories is often – especially in *Midnight All Day* – very comfortable, as his own had become. While Nina in 'With Your Tongue Down My Throat' (LBT) lives on a 'sink' estate and Baxter in 'Flies' (MAD) is unemployed, many of Kureishi's recent protagonists – like Rob in 'Strangers When We Meet' or Aurelia in 'Sucking Stones' (both MAD) – make a good living out of 'the culture industries'. This enables them to inhabit what Nina describes as 'honeyed London' (LBT: 72), areas of the capital only fleetingly glimpsed in *The Buddha* (Pyke's mansion in St John's Wood) or *The Black Album* (Zulma's Knightsbridge flat). Most of the work that such characters produce, however, is – as they themselves recognise –

of little real merit despite its marketability. Much is grudgingly produced simply to support the insatiable demands of growing families. In 'D'Accord, Baby' (LBT), Bill has to shelve his own projects in favour of 'well-paid but journeyman work. Now that Nicola was pregnant he would have to do more of it' (LBT, 57–8). Other artist-protagonists suffer comparable frustrations. Rocco in 'Lately' (LBT) and Marcia in 'Sucking Stones' (MAD) are unfulfilled talents, and Roy of 'In a Blue Time' (LBT) is convinced that his creativity has dried up, an anxiety which afflicts the protagonists of *Intimacy* and *Sleep With Me* as well.

A new emphasis is also apparent in the age group Kureishi has chosen to write about since 1995. The two novels, like most previous work, focused on the joys and tribulations of youth. In Shahid's London it 'was rare to see anyone over forty, as if there were a curfew for older people' (BA, 93). By contrast, the recent writing favours an older set of characters, for whom – like Majid in 'Girl', most young people are simply not 'interesting in themselves any more' (MAD, 97). Many recent protagonists are now, like Kureishi himself, parents. The father–son relationship – a staple theme in his earlier writing – recurs, but it tends to be presented much more from the father's point of view – whether in *My Son the Fanatic* or stories like 'The Flies' (LBT) and 'Strangers When We Meet' (MAD). Many characters in both collections of tales are acutely conscious of the onset of middle age and of its physical symptoms, whether 'greying', sciatica or spreading stomachs. The accumulation of family responsibilities is responded to – particularly in the first collection – with varying degrees of resignation, panic and dismay. The 'blue time' of the title is thus on one level a metaphor for the uncertainties provoked by loss of youth.

The pains of ageing (and growing up) are most apparent in Kureishi's treatment of personal relationships. In the short stories, as in other recent work, mid-life crisis is often expressed in the breakdown of long-term relationships. Whereas in the novels these are presented from the perspective of outside observers, both collections include a number of spine-chilling depictions of failing love, with its attendant bewilderment, deceit and spite, experienced from the inside. Littered with abandoned partners, the short stories are obsessed with the moral dilemmas and emotional consequences (a key word throughout the recent writing) which separation involves. The pain caused both for leavers and those who are left is often far greater than was foreseen, leaving many of Kureishi's recent characters, from the narrator of 'Nightlight' (LBT) to Charles in *Sleep With Me,* in a state of desolation. Children are often pawns in marital strife and far more vulnerable than the teenage Karim in *The Buddha*: devasted young survivors of separation include Nina in 'With Your Tongue Down My Throat' (LBT) and Mikey in 'Morning in the Bowl of Night' (MAD).

Kureishi often represents affective relations as a battlefield without any rules of engagement in his recent writing, in which issues of gender replace those relating to ethnicity as his principal focus.[6] (To this extent, Kureishi is now part of a dominant socio-cultural formation, rather than writing from a 'subaltern' perspective.) To some degree, the stories reflect Kureishi's continuing sympathy for feminist ideas. The motif of the put-upon mother is as strong as ever. 'Girl' and 'Sucking Stones' (both MAD) provide further desolate portraits of isolated older women who (like Margaret in *The Buddha*) have sacrificed their lives to ungrateful husbands and children, graphically illustrating the damage done to some women by conforming to traditional expectations of gender roles. Equally, Kureishi provides many seemingly satiric examples of apparently appalling sexism, such as Roy and Jimmy's exploitation of young women eager to enter the media in 'In a Blue Time' (LBT), which fully justify Nina's complaint in 'With Your Tongue Down My Throat' that: 'Men are pretty selfish bastards who don't understand us' (LBT, 79). The underdevelopment of some men's sense of responsibility is a recurrent theme of the recent writing. As Sophie puts it in *Sleep With Me*: 'It is simple for men to argue that people should follow their passion. But who plans the children's meals, thinks of their health, clothes, schooling?' (SWM, 15). In addition, a critique of 'laddishness' might also be inferred from Kureishi's emphasis on a sour male competitiveness (anticipated at moments in Karim's jealousy of Charlie in *The Buddha*) between friends like Jay and Victor in *Intimacy*. By contrast, feminist ideas are also vindicated in those stories, particularly in *Midnight All Day*, which celebrate the greater role in parenting which is available to contemporary fathers. The many tender portraits in Kureishi's recent writing of men's relations with their young children suggest that the reconfiguration of masculinities in the wake of the Women's Movement has also benefited men.

On the other hand, many of the short stories, or their protagonists at least, express a deeper and more angry vein of the misogyny articulated by flawed characters in the novels like Anwar. This is often expressed in terms of a 'common sense' which suggests that the promiscuous gratification of sexual desire is 'natural' to masculinity. This makes Kureishi's representations of 'laddishness' more ambivalent than has just been suggested. Examples of the explicit anti-feminism articulated by Brownlow in *The Black Album* are more frequent in the recent work, from the opening story of *Love in a Blue Time*, where Roy rails against 'feminist absurdities' (LBT, 15), to 'Sucking Stones', where the successful writer Aurelia dismisses Marcia's feminism as simplistic in itself and irrelevant to contemporary realities (MAD, 130). Avowed feminists, from Deborah in 'With Your Tongue Down My Throat' to Marcia herself are generally represented as more inadequate and foolish than Deedee in *The Black Album*. As striking as the antipathy towards strong women, like Clara in 'In a Blue Time' (LBT), or Susan in *Intimacy*, is the recurrence of 'girl-women' as objects of desire in Kureishi's recent work – in contrast to the two novels, which focus to a large extent on young men's relations with older female mentors.

While it is not always clear whether Kureishi is attempting to provide a critique of patriarchal attitudes or endorsing them, partly because of the variety of predicaments, perspectives and characters represented in the short stories, they nonetheless testify to the pain and confusions entailed by the changing nature of gender relations in the contemporary period. Of a typical social event, the narrator of *Intimacy* observes: 'As usual the women were talking about work and the men about children'

(I, 90), but such adjustments are not without their casualties. One example is the narrator of 'Nightlight' (LBT), who determinedly espouses the role of 'new man' in his marriage: 'For a while he did try to be the sort of man she might countenance ... Soon he didn't know who he was supposed to be. They both got lost' (LBT, 141). Kureishi's stories are riddled with instances of male depression, isolation and anxiety which are the consequence of failed negotiations of the demand for new forms of masculinity. There is an abundance of therapists in the recent fiction, from Feather in 'Lately' (LBT) to Marty in 'Sucking Stones' (MAD) who make a living from damaged men who have been unable to answer the question 'what men are for. Do they serve any useful function these days?' (I, 87; in *The Black Album*, by contrast, therapy and self-help are the preserve of women like Deedee).

Perhaps most contentiously, Kureishi's recent writing implies that one way that men should respond to such developments is by aspiring to some of the freedoms achieved by the Women's Movement. In *Intimacy*, Jay expresses envy about the strides taken by contemporary women and reflects ruefully on men's comparative stasis (I, 54). In 'That Was Then', Nick has written a best-selling memoir which clearly reflects some of Kureishi's new concerns: 'The last chapter was concerned with what men, and fathers, could become, having been released, as women were two decades earlier, from some of their conventional expectations' (MAD, 68). Perhaps the most important such 'conventional expectation' from which women are now deemed to have liberated themselves is discussed in 'Lately' (LBT), where Karen asserts that her sex no longer has any obligation to remain loyal to loveless marriages. Some of Kureishi's tales suggest that this attitude should be copied by men. Time and again, they revolve round the dilemma facing Roger in 'The Umbrella': 'There was no just or objective way to resolve completing claims: those of freedom – his freedom – to live and develop as he liked, against the right of his family to have his dependable presence' (MAD, 186). Time and again it is resolved by the man's departure. From 'Lately' (LBT) to 'Strangers When

We Meet' (MAD), the stories stress the potentially redemptive effects of separation: 'One only sees these things as tragic if one has a certain view of relationships ... That the duration of a relationship is the measure of its success' (LBT, 168).

As such evidence might suggest, Kureishi's recent work is generally darker in tone than his previous writing. Both short story collections, like *Sleep With Me*, are inflected by a millennial gloom, a sense that 'the century is old', as Baxter's neighbour puts it in 'Flies' (LBT, 206). *Midnight All Day* alludes intermittently to the horrors of the twentieth century, with particular reference to the Holocaust and Stalin's purges. The 'blue' mood of Roger, the human-rights activist in 'The Umbrella', is exacerbated by his reflections on the continuing savagery and brutality around the world on the eve of a new millennium. More than anything else, however, it is the sheer unloveliness of so many of Kureishi's characters which accounts for the downbeat tone of the recent work. Every kind of venality is displayed in the short stories, particularly lust, greed and self-importance. Many of their protagonists are chronically dishonest, regularly taking refuge in the belief that lies are justifiable if they spare pain (especially to themselves). Rocco in 'Lately' typifies the widespread conviction that: 'Lying was an underrated and necessary competence' (LBT, 176). To this extent, some of Kureishi's stories evoke the bleaker tales of Joyce's *Dubliners*. Kureishi's London is as specific and grounded as Joyce's Dublin, and both writers stress the paralysis, isolation, instrumental kinds of love and spiritual emptiness which can accompany urban life. (Compare Kureishi's use of Eliot in *Sammy and Rosie*.) Where drink is so often a refuge for Joyce's characters, Kureishi's escape into drugs and, especially, sex. In the recent writing London has become a 'city of love vampires, turning from person to person, hunting the one who will make the difference' (LBT, 142).

However, this is not to suggest that Kureishi's characteristic humour disappears. 'In a Blue Time' (LBT), for example, has several (laddishly) hilarious passages, including the description of Roy's strategies for getting sex from Clara, Jimmy's misremembering of Munday's appointment and Turner's over-hasty disposal of his coke stash. The farce in 'D'Accord, Baby', 'Lately' (both LBT) and 'Four Blue Chairs' (MAD) is equally successful. However, the humour of the short stories, as of other recent writing, is often grotesque, the wit sarcastic, only exacerbating their 'blue' tone. This might support the argument that in some of the stories Kureishi emerges as a satirist of genuine venom. At the launch of *Love in a Blue Time*, he expressed great admiration for Swift and the 'The Tale of the Turd' (LBT), with its distinctly excremental vision,[7] invokes 'A Tale of a Tub'. Some of Kureishi's recent work can certainly be understood as an excoriating attack on the vanities and pretensions of contemporary mores, particularly those of the narrow and self-regarding world of contemporary London 'media-folk'.

In other stories, however, Kureishi's satire has the gentler, more affirmative tone of many of Chekhov's short stories. In both collections, compassion for the characters' suffering mitigates the sometimes harsh depictions of their moral fallibility. In 'D'Accord, Baby', for instance, Bill's vengefulness is softened for the reader by the realisation that 'happiness was beyond him' (LBT, 60). Similarly, the fact that the narrator of 'The Tale of the Turd' is 'crying inside' (LBT, 135) to some degree offsets his unpalatable egotism. Many of Kureishi's tales also register Chekhovian moments of low-key revelation, which galvanise their protagonists towards self-renewal. While often illusory, their attempts at redemption do sometimes succeed. In 'Strangers When We Meet' (MAD), Archie gives up his unsatisfying career in 'property' and in 'Sucking Stones' (MAD), Marcia burns the novel which has taken over her life. For the narrator of 'Nightlight' (LBT), like Jay in *Intimacy*, desire – and the curiosity which it represents – becomes a new *raison d'être*. For other characters, like Parvez in *My Son the Fanatic*, or the narrator of 'The Tale of the Turd' (LBT), bafflement at life's meaning and disappointment in personal relations do not entail resignation to cynicism: 'On, on, one goes, despite everything, not knowing why or how' (LBT, 137). This affirmative emphasis is particularly marked in *Midnight All Day*, in which seven of the ten tales end on a positive note, perhaps marking Kureishi's greater ease with himself after the traumas of the mid-1990s. As Alan puts it in 'Morning in the Bowl of Night': 'From a certain point of view the world was ashes ... But to live was, in some sense, to believe in the future. You couldn't keep returning to the same dirty place' (MAD, 203).

The poignancy of some of Kureishi's stories derives in large measure from his perception of the genuine difficulty of establishing clear moral rules in the contemporary world. (By contrast much of his previous writing positively celebrates moral relativism.) Roy of 'In a Blue Time' regrets that he 'no longer had any clue what social or political obligations he had, nor much idea where such duties could come from' (LBT, 9). The theme of 'how best to live' (LBT, 18) runs through all the recent writing and is taken seriously, both by the writer and many of his protagonists, yet Kureishi is keenly aware that modern society offers none of the moral certainties enjoyed by figures like Swift or philosophical moralists like Montaigne and Pascal, to whom the recent writing refers. A number of possible anchors are considered and dismissed, most obviously the wished-for permanence of affective relationships. Romantic love, however, is too fragile to bear this burden. In 'Flies', for example, its average duration is bleakly estimated at eighteen months (LBT, 197). As in the novels, conventional religion is given short shrift. As Jay in *Intimacy* puts it, 'if I meet anyone religious – and, thankfully, I do only rarely these days – I consider them to be mentally defective and probably in need of therapy' (I, 100). Self-knowledge is difficult to attain; the recent writing is littered with those for whom therapy, for instance, has made no difference. Nor does culture any longer provide the spiritual grounding which it does for Shahid in *The Black Album*. While Bodger in 'Lately' (LBT) defends it in traditional humanist terms and Ian is galvanised by exposure to Rodin in 'Midnight All Day' (MAD), for many characters – from Bill in 'D'Accord, Baby' to Baxter in 'Flies' (both LBT), the 'great tradition' proves useless in their hour of need. The major reason given for this in the recent writing is that culture has at last been entirely subsumed into the market (a culmination of trends which *The Buddha* is already clearly worrying about); as Roy in 'In a Blue Time' reflects: 'Everything was supposed to be the same: commercials, Beethoven's late quartets, pop records, shopfronts, Freud, multi-coloured hair. Greatness, comparison, value, depth: gone, gone, gone' (LBT, 16).

Conventional forms of politics provide no more secure ground for action and moral being than in Kureishi's previous writing. To some extent it is the period of Thatcherism (another way in which the 'blue time' in the title of the first collection of short stories can be understood) which is held responsible for the distressing quality of moral life in Kureishi's stories. All kinds of affective relations have seemingly been contaminated by the ethos of possessive individualism. For example, by the mid-1980s Roy of 'In a Blue Time' 'had cancelled his debts to anyone whose affection failed to yield interest' (LBT, 3). The assimilation of the 'personal' sphere to the mores of the market is equally apparent in 'Lately', where Karen has married Vance for his money and Rocco meditates thus: 'He wanted his freedom; he didn't want Lisa. If he stayed the bills would mount up' (LBT, 176).

It would be consoling to suggest that a clear alternative to such attitudes is offered in some stories at least. As Rocco's hippyish doctor friend Bodger (who is modelled on the compassionate doctors of Chekhov, particularly Samoylenko in 'The Duel') complains: 'People aren't disposable items, are they? It's chilling, Rocco. You sound rational and ruthless at the same time' (LBT, 168). Equally, the narrative voice of certain pieces shines a distinctly ironic light on the Thatcherite values of some characters. In 'In a Blue Time', for instance, Roy irritably dismisses the importuning tramp, much to Jimmy's dismay. That the moral force is with Jimmy is indicated in the narrative comment immediately before this incident that, in grasping after success, Roy 'hadn't considered what he might owe others' (LBT, 10).

Nonetheless, such moments do not amount to an endorsement of Thatcherism's two major opponents, the Left and the bedraggled remnants of the 1960s 'counter-culture'. In the recent writing, Left politics are treated with greater disdain than ever. From the feckless, politically correct Deborah in 'With Your Tongue Down My Throat' (LBT) to the awkward school-teacher Barry in *Sleep With Me*, those who represent the Left are variously puritanical, sad and naive or, in the case of Deborah's lover Howard Coleman and Barry's partner Sophie, as self-seeking as their Thatcherite counterparts. Symptomatically, the former ultra-Left Vincent Ertel of 'D'Accord, Baby' (LBT) has become a Catholic reactionary. Similarly, whereas the 'counter-culture' is largely celebrated in *The Buddha* as having been responsible for major gains in contemporary life, it is now regarded with even greater scepticism than in *The Black Album*. Roy of 'In a Blue Time' represents many characters in dismissing the 'counter-culture' as 'the delinquent dream of his adolescence' (LBT, 38). The collapse of distinctions between 'high' and 'popular' culture, 'fundamentalist' feminisms, the new freedoms of lifestyle – particularly in the areas of sexual choice and experimentation with drugs – are, indeed, regularly deplored.

At times the conflict between characters like Jimmy and Roy in 'In a Blue Time', Rocco and Vance in 'Lately' (both LBT) or Stephen and Barry in *Sleep With Me* involves an explicit contest between the values of the 1960s and the 1980s.[8] In each instance, New Right perspectives provide a biting critique of the selfishness and self-indulgence of latter-day representatives of the 'sixties', of the kind anticipated in Stone's anatomy of Clint's posse in *London Kills Me*. The attitudes and behaviour of Jimmy and Rocco in fact seem, to some degree, to justify Thatcherism as a period of necessary moral cleansing. Indeed, the 'blue mood' of certain characters derives from sorrow that the certainties of the 1980s are no more. Roy, for example,

> had loved that time ... Pretence was discarded ... socialist holiness, talk of 'principle', student clothes, feminist absurdities, and arguments defending regimes – 'flawed experiments' – that his friends wouldn't have been able to live under for five minutes: such pieties were trampled with a Nietzschean pitilessness. It was galvanising. (LBT, 15)

Kureishi further intimates that it has become increasingly difficult to distinguish the values of the 1960s from those of the 1980s. Roy and Jimmy are hard to differentiate in terms of their respective lifestyles and their conduct of personal relations. Rocco and Vance, too, are almost mirror images in these regards. In both *Intimacy* and *Sleep With Me* it is unclear whether the protagonists' decision to follow their own desires mark them as morally admirable or self-obsessed and, in either case, whether they are to be identified as children of the 'counter-culture' or offspring of Thatcherite reaction.

The short stories point to interesting developments in Kureishi's writing. In some ways, the genre seems to suit him better than others he has worked in. His smaller canvases seem more assured, perhaps because the form demands a compression, coherence and focus missing from some of Kureishi's longer texts. Seen as single works, moreover, the multiplicity of narrative voices and mixture of first- and third-person perspectives in each collection produces quite different effects to the novels, which are organised by a single dominant perspective which orders their respective characters' competing discourses hierarchically. To this extent, the collections may represent the ambition to return to the kind of polyphonic, 'collective' writing first attempted in the collages of *Sammy and Rosie*. Moreover, despite their miniaturism, the short stories do not necessarily represent a diminution of Kureishi's ambitions at a thematic level. While focused on the minutiae of intimate relationships, which are rendered more convincingly than in work like *The Black Album*, Kureishi still manages to connect the 'personal' sphere to the public domain, particularly in his explorations of the influence on affective relationships of the mores of the market. To this extent they take the nation's moral temperature in a more economical, implicit and often more telling way than in some of the work considered earlier in this volume.

My Son the Fanatic (1997)

My Son the Fanatic is much the most significant example of Kureishi's enduring interest in issues of race and ethnicity in his recent work. The film script was developed out of the short story of the same name, first published in *The New Yorker* in 1994, before being collected in *Love in a Blue Time*. The film script (and the final film) differs significantly from the short story, perhaps reflecting Kureishi's reconsideration of the problems posed by *The Black Album*'s treatment of similar issues. For example, the location of the film is obviously Bradford, whereas the setting is less clear-cut in the tale, where Parvez looks out of the window 'as if to check that they were still in London' (LBT, 126). Confusingly, however, Bettina is described as living 'outside the town' (LBT, 121). In the tale, the relationships between the principal characters are also plotted differently. Bettina and Parvez's friendship has developed over a number of years and is cemented by the fact that Parvez once rescued her from a violent client – a detail missing from the film script. More important, the relationship never develops a sexual dimension in the original tale. The translation of the story into film further involves the substantial development of the original characters and the introduction of many new ones. Parvez's wife, unnamed in the original text, reappears as Minoo, a complex figure in the film script, though less so in the film itself. In the script Kureishi also turned one of Parvez's anonymous taxi-driving colleagues into a bitter rival, though once again Rashid's role in the film itself is not so significant. The Fingerhuts, the *maulvi* from Lahore, Fizzie and Herr Schitz are all additions to the original tale.[9]

The introduction of these new characters entails a marked expansion of the meanings of the short story. For example, the Bradford settings are used to reconsider broad questions of social deprivation in a manner reminiscent of Kureishi's earlier work. (This perhaps marks a return to the more explicit focus on class issues of Kureishi's early plays.) Some scenes in the script, many of which are not used in the film itself, clearly recall the decayed urban-scapes of the first three films. Many of these issues coalesce around the character of Schitz, the German entrepreneur. On the one hand, he provides a point of comparison with Parvez, reminding the audience that there are different kinds of economic migrant, whose reception by the 'host' society varies according to the migrant's national origin, class and ethnic identity. Schitz enjoys a quite different reception in the working men's club from Parvez. As a developer of shopping centres in this former industrial city, Schitz's presence signals an accelerating shift in British economic life from traditional industries to a service economy, a reorientation which is in part the product of globalisation. Generally identified in the film script simply as 'The German', Schitz represents the growing influence on Britain of Europe, in which a newly united Germany is the economic dynamo and, as such, a potentially oppressive force.

Perhaps the most significant change of emphasis between short story and film script involves the representation of the relationship between father and son and their respective value systems. In the story Ali largely conforms to the stereotypical vision of Muslim 'fundamentalists', being cold, militant, humourless and judgemental. Reprising elements of *The Black Album*'s critique of liberalism, Kureishi generates considerable dramatic irony from the reversal of roles at the end of the story, when the seemingly easygoing Parvez, unable to tolerate Ali's return to his roots – or his bad manners – assaults his son. The impact of the denouement depends, however, on the schematic nature of the opposition between 'good', liberal father and 'bad', illiberal son. In some ways the critique of Islam is even sharper in the film, primarily because of the introduction of the Pakistani *maulvi*. Hypocritical and parasitical, the *maulvi* nonetheless succeeds in galvanising Farid and his friends into direct action against the prostitutes. The vigilantes' violence against the under-age hooker and Farid's own assault on Bettina during the riot lend support to Parvez's disavowal of the seemingly simplistic convictions of Farid's circle, which are further evident in its anti-semitism. As in the novels, gender issues are used to emphasise the regressive nature of the *maulvi*'s religious beliefs. Minoo increasingly takes on the role of servant in her own home after the cleric's arrival, even being required to eat apart from her husband.

However, the treatment of Islam in *My Son the Fanatic* is much more nuanced than all this might suggest and significantly extends *The Black Album* in this respect. In the film script, Farid is drawn in a more complex and sympathetic manner than Ali in the original tale and greater insight is provided into the reasons for his turn to religion. In the first place (though this aspect of the script does not survive into the film), religion provides Farid with an escape route from a lifestyle which earlier threatened to destroy him. (Compare Chad in *The Black Album*; it is Farid's experiments with the drug scene which bring him into contact with Madelaine, making the relationship between the taxi- driver's son and the Police Inspector's daughter more immediately credible in the script than in the film itself.) Secondly, Farid's turning to religion is a credible rebellion against a parent who has anticipated more conventional forms of dissent, such as a career in pop music, by actively encouraging them. Thirdly, Farid's turn to Islam can be understood as a reaction against Parvez's extramarital relationship (of which he has intimations much earlier in the script than in the film itself) and is thus an expression of solidarity with his mother.

As a consequence, there are also major differences between tale and film in terms of their cultural/political meanings. In his introduction to the film script (and as is also suggested in *The Black Album*), Kureishi links the growing appeal of militant brands of Islam to the fact that large numbers of British-Asians continue to exist at the bottom of British society. Parvez's humiliation at 'Manningham's' club is indicative of the hostility of the 'host' culture, which requires him to carry a wooden club for self-protection at work. (The horrifying violence against British-Asian cab drivers is a powerful theme in the essay 'Bradford', which provides *My Son the Fanatic* with many of its details.) In this context, Islam is seen as a legitimate locus of resistance, communal self-help and solidarity. As the older Muslim whom Parvez meets at the mosque argues: 'But … these young people – they're not afraid of the truth. They stand up for things. We never did that' (MSF, 58).

Equally, the moral appeal of Islam is represented more sympathetically in the film script than the original short story. The recurrence of the street of whores as a backdrop in the film, the decadence of the hotel-room scene involving Schitz and Bettina and the orgiastic party to celebrate the acquisition of the businessman's new premises (much more graphically treated in the script than in the final film) are all signs of the decadence which understandably alarms the *maulvi*'s disciples (this dimension is missing from *The Black Album*). Farid's abandonment of his accountancy studies signals his refusal to be part of an economic system in which humans, too, are simply commodities to be bought and sold. Bettina herself recognises the legitimacy of his search for a more spiritual way of living: 'Who can blame the young for believing in something beside money?' (MSF, 53).

Moreover, in the film of *My Son the Fanatic* Parvez is a much more ambivalent representative of liberalism – and thus a less convincing critic of his son's 'fundamentalism' – than in the short story. Parvez is perhaps the most complex and sympathetic character in the film (partly because the role of Bettina is so schematic - she is not much more than the 'tart with a heart'). In part, of course, Parvez's humanity derives precisely from his contradictions and confusions, which are abundant. To begin with, his seemingly liberal attitudes in fact co-exist with unreconstructed conceptions of family roles. He expects unquestioning obedience from his wife, who even before the arrival of the *maulvi* sometimes behaves like a servant – for example, cleaning Parvez's shoes after his first excursion with Bettina – about whom, of course, Parvez never tells Minoo the full truth. (Compare Jay's deception of Susan in *Intimacy*.) In fact, the film script makes much more of Minoo's resentment and frustration at the limitations of her life prior to the *maulvi*'s appearance than the film itself. In this context, there is a crucial difference between the script and the film. The latter chooses not to include the scene in which a drunken Parvez attempts to rape his wife.

From this point on, in the script at least, Minoo's attitudes harden and her return to a strict form of Islam is seen as a form of self-protection.

Parvez is equally patriarchal towards his son, opportunistically citing the Koran to enforce his authority. Perhaps most ironically, his attitude towards Farid's engagement with Madelaine is based on a traditionalist conception of paternal rights. Threatening to 'break open his face until he obeys' (MSF, 30), Parvez complains: 'You go to [others] secretly when I have hand-picked Miss Fingerhut!' (MSF, 38). The limitations of his liberalism are equally clear in Parvez's early investigations into his son's increasingly erratic behaviour. During his attempt to establish Farid's 'normality', Parvez expresses the same kind of homophobia as Haroon in *The Buddha*: 'He used to love his clothes ... I was worried he'd gone homo' (MSF, 35).

Like Amjad in *Borderline* and Nasser in *Laundrette*, Parvez sees Britain rosily as a place of opportunity, the pursuit of which requires cultural 'roots' to be torn up. As he says to Minoo: 'You're not in the village now, this is England. We have to fit in' (LBT, 125). Indeed, Parvez has a blandly affirmative view of the *status quo*, despite its obvious inequalities. Thus, his attitude towards prostitution is that it is a reflection of 'human nature' (MSF, 77), rather than a social problem; and, although exploited himself, Parvez happily takes on the role of pimp for Schitz and his colleagues. As Farid points out, the realities of discrimination mean that in daily life Parvez must rely on obsequiousness to survive. His father's unctuous attitude toward Inspector Fingerhut (in the script, though not the film, Parvez boasts of his police contacts to boost his prestige) and his compliance with Schitz, who consistently patronises Parvez as 'his' little man' – and even on one occasion assaults him – understandably strengthen Farid's determination not to follow the same path.

Ironically, Parvez's liberal ideals leave him one of the most bereft and isolated figures in Kureishi's recent work, abandoned by both son and wife and alienated from former friends like Fizzy. From one perspective, the sacrifices he has been prepared to make for his beliefs bespeak a nobility of soul which reinforces the authority of his liberal perspectives. Yet they also bespeak an inability to compromise (or 'fanaticism') which is comparable to his opponents'. As in the ending of *The Black Album*, Parvez's predicament exemplifies Kureishi's conviction of the difficulties of inhabiting the 'in-between' state of cultural hybridity that Farid rails against. Ground between the hostility and indifference of the 'host' society on the one hand and the surly certainties of the *maulvi*'s followers on the other, Parvez is in the end as pathetic as he is tragic. As this might suggest, in contrast to the evasive end of *The Black Album*, *My Son the Fanatic* is more nuanced and obviously troubled in its treatment of the issues raised by 'the politics of recognition'.

The transition from short story to film is partly mediated by means of an extended engagement with Martin Scorsese's *Taxi Driver* (1976), a film much admired by Chili in *The Black Album* and which his brother Shahid watches in the hope that it will prepare him for life in London. (In *The Buddha*, Karim attends a season of Scorsese's films at the ICA.) Most obviously, Parvez and Travis Bickle (Robert de Niro) share the same job and both are isolated figures, alienated from their workmates. The principal female role in both films is a prostitute with whom the male lead falls in love and whom he seeks to redeem. Certain characters and incidents in *My Son the Fanatic* have their precedents in Scorsese's work. For example, both films feature an angry hooker who appears at intervals and, early on in each, a prostitute and client have sex in the rear of the cab, causing the respective drivers great concern about their upholstery.

Three of Scorsese's central themes recur in *My Son the Fanatic*. Firstly, *Taxi Driver* emphasises the racial divisions of New York, the city in which it is set. Travis's colleagues are reluctant to drive in Harlem, which Dough-Boy describes as 'fucking Mau-Mau land'. At one point Travis is surrounded by a gang of black youths who attack his car (this perhaps also provides the precedent for *Laundrette*, when Johnny's gang ambush Salim's vehicle). At another moment, Travis picks up a fare (played by Scorsese himself) who is on his way to kill his wife for having an affair with a 'nigger' (compare Parvez and

Bettina.) Secondly, Scorsese's film is preoccupied by questions of belonging. Travis is a Vietnam veteran who has returned to a city where his sense of displacement generates paranoid tendencies. Thirdly, *Taxi Driver* is also concerned with moral fanaticism. Like Farid rather than Parvez, Travis is disgusted by the degeneracy of New York. In his eyes, it is 'like an open sewer' and he hopes that someone 'will flush it right down the fucking toilet'. Travis, too, sees the sex industry as the most striking symbol of corruption. Those who work in it (Easy apart) are 'scum of the earth' and his 'cleansing' mission is directed at them.

The influence of *Taxi Driver* on *My Son the Fanatic* is also evident at the level of style. Their respective depictions of New York and Bradford are largely naturalistic, with the 'mean streets' of each location foregrounded (more so in Kureishi's script, perhaps, than the film). However, this is counterbalanced by an eye for the beauty of urban-scapes in each work. When Parvez drives at night, his city is often made hauntingly lovely by the distorting lens of his rain-swept windscreen. (Travis's night drives produce similar effects, making *Taxi Driver*, too, a kind of nocturne.) In both works, the sound-track is critically important. However, whereas Scorsese relies on an at times enervatingly moody and downbeat jazz track, Kureishi draws on a range of genres (including jazz – Parvez is obsessed by Louis Armstrong), in the manner of *London Kills Me*, reflecting the more varied tonal palette of *My Son the Fanatic* compared with *Taxi Driver*.

Despite the serious issues it addresses, *My Son the Fanatic* is a much more tender, human and humorous film than the portentously sombre *Taxi Driver*, perhaps ultimately because of the different national, social and cultural contexts in which each work is situated. There is genuine comedy in the scene where Parvez discovers the *maulvi* surreptitiously watching TV cartoons, and in his anxious search for evidence of his son's substance abuse. Even as their relationship declines, there are moments of real poignancy between Parvez and Minoo, for example when he beguiles her into laughing at his imitation of the *maulvi*. Such

touches help to make *My Son the Fanatic* possibly the most
satisfying and complex of Kureishi's films at the aesthetic and
psychological levels and the most nuanced and penetrating in its
cultural politics. Less sentimental than *Laundrette,* less fractured
than *Sammy and Rosie,* more engaging than *London Kills Me,*
My Son the Fanatic thoroughly vindicated Kureishi's return to
scriptwriting.

Intimacy (1998)

Intimacy has proved the most contentious of Kureishi's recent
works because it has been taken by many observers as an
opportunistic, explicit and hostile account of the breakdown of
his relationship with his former partner Tracey Scoffield. *Time
Out* described the narrative as 'scaldingly personal' and in *The
Observer,* Cressida Connolly asserted that what she saw as the
repugnancy of the text was due to the fact that 'Kureishi's own
life is known to mirror the events he describes.'[10] As was
indicated in Chapter 1, Scoffield herself scoffed at the idea that
Intimacy was fiction. The novella itself seems to lend support to
such interpretations. For example, the writer-protagonist Jay
comments that 'I find myself putting more of myself into the
stories than formerly' (I, 35).

Further encouragement to read *Intimacy* as a species of
autobiography[11] is provided by some of its intertexts, notably its
engagement with the genre of 'male testimonial', the recent
emergence of which is one manifestation of a contemporary
'crisis of masculinity' that has been detected by many on-
lookers.[12] At the Purcell Room reading of *Intimacy* in June 1998,
Kureishi's moderator Blake Morrison (the choice of whom for
this role seemed designed to emphasise the non-fictional aspects
of *Intimacy*) observed that in keeping with his own contribution
to the genre, *And When Did You Last See Your Father?* (1993),
Intimacy was primarily 'a book about a man's problems'. While
mainly engaging with such problems in the context of the
conduct of sexual relationships, the novella addresses other

staples of 'male testimonial' such as the changing nature of relations between fathers and their male children in particular.

The most explicit citation of this sort is of Nick Hornby's *Fever Pitch* (1992); Jay's anxiety that, under the influence of some future stepfather, his sons may (like Hornby) become Arsenal addicts,[13] recalls Hornby's own anxieties about the footballing loyalties which his imagined children might develop in the event of a separation.[14] Other references to 'male testimonial' are more implicit. *And When Did You Last See Your Father?* comes to mind most obviously when Jay meets a lost young man in a bar during his search for Nina and in a roundabout way asks him when he last saw his father (I, 106). Other elements of Morrison's text which recur in *Intimacy* include the theme of a father's death, reflections on former loves, the potential of therapy for men, even explicit scenes of masturbation. By contrast, insofar as Jay's narrative is addressed partly to his son (I, 91), *Intimacy* has parallels with Fergal Keane's contribution to 'male testimonial', *Letter to Daniel: Despatches From the Heart* (1996).

However, *Intimacy* is less transparently documentary than some responses have suggested. In the first place, the differences between the details of Jay's life and Kureishi's are sometimes striking. Jay works exclusively in the visual media (and his projects bear little resemblance to any of Kureishi's films). Kureishi's father did not work at Scotland Yard and he has a sister rather than a brother like Jay. There are also obvious marks of aesthetic shaping in *Intimacy*, notably the non-chronological sequencing of events at the end. As Jay observes knowingly: 'Organization in a work is more important than people realize' (I, 36). At the Purcell Room reading Kureishi asserted that, while he had used his own experience, he had also drawn on other people's and, as appropriate, 'made it up'. He also claimed that the narrative had intially been written in the third person, before being changed to first person to achieve the aesthetic effects he was after. Kureishi insisted that for these reasons *Intimacy* was to be understood as 'an artificial construct ... a work of fiction'. It might, then, be read more productively alongside fictional explorations of contemporary masculinity like Will Self's *Cock and Bull* (1992), Tony Parsons's *Man and Boy* (1999) and Mike Gayle's *Mr Commitment* (2000).

Whether or not one interprets Kureishi's comments as a guilty rationalisation after the rough initial reception of his text, like 'male testimonial' and its fictional analogues, *Intimacy* draws heavily on the conventions of feminist testimonial and fiction. At one point, Jay describes how he has a series of notebooks in which he intends to keep 'significant fragments' relating to his life, work and thoughts (I, 48). This, it might be argued, invokes Doris Lessing's *The Golden Notebook* (1962), a feminist classic which was obviously on Kureishi's mind as he wrote the first collection of short stories. (Laura takes up Lessing's novel in 'Blue, Blue Pictures of You' and reading it prompts her to radically alter her life.) The correspondences between the two texts are partly stylistic. The flat, even numb, realism of Jay's account recalls the diaristic texture of so much of Lessing's novel and the sometimes fragmentary nature of his narrative recalls Anna's Blue Notebook in particular. At the same time, both works are intensely self-conscious about their status as texts, the process of writing and the relation between fiction and visual media and, arguably, each work subordinates plot and character to ideas.

The thematic parallels are equally obvious. The central protagonist in each novel is a writer who suffers from creative block and Anna's relationship with Molly is reworked in Jay and Victor's friendship. The discussions of issues like popular culture, communism and psychoanalysis in *The Golden Notebook* are recalled in Jay's musings on these very topics and both texts consider nervous breakdown as a route to personal renewal. Each work is inflected by a strong current of existentialism: the notebooks kept by both Anna and Jay invoke those of Camus, whom each admires.[15] Above all, both writers address the state of gender relations contemporary to them, focusing on long-term relationships and the conventions and expectations surrounding these. Like Ella in Anna's novel, who leaves 'the man who had suffocated her, imprisoned her, apparently took away her will',[16] Jay embarks on a journey of conscious self-reinvention as 'someone else' (I, 77) which ends in liberation from a stifling partner. Of most relevance in connection with the ethics of Jay's action, perhaps, is Marion, who in order to become a 'free' woman leaves not just her husband but, like Jay, her children too.

All the same, the relationship of *Intimacy* to feminist works like *The Golden Notebook* is deeply ambivalent. It could even be argued that *Intimacy* is an opportunistic appropriation of a 'subaltern' mode of writing by a member of the dominant gender to shore up challenges to its power. It is significant that the single book that Jay takes with him when he leaves his wife is a volume of Strindberg plays. Many of his attitudes to women are vengefully misogynistic or transparently adolescent. At one point Jay even applauds his uncle's segregated household in Pakistan as a model to follow in the regulation of the gender economy at home. Such evidence suggests that *Intimacy* can be read as a reassertion of traditional forms of patriarchal masculinity. To this extent, it could be placed in the archive of what Ros Coward has described as the literature of 'male grievance', a strand of 'male testimonial' that aims at 'a total reversal of the feminist project'.[17]

By contrast, one could suggest that *Intimacy* in fact corroborates feminist ideas by providing a deeply ironic vision of contemporary masculinity. Such an interpretation is certainly liable to challenge. A reviewer in *The Sunday Telegraph* complained that *Intimacy* was 'deeply irritating, and finally dull', primarily because 'the novel is sucked with claustrophobic intimacy into the viewpoint of its hero: there is no space here for irony.'[18] One might, however, argue that such space does exist, allowing irony to be expressed in two principal ways. The first of these might be described as 'objective' insofar as Jay consistently compares his behaviour and attitudes with those of other characters, especially his father and his friend Asif, who each provide critical counter-perspectives to his views. Asif's condemnation of Jay's behaviour is voiced directly and is all the more effective for coming from a close friend whose gentle humanity and integrity is never questioned. Asif strips Jay's behaviour of all its seemingly pretentious philosophical justifications and reduces his motivation for leaving Susan to a desire for new sexual excitements. Without portentous moralising and without sentimentalising what it involves, Asif's experience demonstrates that marriage is perfectly capable of providing the satisfactions which Jay claims to crave, including intimacy. While his beloved father (whose experience of marriage, at least in later life, corresponds to Asif's) is a necessarily silent presence, Jay is aware that, according to his parent's values, his behaviour to Susan is cruel and cowardly.

Perhaps the most interesting instance of this kind of counter-perspective, however, comes from Susan herself. To begin with, insofar as she is unquestionably the victim of a cowardly act of abandonment (even at the end, when Jay finally plucks up the courage to inform her of his entanglement with another woman, he immediately denies that Susan is going to lose him), the reader's sympathy is with her. However much Jay attempts to sway the reader's responses by insisting on her shortcomings, Susan emerges from Jay's account as anything but the monster he claims she is. Over-extended by her job and the stresses of raising two small boys, she still rouses herself unhesitatingly at the end of the narrative to care for her wounded partner. But Susan is not simply a passive victim, whose principal 'crime' is to have grown older and thereby to have come to belong to 'a different order of life' (I, 81). Echoing some of the sentiments expressed by Changez in *The Buddha* (215) and, indeed, Riaz in *The Black Album* (199), she provides one of the most penetrating critiques of the attitudes informing Jay's behaviour although, interestingly, its terms of reference are not gender-specific. As he recalls:

> She talks of a Thatcherism of the soul that imagines that people are not dependent on one another. In love, these days, it is a free market; browse and buy, pick and choose, rent and reject, as you like. There's no sexual and social security; everyone has to take care of themselves, or not. Fulfilment, self-expression and 'creativity' are the only values. (I, 52–3)

One might further argue that ironic distance *vis-à-vis* Jay is evident in more implicit but equally effective ways. Jay must surely alienate all but the most obstinate defenders of patriarchy by his excessive attitudes; he meditates seducing his best friend's wife and pursues an affair while Susan is still in hospital with their first child, taking the celebratory bottle of champagne his father-in-law has provided to oil his illicit encounter. Jay is at times pathological in his egotism. At one point he comments: 'It would be dispiriting if my departure went unnoticed' (I, 50). He packs a photo of his children only as an afterthought. His constantly parades his crassness in mirthless, shallow aphorism. For example: 'How do I like to write? With a soft pencil and a hard dick – not the other way round' (I, 47). Despite his patronising attitude towards Nina – he describes her as one of the 'uneducated educated' (I, 99) – Jay is himself not as cultured as he thinks; for example he misattributes a classical epigram about post-coital tristesse to D. H. Lawrence. Furthermore, Jay is a self-confessed serial liar. The fact that *Billy Liar* is a favourite film inevitably prompts questions about the degree to which his narrative is an 'inventory' or, indeed, an *invent*ory. There are clear signs that Jay is not telling the whole story to the reader any more than he does to his therapist: 'I had decided to confess *all*, to offer a *few* secrets without inhibition' (I, 73, my emphasis).

Finally, Jay's narrative is riddled with evidence of persisting confusions which belie his claims to have completed the existential journey to self-knowledge through experience and suffering (I, 110, 116) on which his presumed authority as a narrator largely depends. In contrast to the progress made by the protagonists of *The Golden Notebook*, Jay remains stuck in his attitudes, especially in regard to intimacy. On the one hand, Nina seemingly represents the possibilities of 'a tender and complete intimacy' (I, 59) which he feels is no longer possible with Susan. Yet he is also keen to keep Nina at arm's length (while also attempting to attract her by seeming unavailable) to the point of driving her away. His desire for intimacy is also called into question by the fact that he has chosen for his soul-mate someone who is so evidently not his equal in intellect or life-experience. Jay himself stresses how child-like Nina is, to the extent of describing her as 'a part-woman' (I, 111). The shallowness of Jay's new attachment is indicated in the course of his search for her at the end of the novella. Jay stumbles into a club where he is sidetracked by a chance encounter with a woman dancing on her own: 'I imagine going home with her. If she says yes, I will go' (I, 112). Conversely, of course, Jay represents his life with Susan as too intimate, complaining that his relationship has failed primarily because his wife is not detached enough. He insists that what he aspires to is an attachment characterised by 'kind indifference' (I, 83). Seen in the light of such evidence, perhaps *Intimacy*'s real message is contained in Asif's retort when Jay tries to persuade him that women 'prefer mature men': 'Does such a thing exist?' (I, 30).

Like many examples of 'male testimonial' and fictional accounts of contemporary masculinity, it remains unclear whether *Intimacy* is an affirmation of feminist thinking or a critique of it. However, in keeping with the emphasis of his earlier writing on the virtues of hybridity and the inhabitation of 'in-between' spaces in other contexts, it may be that Kureishi is seeking to transcend an either/or position in his vision of contemporary gender relations. As with a distinguished tradition of unreliable first-person narrators, from Chaucer's Wife of Bath (and Chaucer's attitude to feminist ideas is no more straightforward than Kureishi's) through Swift's Gulliver to Conrad's Marlow, it is difficult to judge exactly how consistently ironic Jay's (self-)presentation is intended to be. (This raises another important point. Had *Intimacy*, which is not all that much longer than some of the short stories, been published in either collection, it is doubtful whether Jay would have been so readily identified with Kureishi himself; rather he would probably have been taken as one more of the short stories' characteristically flawed and unreliable first-person narrators.)

Indeed, precisely because of its unresolved ambivalences, *Intimacy* might in fact represent a particularly honest account of the confusing predicament of modern men. His at times lacerating self-criticism, his reporting of Susan's criticisms of his tyrannical behaviour, his unresolved feelings towards her, his repeated expressions of loneliness and fear mark him as anything but an unthinking *machisto*. Like Lessing's *Golden Notebook*, *Intimacy* can be read in part as a record of the 'emotions of aggression, hostility, resentment'[19] generated by a specific phase in the evolution of contemporary gender relations. Though she rightly disavowed the criticism that recording such emotions in *The Golden Notebook* made her a 'man-hater', Lessing's text is also too ambivalent to be taken in any straightforward way as what she called a 'trumpet for Women's Liberation'.[20] (Anna's obsession with traditional kinds of 'real men', and her obvious homophobia, which are morally suspect but psychologically credible, have parallels with some of Jay's more unsavoury attitudes.)

Similarly, Kureishi's text may be too complex to be considered simply as a symptom of what Susan Faludi described at the beginning of the 1990s as a growing 'backlash' against the Women's Movement.[21] It is not just the claustrophobic, present-tense, first-person narration which forces the reader to see things to some degree from Jay's perspective. His predicament involves dilemmas which cannot easily be resolved, given his conviction that his relationship has irrevocably broken down. Jay's observation that the traditional rules governing relationships have lost their force cannot be seen simply as a rationalisation for what he is about to do to Susan. While his father's certainties about what duty involves certainly provide a critical perspective on Jay's behaviour, they are clearly more sustainable in the earlier era to which his parent's marriage belongs. In any case, Jay's parents' experience suggests that observing proprieties may not necessarily be the best way forward. Like many of the protagonists of early feminist fiction and testimonial (and of Kureishi's earlier work), his mother has been reduced to what he calls a 'lump of living death' (I, 45) for much of her marriage by choosing the path of conformity.

Certainly, *Intimacy*'s unflinching treatment of such issues compares favourably with other examples of 'male testimonial'.

Paradoxically, the genre often plays down discussion of long-term sexual relationships. In *Fever Pitch*, Hornby is without a partner for many of the years covered in the book and in *And When Did You Last See Your Father?* Morrison barely mentions his wife. Each writer's redemptive vision of contemporary masculinity is effected through a concentration on the working-through of their relationships with their fathers, a focus much more amenable to the idea that the 'new man' is indeed emerging. Even more than Hornby's and Morrison's texts, *Intimacy* might thus be taken as partial corroboration of certain 'post-feminist' works, such as Susan Faludi's *Stiffed* and Ros Coward's *Sacred Cows* (both 1999), which diverge significantly from their authors' earlier work in criticising feminism from the point of view of its failure to register sufficiently some of the consequences of the Women's Movement's successes for contemporary men. As was seen in the first section of this chapter, Nick in 'That Was Then' has written a best-selling 'male testimonial' outlining what men 'could become, having been released … from some of their conventional expectations' (MAD, 68). In this respect, the fact that Jay's notebooks remain largely blank perhaps suggests that for Kureishi a satisfactory script of contemporary masculinity is as yet unwritable.[22] Nonetheless, *Intimacy* contributes to making such a script more feasible.

Sleep With Me (1999)

Sleep With Me, Kureishi's first original play for sixteen years,[23] explores the experiences of some forty-something former university friends weekending at the country retreat of one of their number, the successful writer Stephen. It thus belongs partly to a genre which includes Lawrence Kasdan's *The Big Chill* (1983) and its British spin-off, Kenneth Branagh's *Peter's Friends* (1992). As in these works, the reunion in *Sleep With Me* occasions a sometimes disobliging comparison of the group's life experiences and provokes significant shifts in their relationships. The main plot-line involves Stephen's deciding to leave his partner Julie and two children for a much younger woman – a situation with obvious parallels to Jay's in *Intimacy*. Mirroring this is Sophie's dissatisfaction with Barry, which almost provokes a similar separation.

As in the films mentioned above, personal relations in *Sleep With Me* are intertwined with broader cultural/political issues, insofar as memories of the radicalism and experimental lifestyles of student days initiate a critique of the 'realism' and routine of middle age – and vice versa. The play's country house setting also invokes 'condition of England' drama such as Shaw's *Heartbreak House* (1919) or Priestley's *An Inspector Calls* (1947). Though there is more explicit discussion of class than in most of his other recent writing, Kureishi's primary focus is again on gender issues. At one point Charles summarises a newspaper article about the rising rate of divorce and *Sleep With Me* attempts to put flesh on these cold statistics of marital breakdown in contemporary life, covering much of the same ground as *Intimacy*. For example, Stephen's predicament is related to deep-rooted changes in attitudes which have made the spirit of the age inimical to marriage. Meanwhile the play reprises *The Black Album* in set-piece debates about the inequalities of educational provision and the effects and purpose of popular culture. These help pattern the characters' relationships and the dramatic developments which they involve. The antagonism between Stephen and Barry is as much due to ideological differences as their competing claims on Sophie, and onto the sexual rivalry between Stephen and Russell, Kureishi maps a conflict between 'serious' writer and media mogul.

More obviously than is the case with *Intimacy*, *Sleep With Me*'s savagely naturalistic account of 'the battle of the sexes' owes something to Strindberg in its verbal violence and claustrophobic intensity.[24] The unexpected reconciliation between Barry and Sophie recalls the denouement of *The Dance of Death* and Stephen's accident with his eye (SWM, 41) invokes Jean's in *Miss Julie*. (It is probably no coincidence that Stephen's wife is called Julie.) However, Kureishi's treatment of gender conflict is also shaped by similar influences to his last play, *Birds of*

Passage (1983), though the balance between them is somewhat different. The clash of ideas which typifies agitprop is reflected in the polarised exchanges on various social problems. If the schematic outlines of characters like Barry and Russell also hark back to 'fringe', however, they may equally reflect the continuing appeal of Joe Orton. The naive but scheming Lorraine, for instance, could come from any one of several Orton plays, many of which anticipate the ambivalence of *Sleep With Me* in being simultaneously scathing about, and complicit in, the amorality which they anatomise. Stephen's assault on Russell (which echoes Truscott's similarly unexpected attack on Hal in *Loot*), Barry's nudity (like Nick or Sergeant Match's in *What the Butler Saw*), the oral sex and noisy lovemaking all recall Orton's desire to assault bourgeois notions of decorum. His influence is also evident in the farce elements in *Sleep With Me*, which include Barry's misadventures in the river and his greater concern for the cocaine which is scattered in the course of Stephen's assault than for either protagonist. Finally, Orton's spirit informs the would-be polished, aphoristic quality of so many of Kureishi's characters' remarks.

Chekhov, however, is once again the dominant influence.[25] The setting invokes the opening scenes of both *Uncle Vanya* and *Ivanov* and Stephen is partly modelled on Ivanov, who is similarly unhappy in his marriage and also loves a much younger woman. Like Ivanov, Stephen is approaching middle age, is world-weary and has lost his former social ideals. Like Ivanov's wife, Julie reminds her husband of the many depressions she has helped him through, even as he plans his desertion. As in *Ivanov*, *Sleep With Me* turns on the unexpected arrival of the woman with whom the protagonist has become involved, and the central moral issue in Chekhov's play is reiterated: as Sasha puts it to Ivanov: 'Are you to blame because you've stopped loving your wife?'[26]

There are strong echoes of *The Seagull*, too, in *Sleep With Me*. Stephen resembles Trigorin in that both are successful writers without being accepted as major talents. Both are driven, insecure philanderers who become infatuated with a much younger woman. Like Trepliov, moreover, Stephen has lost confidence in his creative powers and expresses similar sentiments of self-loathing. *The Seagull* provides a precedent for the self-conscious debate about the purpose of art in *Sleep With Me*, with the claims for different kinds of culture being advanced by Trigorin and Trepliov who, like Stephen and Russell, are also rivals in love.[27] (Indeed, one might argue that, insofar as *Sleep With Me* is a play of debate, it is Chekhov as much as 'fringe' which provides the model.) The uxorious, sententious and harassed Barry is prefigured in *The Seagull*'s Medviedenko (who also complains repeatedly of the hardships of teaching). Sophie's disillusion with domesticity and unrequited yearning for another man has parallels with Masha's and Charles has much in common with Sorin – both are bored and uncomfortable in the country, both are foolish, unsuccessful in love and parasitic (though he also resembles Ivanov's steward Borkin in some of these respects). As in *The Seagull* (and most of Chekhov's other plays), the tone of *Sleep With Me* is often melancholy: Kureishi's characters often express a comparable regret to Chekhov's for wasted lives and wrong choices made.

Nonetheless, the differences between *Sleep With Me* and Kureishi's previous drama are also striking. It is a much darker, more cynical piece than any of the earlier plays. More than anything else, this is due to the unappetising nature of all the play's characters and their attitudes.[28] Again, *Ivanov* is a useful point of comparison. Shabyelsky complains that everyone around him is 'so low and small-minded and dull-witted',[29] a judgement which is equally applicable to Stephen's friends. The latter are, however, more selfish, narcissistic, dishonest with themselves and others, and chronically manipulative than Shabyelsky's circle. While Lvov comments of his friend that he has never seen 'so much heartless egoism, such cold humanity' in a man, and complains directly to Ivanov about the latter's 'beastly cynicism',[30] Ivanov is substantially redeemed by his passion, his effort to dissuade Sasha from marriage and the tortured conscience which leads to his suicide. *Sleep With Me*'s bleakness also derives from the lack of alternatives to the world it depicts. There is no equivalent of the compassionately wise doctor Dorn in *The Seagull*, or even his more brutally honest equivalent Lvov, to provide a perspective which contains the outlines of a restorative vision. Nor is there any cathartic revelation of truths which might lead to redemption. While Anna Petrovna learns all about her husband's behaviour in *Ivanov*, Anna's real relation to Stephen remains concealed from their respective partners at the end of *Sleep With Me* – following the pattern of *Intimacy*.

Finally, despite the ambivalence of Kureishi's previous plays about some of the claims of the Left and the 'counter-culture', they are nonetheless clearly examples of social protest. In *Sleep With Me*, as in other recent writing, the radicalism of the 1960s and 1970s is represented as both an unmitigated failure and as intrinsically mistaken in its analyses. Sophie, a disappointed feminist, tries to jump ship from both her husband and career in social work to Russell and his glib media world. While Barry's self-deprecation and misadventures make him one of the more sympathetic characters in the play, Stephen and Russell's hip world makes Barry seem simply out of date; like David's in *Birds Of Passage* or Gayev's in Chekhov's *The Cherry Orchard*, his politics are a throw-back to an era of social relations which has been largely superseded (Lorraine has the use of a convertible and holidays in Umbria and Antigua). Barry is also both a bore and hypocrital in his pursuit of Lorraine and it is little surprise that Sophie struggles to escape him. This leaves no alternative to the dog-eat-dog ethos of which, for all their other differences, Stephen and Russell are equally representative.

Despite the enthusiasm and energy with which Kureishi returned to writing drama, *Sleep With Me* was badly received. Indeed, the piece elicited probably the worst set of reviews that Kureishi has ever received, certainly since *London Kills Me*. *The Independent on Sunday* described it as 'this cringe-making event' and lambasted Kureishi's 'emotional banalities', '[m]irth-less aphorisms' and reliance on stereotypes.[31] *The Observer* was even more scathing: 'Kureishi marshals every cliche known to psychobabble, and then some ... At one point, his alter ego, Stephen (Sean Chapman), is asked what a writer knows of life.

"No idea about anything," he replies. "None at all." Enough said.'[32]

While *Sleep With Me* was by no means as bad as such reviews suggested (and on the evidence of the two performances that I attended, at the beginning and end of the run, the ordinary public thoroughly enjoyed itself), it was certainly not a success. Perhaps the principal reason was that, as with *Sammy and Rosie* and *The Black Album*, the varied dramatic sources and influences on the play work against each other. Such tensions are most obvious in the area of characterisation, where the tendency of 'fringe' and Orton towards caricature conflicts with the emphasis on psychological depth and moral complexity in Chekhov, which is instantiated in Ivanov's view that 'we all have too many wheels, and screws, and valves inside of us to be judged by first impressions or by a few external traits'.[33] *Sleep With Me* is unable to elicit the kind of interest and compassion which Chekhov does because Kureishi's characters are too schematic: while they have secrets, they lack depth – a serious problem in a full-length play. Stephen remains throughout an arrogant, deeply insensitive, serial adulterer. Anna has much less complexity and what Stephen calls 'grace' than counterparts like Nina in *The Seagull* or Sasha in *Ivanov*, being ignorant and lacking in empathy for others. Even Julie elicits little sympathy. Her constant nagging of Stephen, her snobbery towards Barry and Sophie, her exploitation of Lorraine and her greedy consumerism make her a victim towards whom the onlooker is likely to be largely indifferent, if not actually hostile – in contrast to the sympathy one feels for Ivanov's wife Anna Petrovna.

On the other hand, *Sleep With Me* fails to deliver the best effects of Kureishi's other dramatic influences. In this instance, at least, his aphorisms lack the wit and penetration of Orton's. Equally, Kureishi's play fails to match Strindberg's often grotesquely comic tone because much of the humour of *Sleep With Me*, like Barry's misadventures with his clothes, is laboured and obvious. Conversely, the attempts at critical realism are not altogether successful, the characters being from too narrow a social range for the piece to function as a genuine 'condition of

England' play. Topics such as the role of Left thinking in the aftermath of Thatcherism, or the competing claims of 'high' and 'mass' culture, are sufficiently well-rehearsed as to need much fresher treatment than Kureishi provides to make *Sleep With Me* a play of innovative debate. Finally, in its discussion of gender, more specifically, the play lacks Strindberg's even distribution of power between the sexes, being much too loaded in favour of Stephen.

Sleep With Me has the unhappy feel of one of those works so often referred to in the short stories, which is dashed off by unwilling creators under the exigency of financial pressures. Whatever the reason, Kureishi's rustiness in the craft of drama was obvious. As Robert remarks in 'Midnight All Day', perhaps reflecting Kureishi's own rueful recognition of the fact, 'the theatre is not a profession you can return to at will' (MAD, 46).

Conclusion

As already suggested, Kureishi's recent work involves some significant differences of emphasis from his previous writing, particularly in relation to his hitherto characteristic preoccupation with issues of race and ethnicity. To this extent, it marks a further stage in his disavowal of the 'burden of representation'. Equally, it testifies to Kureishi's recognition that he needed to develop as an artist. Some critics were becoming tired of Kureishi's recycling and revisions of previous work. Of *The Buddha*, for example, Marc Poree complained: 'Why does Kureishi write about the same subjects over and over again?'[34] After *The Black Album*, Kureishi himself acknowledged the need to plough new furrows: 'I think that many of the immigrant stories that I wanted to tell … I've kind of done in different ways already.'[35] More contentiously, perhaps, one might relate Kureishi's turning away from his habitual subject matter to his perception that issues of race and ethnicity have become less pressing than they were in the 1970s and 1980s. For instance, in a recent *Guardian* piece, Kureishi commented that although racism would probably never disappear: 'The whole country has become much more liberal. I feel much more optimistic than before ... [racism is] not tolerated in institutions and that's the most important thing.'[36]

Nonetheless, the reception of Kureishi's new work has been mixed, for a variety of reasons. For example, Sukhdev Sandhu's review essay on *Midnight All Day* suggests that the collection 'represents – along with *Love in a Blue Time* (1997) and *Intimacy* (1998) – the third instalment in the ongoing decline of a once vital writer.'[37] While Sandhu ostensibly concentrates on the aesthetic (he is particularly harsh on Kureishi's recent prose style) and moral shortcomings which have led to the 'impasse' in which Kureishi now supposedly finds himself, it is difficult not to relate his stance to Kureishi's perceived abandonment of issues of ethnicity. A good three-quarters of the essay is about how Kureishi's earlier work played such an enabling part in giving second- and third-generation British-Asians cultural self-confidence. (Curiously, however, Sandhu makes no reference to *My Son the Fanatic* in his account of Kureishi's recent output.) This suggests, if not that Kureishi has a duty to stick to the subjects which first brought him to attention, at least regret that he has not done so.

Some other hostile accounts of the work covered in this chapter are equally suspect, especially those which imply that Kureishi has written about things which he ought not to have done. Some of the reviews of both *Intimacy* and *Sleep with Me*, particularly, seemed primarily preoccupied with scoring moral points off Kureishi the man. Thus, *The Observer* commented of the latter piece:

> In fact, it is a recycled version of his recent novel *Intimacy*, continuing his apparent need for public self-flagellation after his own abandonment of his partner and small children ... Kureishi should really bore a shrink to death rather than inflict his guilty private demons on National Theatre audiences.[38]

To raise the point about originality seems legitimate – and the review is probably right in this respect. To abuse Kureishi in such an *ad hominem* way certainly is not. To make judgements of the sort described above presumes a knowledge of the facts which it is unlikely that anyone except Kureishi and his former partner could have. Such responses do not exhaust the negative reactions to the recent work, however. As has been seen, objections have been made to the claustrophobic nature of the narrative mode of *Intimacy*. Of *Midnight All Day*, James Hopkins complained that 'it's hard not to tire of the cynicism or the fact that the characters are so similar'.[39]

Nonetheless, there has also been abundant praise for the recent work. While finding some of the stories in *Love in a Blue Time* 'facile or over-explicit', Maya Jaggi praised others for their 'insistent observation of the present' and concluded that 'his distinctive voice has acquired a new wistfulness'.[40] Suzanne Moore lauded *Intimacy* on the grounds that 'Kureishi is doing no more than document how it feels to fall out of love with someone ... His real subject, why men leave women, is surely immensely important and relevant.'[41] *The Guardian* commended *My Son the Fanatic* for creating 'characters of great richness and originality' and concluded that 'it brings dramatic and cinematic skill to bear on difficult questions with an edge and spirit of social inquiry that should be a staple of a healthy domestic cinema.'[42] Of *Midnight All Day*, Paul Binding argues that Kureishi 'wields a singularly pure and classical style' and that in finding new topics to write about, he is 'refining, not abjuring, his art'.[43] Hugo Barnacle concludes that Kureishi is 'working hard to develop a worthwhile neo-Chekhovian manner' in his recent work and that *Midnight All Day* 'is a big improvement' on the first collection.[44] Tom Charity has commented that 'the strongest attribute of his recent work is precisely its humanity.'[45]

Taken as a whole, these reviews perhaps corroborate David Robson's argument that in the recent work Kureishi reveals himself to be 'a frustratingly uneven writer, capable of real brilliance, but prone to nervous introspection'.[46] However, they also have important implications for Kureishi's status as a 'world writer'. *My Son the Fanatic* aside, this ascription comes under pressure from two directions as far as the texts covered in this chapter are concerned. On the one hand, the strong streak of existential thinking throughout the recent work (many of the canonical philosophers, from Kierkegaard to Camus, are invoked in one work or another) pushes Kureishi in the direction of something more (putatively) 'universal' than is the case with his earlier writing. On the other hand, his close engagement with the narrow world of west London media folk pushes him in a quite contrary direction, a tendency which is reinforced if one follows some critics in seeing most of the recent work as a species of autobiography. James Hopkins, for example, argues that 'Kureishi's approach is now not so much minimalist as miniaturist: the world has shrunk to the size of his own concerns.'[47] Either or both of these emphases (they are not necessarily mutually exclusive) severely compromises Kureishi's identity as a 'world writer' as defined in Chapter 1 (while opening him up to different kinds of critical contextualisation).

Critical overview and conclusion

Introduction: Kureishi's place in cultural tradition

It would clearly be premature to attempt definitive judgements of Kureishi's status as a writer. He is still only in his mid-forties and, other things being equal, has a long and productive career ahead of him. What weight the texts and interests which have thus far brought him to public attention will have in his completed canon can only, therefore, be conjectured.[1] In focusing primarily on providing an overview and critical evaluation of Kureishi's treatment of issues of ethnicity and diaspora, national identity and cultural belonging, then, this concluding chapter can be no more than an interim report on his output to date.

What already seems clear, however, is that even if he were never to return to 'immigrant stories', Kureishi's status as a 'contemporary world writer' is probably assured. While – as previous chapters have indicated – by no means all of Kureishi's work has been unanimously well received, certain texts – notably *Laundrette* (nominated for an Oscar) and *The Buddha* (which has sold more than half a million copies and been translated into more than twenty languages) – have earned popular acclaim around the world. Signs of the critical esteem in which some of his writing is held are also abundant. In 1997 *The Buddha* – winner of the Whitbread Award for Best First Novel in 1990 – appeared on the French *agrégation* university syllabus in English literature (a rough national equivalent of the MA in Britain). In 1999 there was a retrospective season of his films at the National Film Theatre in London. He has been hailed by such leading contemporary critics as Spivak and Stuart Hall for adumbrating the emergence of important new kinds of cultural politics.[2] Colin MacCabe, former head of research at the British Film Institute and now once more a Professor of English, has praised him as one of the most important writers of the last twenty-five years.[3] Fellow-writers have, at times, been equally enthusiastic. Rushdie has praised *Laundrette* as 'one of the finest works of art to emerge from the new generation of black British writers'.[4]

Kureishi's *oeuvre* is likely to have historic importance as one of the first substantial bodies of cultural work produced by a British-born descendant of the nation's minorities of 'New Commonwealth' origin. More specifically, Sukhdev Sandhu argues, Kureishi 'offered for the first time a recognisable portrait of British Asian life',[5] which has proved powerfully enabling as regards the subsequent emergence in the 1990s of a distinctively British-Asian contribution to cultural production in the UK. From the visual arts (Anish Kapoor, Chila Burman) to popular music (Nitin Sawhney, Asian Dub Foundation, Talvin Singh, Cornershop) to television (*King of the Ghetto, Goodness Gracious Me*), film (*Bhaji on the Beach* and *East is East*), dance (Shobana Jeyasingh, Akram Khan, Mavin Khoo) and literature (Shyama Perera, Meera Syal, Atima Srivastava, Bidisha) this has a higher profile than ever before at the turn of the new century and is now receiving both popular and critical acclaim.[6]

As Cornershop's homage on the B-side of their first single, 'Hanif Kureishi Scene' suggests,[7] Kureishi has acted as a path-finder for this explosion of British-Asian cultural expression in a number of domains. The plays of Harwant Bains (*Fighting Kite* at Stratford East in 1987, *Blood* at the Royal Court in 1989); Parv Bancil (*Crazyhorse* at Battersea Arts Centre in 1997, *Made in England* at the Etcetera, Camden in 1998, *Bollywood or Bust ... Innit!*, at the Watermans, Brentford, 1999); and Ayub Khan-Din (Sammy in *Sammy and Rosie*), whose *East is East* was a major critical hit at the Royal Court in 1997, has all emerged in the wake of the success of Kureishi's early drama. In cinema, David Attwood's *Wild West* (Channel 4, 1992, written by Harwant

Bains), Gurinder Chadha's *Bhaji on the Beach* (1993, written by Meera Syal – Rani in *Sammy and Rosie*) – and Damien O'Donnell's film of Khan-Din's *East is East* (1999) have thrived in the cultural space opened up by *Laundrette* and *Sammy and Rosie*. In *East is East*, probably the most successful of these films, critically and commercially, Kureishi's influence is particularly marked. Like *The Buddha*, it is a 'coming of age' text set in the 1970s and draws heavily on pop music of the time. It, too, explores the internal dynamics of a mixed-race family (albeit in northern England) and its relation to wider society. Khan-Din's film also 'borrows' more specifically from Kureishi's work. The scene where Peggy is mounted by a large, unruly hound is clearly adapted from Karim's humiliation by Hairy Back's Great Dane. Indeed, the film version of *East is East* adds a whole narrative strand absent in the play which revolves round a cross-race gay relationship of the kind first explored in *Laundrette*.

In fiction, too, a new generation of British-Asian writers has followed on from Kureishi. Several appeared at the 'Continental Drift: Asian Writing in Transit' conference at the Royal Festival Hall in London in 1999, which brought together writers of South Asian origin now living in different parts of the world for readings and critical discussions. I asked some of the figures at this event to comment on the relationship of Kureishi's work to their own. Shyama Perera was most enthusiastic, acknowledging that Kureishi's success had been a major inspiration behind her own decision to become a writer. More particularly, she described *Intimacy* as the 'provocation' for her second novel, *Bitter Sweet Symphony* (2000; Perera's work explores the abandonment by her white partner of the British-Asian Nina – Jay's lover has the same name – from her point of view and Kureishi is mentioned in the text). Atima Srivastava was also complimentary, suggesting that both *Laundrette* and *The Buddha* were landmarks in terms of making Asian Britain available as a subject to write about. Perera's *Haven't Stopped Dancing Yet* and Srivastava's *Looking for Maya* (both 1999) have many similarities with (as well as, particularly in regard to gender issues, some significant differences from) *The Buddha*. Each is a

first-person *Bildungsroman* involving a British-Asian protagon-
ist coming of age in London. Meera Syal, too, acknowledged *The
Buddha* as an enabling precedent for her acclaimed first novel
Anita and Me (1997) though she, too, stressed the differences
(notably in the semi-rural Midlands setting and, again, in her
treatment of gender issues) between Kureishi's novel and her
own first-person narrative about growing up in 1960s and 1970s
England. However, Kureishi's influence extends beyond recent
British-Asian fiction. Insofar as *The Buddha* informs Nick
Hornby's *Fever Pitch*, it has helped to seed the increasingly
popular genre of 'male testimonial'. (Both are preoccupied by
the lure of London for suburban youth, the search for a new
'family' after parental separation, father–son relationships, and
both are mapped in relation to 1970s pop.) And at a reading in
London in 2001, the Black-British novelist of Nigerian extrac-
tion, Deran Adebayo, acclaimed *Laundrette* as the inspiration
for his decision to become a writer.

By contrast, it is also important to recognise that for many
British-Asian cultural producers, Kureishi's work has not
necessarily provided such positive inspiration. This reinforces
the wisdom of approaching with caution the kind of claim made
by Berthold Schoene that '[o]ver the last two decades Kureishi
has established himself as a cultural spokesman of the Asian/
Pakistani community in Britain'.[8] While Parv Bancil, for
example, 'loved' *The Buddha*, he felt that earlier work like *Birds
of Passage* did not really speak to him; first, because it did not
sufficiently reflect the realities of inner-city Asian Britain as he
knew them and, secondly, because it was directed too much at a
'white' audience. Bancil's own work for the theatre, by contrast,
was – at least to begin with – intended primarily for the specific
West London British-Asian community he grew up in.[9] The
film-maker Gurinder Chadha has complained that Kureishi is
'quite isolated from the Asian side of himself. If there's one
criticism of him, it's that he's used that side of him without real
cultural integrity'.[10] At the 'Continental Drift' event, Bidisha,
author of *Seahorses* (1998) and *Too Fast to Live* (2000), was
much less enthusiastic than either Perera or Srivastava, accusing

Kureishi variously of being sexist, politically conservative, an insufficiently good stylist and opportunistic in his uses of British-Asian experience. Nonetheless, implicit in all three responses, perhaps, is a backhanded acknowledgement of Kureishi's achievement, in that he has at least provided a model to kick against.

Kureishi and the politics of cultural hybridity

Kureishi's status can also be measured in the growing volume of critical attention that he is now receiving. As befits a 'contemporary world writer', such interest is world-wide, extending on one axis from Texas to Taiwan, on another from Manchester to Melbourne. Indeed, a good two-thirds of the critical writing on Kureishi has originated outside Britain. The films were the first of his works to attract attention, with articles beginning to appear in the second half of the 1980s. The first article on Kureishi's fiction was published in 1992. Since then, as the select bibliography to this volume attests, an ever-increasing amount of critical material has been published, with the first monograph on Kureishi's (first two) films, by Ines Böhner (in German) appearing in 1996. Marc Porée's monograph on *The Buddha* came out the following year and in 1998 Kenneth Kaleta produced the first overview of Kureishi's career to date. Such attention has, however, been unevenly distributed. *Laundrette, Sammy and Rosie* and *The Buddha* are the focus of some ninety per cent of the critical writing. By comparison, the plays and (more understandably) the work discussed in Chapter 5 of this volume, aside from *Love in a Blue Time*, have thus far received little attention.

Although only a relatively narrow spectrum of Kureishi's work has been engaged with to date, there is considerable variety in both the methodological approaches employed and range of issues addressed. Kureishi criticism ranges from fairly traditional (though, of course, necessary) kinds of content and formal analysis, through various cultural-historical contextualisations to sometimes highly theorised discussions grounded in the conceptual frameworks of Cultural Studies, gender studies, film studies, postmodernism and minoritarian/postcolonial theory. In terms of issues addressed, there is an equal range, from discussions of rage and of diet to analysis of his working practices and processes of composition, his onomastics, gender issues and Kureishi's use of pop. Thus far, however, Kureishi criticism has focused predominantly on his treatment of the complex nexus of individual, racial, ethnic, (sub-)cultural and national forms of identity and belonging. The more specifically political implications of Kureishi's work in this regard have perhaps excited the most intense discussion and the rest of this concluding chapter will therefore be devoted to a review of this aspect of the critical debate, supplementing it where appropriate. The main points of contention have been over the degree of Kureishi's espousal of 'hybridity', both as a cultural strategy and as a socio-political ideal – and over the extent to which his engagements with 'hybridity' are politically enabling and progressive or otherwise.

The claims which have been made for (and against) 'hybridity' in contemporary cultural theory are abundant and substantial, though such has been the proliferation in the usage of the concept – and of its cognates, such as 'in-betweeness' – that it has been in danger of becoming either 'vacuous' or a 'cant' term.[11] For this reason alone it may be worth subjecting it to closer scrutiny than has generally been the case in Kureishi criticism. Perhaps fittingly, 'hybridity' is a highly fissile and unstable concept, with a history which long predates, and complicates, its formulations in contemporary cultural theory. As Robert Young notes in his genealogy of the term in *Colonial Desire*: 'Hybridity is ... itself a hybrid concept.'[12] Young's proposition is amply borne out by Monika Fludernik's patient tracking of the wide variety of sometimes conflictual meanings and applications even in the single example of the work of Homi Bhabha, one of its most influential proponents.[13] Rather than attempting an exhaustive survey of the concept's multiple meanings, it may be more productive to isolate a few of its aspects in a range of contemporary cultural theory and criticism which have particular relevance to Kureishi's work. To begin with, the focus will be on some positive accounts of 'hybridity'.

One of the most enthusiastic accounts of 'hybridity' comes in Salman Rushdie's famous defence of his most notorious novel:

> The Satanic Verses celebrates hybridity, impurity, inter-mingling, the transformation that comes of new and un-expected combinations of human beings, cultures, ideas, politics, movies, songs. It rejoices in mongrelization and fears the absolutism of the Pure. Mélange, hotchpotch, a bit of this and a bit of that is how newness enters the world. It is the great possibility that mass migration gives the world, and I have tried to embrace it. The Satanic Verses is for change-by-fusion, change-by-conjoining. It is a love song to our mongrel selves.[14]

Here, 'hybridity' is conceived as a dialectical and processual movement, whereby two (or more) initially separate and different traditions, identities or cultures combine to produce a new, third, term.

Rushdie's syncretising model of 'hybridity' can be claimed as politically progressive in a number of ways. First of all, as Chapter 4 indicated, it overturns the binary structure of opposition between different cultures and cultural traditions, thus potentially diminishing possible hostilities between them. In this regard, 'hybridity' involves a critique of the 'Purities' around which minoritarian cultural nationalism mobilises as much as those of the dominant or 'host' society. In the context of the latter, more specifically, it obviously resists discourses of contemporary inter-cultural relations which insist that mergings between different cultures are undesirable, divisive and socially degenerative in tendency because of ontologically-grounded differences between the cultures involved. (Such discourses, which tend to bar 'outsiders' from access to membership of the nation, are generally associated with the far Right, for instance, apartheid regimes. 'Hairy Back' in The Buddha exemplifies this position.) Secondly, it resists the assimilationist tendencies of some (usually centre-right) discourses of contemporary inter-cultural relations, which require minorities to surrender their culture of origin and adopt the norms and practices of the 'host' society. (While this admits the possibility that minorities can gain access to citizenship, 'hybridity' *per se* tends to be conceived of as an impediment to full integration.[15] Such a vision informs the attitudes of Jean and Ted at the outset of *The Buddha*.) Thirdly, by contrast, Rushdie's model of 'hybridity' also resists the exoticism of some (usually Left-liberal) discourses which encourage minorities to cling to the traditions of their culture of origin. (These tend to see 'hybridity' as a disabling loss of 'authenticity'. Shadwell assumes this posture in *The Buddha*.) Finally, it resists certain liberal 'multi-culturalist'[16] discourses which – while paying lip service to respect for cultural difference, reinscribe the authority of the 'centre', whether as the privileged term ('first among equals') or as the necessary guarantor of the nation's cultural diversity. (This is Helen's position in *The Buddha*.)

While reinforcing the political thrust of Rushdie's model of 'hybridity',[17] Homi Bhabha's work theorises the concept in somewhat different ways. Drawing on Derrida's theories of *différance* and Lacanian psychoanalysis, he argues that any given kind of identity is 'hybrid' insofar as it is necessarily linked differentially to – and therefore partly constituted by – what it is not. As 'Remembering Fanon' puts it, 'identity is only ever possible in the *negation* of any sense of originality or plenitude, through the principle of displacement and differentiation ... that always renders it a liminal reality'.[18] The implications of this for both colonial and post-colonial/diasporic social relations are crucial insofar as it entails that 'the traditional grounds of racial identity are dispersed, whenever they are found to rest in the narcissistic myths of Negritude or White cultural supremacy.'[19] (Compare the implications of the way Karim and Charlie 'mirror' each other as ethnically-marked individuals in *The Buddha*.) However, while this corroborates Rushdie's conception of 'hybridity' as an assault on the 'Purities' claimed by either centre or margin (more specifically, either western 'host' culture or migrant 'culture of origin'), there is a crucial distinction between Rushdie and Bhabha's models. In Bhabha's, differences between the terms or cultures in question are *not* sublated through a dialectical progression into a newly-synthesised 'third term'. Rather, the first two terms continue to exist in a complementary relationship (usually of productive tension).[20]

Stuart Hall complicates Bhabha's model of 'hybridity' by extending it beyond the purview of race relations to incorporate other kinds of identity and (self-)identification such as gender, class and sexuality. If centre and periphery still largely survive in Bhabha's scheme, although not necessarily always in the anatagonistic relationship proposed in an earlier phase of post-colonial criticism, such differentiations become harder to sustain in Hall's work. According to Hall, all *individual* identities are always already decentred by differential negotiations *across as well as within* conventional centre/periphery divides (thus a middle-class, gay, black man belongs to the margin by virtue of ethnicity and sexuality but to the centre by virtue of class and gender). Consequently, in Hall's view, it is crucial to develop a cultural politics which

> is able to address people through the multiple identities which they have - understanding that those identities do not remain the same, that they are frequently contra-dictory, that they cross-cut one another, that they tend to locate us differently at different moments ... In order to conduct [this] politics really we have to live outside of the dream [of identity as ontologically grounded and fully self-present], to wake up, to grow up, to come into the world of contradiction.[21]

The kind of cultural politics which Hall advocates can therefore only be conducted according to the logic of the Gramscian 'war of position', on the basis of temporary, strategic alliances aimed at the achievement of determinate and often 'local' ends. In practice, however, Hall's conception of 'hybridity' primarily enables social alliances in which *marginalised* formations are 'linked through their *differences*, through the dislocations between them, rather than through their similarity, correspon-dence or identity'.[22] As with Bhabha, there is no question of sublating such differences into the kind of synthesis represented by Rushdie's model.

'Hybridity' is often seen as an effect of 'hybridisation' in contemporary cultural theory. While the latter is sometimes seen as an immanent historical process without an intending subject (it simply happens whenever different cultures come into contact, even when relations of domination are not involved), in the work of Homi Bhabha (following Bakhtin's *Dialogic Imagination*), especially,[23] it is more commonly described as an intentional act of appropriation of the symbols and narratives of the dominant culture and their reinscription by the (formerly) marginalised. As Ashcroft, Griffiths and Tiffin put it: 'Received [cultural] history is tampered with, rewritten, and realigned from the point of view of the victims of its destructive progress'.[24] It is this intentional kind of 'hybridisation' which primarily represents what Rushdie has famously described as the act of 'writing back' to the former imperial power.[25]

Kureishi's work bears a complex and ambivalent relationship to these various positive definitions of 'hybridity'. Amongst those who have most enthusiastically responded to Kureishi's perceived espousal of the concept are Gayatri Spivak and Stuart Hall, who use Kureishi's films to illustrate some of the thematic meanings just discussed,[26] and A. Robert Lee, Schoene and Yu-Cheng Lee, who do so in relation to *The Buddha*. For all these figures, Kureishi is the 'herald'[27] of new, liberating models of identity which confound singular and hierarchically organised models of (self-)identification of the kinds discussed in Chapters 3 and 4. (As suggested there, these can be coded positively or negatively and both modes are to be found in the 'host' society's and minoritarian cultural politics alike.) Thus, according to Schoene, Karim constitutes a 'a radically deconstructive presence in a world obsessed with clear-cut definitions of cultural or ethnic identity'.[28] Similarly, Yu-Cheng Lee sees 'hybridity' as offering figures like Karim a way of transcending 'forces that endeavour to confine him within the policed borders of definition of his ethnic and cultural belonging [which are] carefully mapped out for him'.[29]

Kureishi's work also at times lends comfort to Hall's vision of 'hybridity' as enabling solidarities both between different ethnic minorities (the burgeoning friendship between Danny and Rafi in *Sammy and Rosie*, for example) and between these and other social groups which are oppressed or disadvantaged on different grounds. For instance, Spivak and Mohanram emphasise the way that Kureishi maps the categories of gender/sexuality/race onto each other in his first two films, so that metaphorically, at least, these terms can seem to be 'equivalent', if not substitutible, for one another. Moreover, the thematics of homo- and bi-sexuality which run through Kureishi's *oeuvre* do not simply problematise dominant discourses of 'normal' and 'perverse' sexuality, but of national belonging, too. As Chapter 4 suggested, it is sometimes possible to see this palimpsestic process extending to the relationship between class and ethnic identities, too. At one moment in *The Buddha*, Karim likens his entrance into a new class milieu to the learning of a second language, so that the trajectory of the immigrant and the up-wardly thrusting 'New Man' become entwined. To all this one might add that Kureishi's work also provides several instances of different kinds of minority productively engaging together. Both *Sammy and Rosie* and *London Kills Me*, for example, represent communities based on solidarity between various 'new social movements'.

At the level of form, the case has also been made that Kureishi's writing at times exemplifies the kind of 'hybridity' elaborated by Rushdie. Thus Chapter 4 explored the relation of *The Buddha* to the conventions of subcontinental orature. Alamgir Hashmi proposes that Kureishi mingles British, Asian and 'expatriate-Asian' narrative traditions in the novel[30] and Nahem Yousaf makes interesting claims about Kureishi's film style in this respect. He argues that the fragmentary, dialogic nature of *Sammy and Rosie*, in particular, is a 'response to the "structure" of the Asian community as a *bricolage*', which corroborates Kobena Mercer's argument that 'hybrid' forms have, of necessity, developed in response to the 'diverse and complex qualities of our British blackness – our differentiated specificity as a diaspora people'.[31] To this one might add that there is abundant evidence of Kureishi's 'hybridisation' of the symbols and narratives of the dominant culture. As Chapter 3 argued, Kureishi's films adapt many of the tropes of 'Heritage' and 'Raj Revival' cinema in a counter-hegemonic way. Similarly, there is a persistent engagement throughout his work with 'colonial discourse', notably the work of Kipling and Forster, which is motivated by a desire to reinscribe the experience of the (formerly) colonised in a fuller, more empowering and less distorted way than in these originals. Equally, Kureishi 'hybrid-ises' a range of work with no obvious connection to colonialism, from Chekhov to Salinger, to provide cultural space from within which to represent minority experience.[32]

At the same time, Kureishi's work does not consistently instantiate all of these positive accounts of 'hybridity'. As Chapter 1 argued, he does not juxtapose and/or synthesize western and non-western narrative traditions to anything like the degree that figures like Rushdie or Derek Walcott do. There are very few allusions to non-western texts in his corpus and Kureishi rarely uses either non-standard English or diction from other languages – and even more rarely leaves the latter untrans-lated. As Chapter 3 suggested, the experimental quality of his films might be more convincingly explained in terms of their engagement with (post)Modernist ideas of collage and/or the adaptation of the conventions of the 'fringe' theatre in which Kureishi cut his teeth as a writer. Equally, the oral qualities of *The Buddha* can be explained in terms of his recourse to western confessional modes of the kind represented by *The Catcher in the Rye*; and the mixing of 'high' and 'popular' forms so characteristic of Kureishi's writing is, of course, as much a staple of postmodernism and as of postcolonialism. Finally, the pastiche of Chekhov and Orton in *Sleep With Me*, at least, may be just that; in the absence of any engagement with issues of ethnicity, it cannot necessarily be attributed the motivation of postcolonial forms of 'hybridisation'.

Indeed, it could be argued that despite his avowed ambition to be a 'cultural translator', Kureishi has a limited interest in 'hybridity'. A significant minority of his critics has questioned how deeply Kureishi is preoccupied by issues of race, ethnicity and inter-cultural relations, let alone by any desire to polemicise on behalf of 'hybridity'. Manferlotti, for example, alludes to 'his perhaps unconscious debunking of the whole inter-ethnical question'.[33] Helbig argues that in *The Buddha*, Karim is 'notoriously unconcerned about his ethnic background', one sign of which is that – with a couple of exceptions (Hendrix, the Jackson Five) – Karim 'listens exclusively to what must be called "white" music'.[34] Indeed, Helbig finds it

> almost unbelievable that Kureishi should omit precisely the one McCartney song which brings up the issue of immigration. The song, 'Get Back,' had originally been planned as a satire on the British immigration laws, so the refrain line 'Get back to where you once belonged' made a bitter comment on populist prejudices against ethnic minorities.[35]

Moreover, insofar as the strategy of 'hybridity' espoused by characters like Karim aims, in A. Robert Lee's words, to 'elude definition by any one, all-purpose, determinant, be it "colour" or anything else', one can infer their desire, as Schoene puts it, to inhabit 'an ethnicity-free no-man's-land'.[36] Kureishi's increasing focus on issues other than ethnicity in much of the work discussed in Chapter 5 might support the view that this is his desire, too.

Even if one was not to go this far, there is certainly abundant evidence of scepticism about 'hybridity' in Kureishi's work. In the first instance this derives from his insistence on respect for heterogeneity, particularly the diversity of minority experience. As suggested in Chapter 1, Kureishi is always scrupulous in presenting Asian Britain as a patchwork of peoples from diverse parts of the subcontinent, with different languages, religions and values. To conflate new migrants with British-born members of the community, or to assume that different generations or genders within Asian Britain necessarily have common interests is bad enough, but to assume that there is some intrinsic common ground between Asian Britain and the country's populations of African or Caribbean origin is, he implies, to reproduce the vulgar perception of the dominant culture that such peoples are 'all the same'.

Such misgivings underlie Kureishi's concern that social alliances based upon the principle of 'hybridity' can be just as coercive as those organised around putatively singular identities. His writing discusses a range of formations which might be (or once have been) considered 'hybrid'. In *The Buddha*, most obviously, Karim recognises that, in theory, the category 'Black' is a mode of identification which could unite all ethnic minorities against a common oppressor. *The Black Album* accepts that in theory Islam offers a common mode of identitification for people from a whole range of different national and cultural backgrounds. The Left is also acknowledged as having been an important focus in the creation of a 'long front' of different kinds of oppressed constituencies against the dominant order. Even Thatcher's enterprise culture, so enthusiastically embraced by Nasser in *Laundrette*, promised a new (if spurious) kind of community embracing all sectors of society. Kureishi's scepticism about all of these formations is based primarily on a conviction that their conception of a 'common culture' is achieved at the cost of denigration of, or blindness to, difference. Thus, in 'Old Left' politics, according to several of his works, racial, gender and sexual differences are subsumed under the rubric of class. Not only does this tend to discount these other identities but it even reorganises them in a new hierarchy in which (the working) class is the privileged term. Equally, what Karim objects to in Tracey's 'Black' politics is its tendency to assume that 'all minority groups are oppressed equally in the same way'.[37] By contrast, as Allie observes: 'At least the blacks have a history of slavery. The Indians were kicked out of Uganda. There was reason for bitterness. But no-one put people like you and me into camps, and no-one will' (BS, 267–8).

As often as not, Kureishi's writing stresses that the differences between different kinds of marginal constituencies override the imperative of solidarity, even in the context of minority (sub-)cultures which are seemingly closely aligned. As was seen in Chapter 4, Anwar hates all Hindus (while invoking the example of Gandhi in his hunger strike to reassert his patriarchal authority over Jamila) and Changez repeatedly denounces Pakistanis. Even Rani's lesbian relationship with Vivia in *Sammy and Rosie* raises uncomfortable issues in terms of the power relations between the (voluble) British-Asian and (relatively silent) Black-British woman. In Kureishi's work, middle-class members of minorities often take advantage of their own people as well as of the white working class and there is as much class snobbery within Asian Britain as in mainstream society. Similar dislocations are evident in relationships which cross ethnicity lines. White women are as often exploiters of, as exploited by, minority males in Kureishi's writing. As Susan's friendship with Amina in *Borderline* implies, the conjunction of mainstream feminism with 'minoritarianism' is particularly fraught (though it is much too simple to write Kureishi off as a misogynist, even if one confines oneself to the texts discussed in Chapter 5). Riaz, like many British Asians in his writing, is homophobic – as is Karim himself, at times, despite his bisexuality (BS, 150) and both Anwar and Amjad in *Borderline* are deeply patriarchal. By contrast, the mutual hatred between Karim and Heater – 'the symbol of the masses' (BS, 175) – or the socialist Hussein's suspicion of Johnny in *Laundrette*, suggests the difficulties of aligning class and ethnic politics.

Kureishi's work also dampens the ardour of some of the more enthusiastic proponents of 'hybridity' insofar as the desire for it is often in practice overwhelmed by a variety of majority and minority particularisms. As Hashmi argues, for many of Kureishi's characters the '*black-and-white* aspect of the social reality literally reduces them to certain roles which, howsoever they may modify them, they cannot reject or transcend'.[38] As this suggests, it is one thing to claim 'hybridity', another to have that claim accepted or even tolerated by either or both of the cultural formations between which one is wishing to negotiate. *The Black Album* is perhaps most pessimistic in this respect:

> [Shahid] had noticed, during the days that he'd walked around the area, that the races were divided. The black kids stuck with each other, the Pakistanis went to one another's houses, the Bengalis knew each other from way back, and the whites, too. Even if there was no hostility between

groups – and there was plenty ... there was little mixing.
And would things change? Why should they? A few
individuals would make the effort, but wasn't the world
breaking into political and religious tribes? The divisions
were taken for granted, each to his own. (BA, 111)

John Ball rightly suggests that Kureishi's work often 'qualifies
and ironises the author's ... constructions of London as an enabling space inclusive of peoples and processes that represent "the
world"'.[39] A. Robert Lee makes a similar point about the inner
city, a favoured symbol of 'hybridity' in Kureishi's writing:
'Ethnic intercommunalism can flourish, as in Moss Side or Brent,
or turn divisive, as between Sikhs and Muslims in Slough and
Southall.'[40]

Even for those who seem to successfully evade the demand
for 'Purities' made by both majoritarian or minoritarian cultures,
Kureishi's writing suggests, there is often a heavy price to pay.
The author himself has recently disavowed earlier statements to
the contrary (see Chapter 1) in denying that he has been in any
way disadvantaged by the predicament of 'in-betweenness'.
Thus, he complained to Kaleta: 'Critics have written that I'm
caught between two cultures. I'm not ... I've made it in
England.'[41] However, his work itself often corroborates Salman
Rushdie's perception that: 'Sometimes we feel that we straddle
two cultures; at other times, that we fall between two stools.'[42]
For much of the early part of The Black Album, the largely
assimilated Shahid nonetheless feels himself to be 'invisible' in
London and his predicament at the end of the text is clearly
deeply uncertain and painful, despite the temporary relief of
reconciliation with Deedee. Even The Buddha ends with a
strongly melancholic undercurrent, which flows against its
characteristic optimism about the liberating potential of plural
and partial identities. This perhaps explains why physical escape
is often apparently the only viable option for Kureishi's
'in-between' protagonists, from Haroon in Borderline to Shahid
in The Black Album.

It should be noted in passing that Kureishi's enthusiasm for
other kinds of 'hybridity' is also often qualified. While multiform

sexuality is often celebrated, it is clearly no guarantee of political correctness, as Pyke's exploitation of Karim makes clear. Equally, as was seen in Chapter 5, much of the recent writing deplores the collapse of distinctions between 'high' and 'popular' cultural forms as evidence of the triumph of the market and its takeover of one of the last traditional sites of resistance to capitalism.

As was suggested earlier, while 'hybridity' has generally been presented in a positive light in contemporary cultural theory and criticism, it has also been viewed sceptically. This is not just because the very heterogeneity of its possible applications is such that 'hybridity' and its cognates sometimes appear to be in danger of losing any conceptual force. As Kureishi's writing suggests, individuals, relationships, groups and nations may all exhibit 'hybridity' in ways and to degrees which are not necessarily equivalent. Aspects of personal identity as diverse as place of habitation (London, suburbia, even West Kensington, are all 'interstitial' to differing degrees), class and sexuality may involve incommensurable kinds of 'hybridity'. Nor is it simply because there is a danger that 'hybridity' may itself become essentialised, in binary opposition to both 'host' culture and culture 'of origin' which in the process are illegitimately (re)constructed as singular, stable and 'pure' (paradoxically, 'hybridity' can thus lead to new dualisms).[43]

Rather, scepticism about 'hybridity' has been most forcefully expressed on political grounds. Some 'minoritarian' critics have argued that the rise of the concept accompanies the 'decline of "politics"' *tout court*.[44] Ella Shohat argues more moderately that 'celebration of syncretism and hybridity per se, if not articulated in conjunction with questions of hegemony and neo-colonial power relations, runs the risk of appearing to sanctify the *fait accompli* of [neo-]colonial violence.'[45] This reminds one that 'hybridity' has been at least as much a strategy of power exercised by the dominant culture as one of resistance by the subordinate. As earlier chapters have suggested, colonial policy was often concerned to produce compliant mimic men amongst the native populations by processes of 'hybridisation', acculturation and 'filtration'. The same process has, however, long been observable *within* Britain. In *On the Study of Celtic Literature* (1867), Matthew Arnold (who was seminal in the development of English studies) recommended the extinguishing of Welsh as a language in order to facilitate the principality's fusion with (in other words, submergence within) English culture. Conversely, he also embraced 'Celticism' ('Celts' can be understood to some degree as a Victorian equivalent of today's metropolitan minorities) as a means of leavening (or 'hybridising') the dull Saxonism of English culture (and in the process, of course, improving the efficacy of British control over its first and oldest colonial possession, 'Celtic' Ireland).[46] Thus, in contrast to Schoene's reading of Kureishi, which stresses how the author reveals 'the gaping void at the disheartened core of middle-class suburban Englishness',[47] one might see the 'centre's' selective appropriation of 'alien' cultures – in the form of Kureishi's own work, too – not as a symptom of 'lack', but of a confidently enduring neo-colonial mentality.

Moreover, if one understands globalisation as a reconstituted form of imperialism, the increasing 'hybridity' which many observers detect coming in its wake may be seen at least in part as a reinscription of this former colonial strategy. Not only does 'hybridity' become a means to acculturate the contemporary non-western world to the dominant norms and practices of the West, but in the view of critics like Yousaf, the 'positive' valuation of both cultural difference and 'hybridity' on the part of the 'host' culture is inextricably tied up with its value as a commodity within this new economic dispensation.[48] Insofar as capitalism is organised around the need to restlessly produce new commodities, and to extend its markets, so there is a tendency for both to become ever more 'hybridised'.[49] From this perspective, 'contemporary world writing' (and, indeed, more ostensibly oppositional kinds of postcolonial literature) is not so much an answering back to the centre, but a response to its demand for new kinds of niche product which it can also then re-export to the non-western world – or even a form of telling the West what it wants to hear about the non-western 'Other' in the comfort of its own languages.[50]

To some recent critics – they are usually Marxist or cultural nationalist or both – 'hybridity' can therefore be positively reactionary in its implications and effects. Aijaz Ahmad has bitterly criticised Salman Rushdie's cosmopolitan 'unrootedness' as, at best, a form of political evasion.[51] What lies behind such arguments is profound scepticism about the effectiveness of 'hybridity' in comparison with traditional kinds of political opposition to the injustices of the 'New World Order', whether in the form of class-based or cultural nationalist politics.[52] Even if one does not go this far, as Flint points out, mobilisations around multiple identities may be precarious ground on which to organise politically. If 'the problematics of being able to place oneself within a shifting culture … unsettle easy placements of centre and periphery',[53] they also make the 'centre' an elusive target, as Rushdie himself seems to confirm: 'If you look at any majority group it very quickly disintegrates … perhaps we are all members of exception groups [*sic*] … all societies are at least multi-sub-cultural, and most of us belong to more than one of this infinite variety of sub-cultures.'[54]

Once again, Kureishi's relationship to these negative accounts of 'hybridity' is divided and ambivalent. He himself lends weight to those who might doubt the conceptual purchase of the term, arguing that 'hybridity' is a constant feature of all human culture and not the exclusive property of minoritarian or post-colonial cultures: 'There are new hybridities and fusions … which are springing up all the time. As long as people from different worlds or different aspects of the same world mix together, there will be new forms and new hybrids.'[55] By contrast, he has also acknowledged the tendency to the commodification of ethnicity and 'hybridity' alike in arguing that 'our specific cultural inheritance … is often used by the owners of the media only in very specific ways … When the BBC or Channel 4 need an Asian they get us in and we do whatever we do.'[56] His writing repeatedly refers to this sort of commodification. For example, in *The Black Album*, Karim has exploited his 'hybridity' to become a successful actor and the high regard of sections of the majority culture for 'ethnic' products, from food to interior furnishings, is a consistent theme across Kureishi's *oeuvre*.

Moreover, his writing seems at times to corroborate the argument that the 'hybridisation' effected by the forces of globalisation may in practice mean nothing more than the reconstitution of older hierarchies, social divisions and physical boundaries within the more compressed space of the 'host' cultures of the West. Kureishi's London reproduces in microcosm the geographical differentiations of the former empire, with a variety of minorities located in often quite distinct areas or ghettos (Bangladeshis in East London, Sikhs in Southall, Africans in New Cross, Jamaicans in Brixton). So when Ball comments that London 'replicates within its borders the world's spatial patterning',[57] it is as well to remember that this patterning is partly a product of the long history of Western dominion overseas, which is now being replicated 'at home' in the system of 'domestic colonialism'.

Kureishi also constantly registers the centre's success in having its demand for 'hybridity' answered by minorities. Indeed, many of his least sympathetic Asian and British-Asian characters are distinctly 'hybrid'. In the first place, members of the national bourgeoisie of their countries of origin like Rafi in *Sammy and Rosie* are often highly 'hybridised'. The Cambridge-educated Rafi's cosmopolitan liberalism is no obstacle to his programmes of political oppression at home nor, indeed, to his traditionalist and oppressive conceptions of gender roles. There is a long line of similarly 'hybridised' and, in certain respects, equally unpleasant minority businessmen in Kureishi's work, from Haroon's father in *Borderline* to Salim in *Laundrette* and Nina's father in 'With Your Tongue Down My Throat' (LBT), who nonetheless cannot by any means be considered *fully* assimilated to the dominant culture. In such instances 'hybridity' provides a passage to a position of power (whether within the 'host' country or their country of origin) from which they often act as oppressors, even towards those in their own communities. While it is little suprise that an entrepreneur like Nasser in *Laundrette* is such an enthusiast for 'hybridity', those who are more distanced from ownership of the means of production, distribution and exchange, like the Jamaicans whom he employs to evict the squatters, experience the benefits of 'hybridity' to a far lesser degree.

However, Kureishi's work might itself be deemed vulnerable to some of the charges which have been brought against 'hybridity'. While Ahmad's critique is directed against more obviously postcolonial figures like Rushdie, it might also have some purchase in connection with writing like Kureishi's. In the first place, 'hybridity' rarely disturbs class hierarchies in Kureishi's work, as the failures of the various alliances based in the 'new social movements' in his films and novels suggest. In any case, it could be claimed, it tends overwhelmingly to be explored in terms of individuals rather than through forms of social solidarity. In certain texts, moreover, it is arguable that 'hybridity' is primarily tied up with issues of lifestyle, pleasure, consumption and self-advancement rather than with forms of political resistance. As several critics note, Karim chooses not to go on Jamila's march, dedicating himself to his art (and, more immediately, his love life) rather than engaging in political action. While he disdains binaries, the reality is that the politics of racism (and anti-racism) thrives on them. (Compare Haroon's stance in *Borderline*.) To this extent, Kureishi might seem to justify Sanjay Sharma's anxiety about 'the danger of sliding into an endless postmodern play on difference'.[58] It might further be argued that Kureishi's 'cultural translations' work overwhelmingly in one direction, characteristically making available, or even commodifying, British-Asian experience for a predominantly 'white' audience. As was argued in Chapter 2, from the outset of his career he has chosen to work in institutions which are in practice geared to an ethnically majoritarian audience.

As was seen in the introductory section of this chapter, some observers have questioned the integrity of Kureishi's use of British-Asian experience in his work. Behind some such criticisms lies a perception that, far from embracing any progressively 'hybrid' perspective, let alone taking up more obviously or traditionally oppositional positions, Kureishi's vision of

Asian Britain is 'assimilated' to the extent that it is indistinguishable from the dominant gaze of the dominant ethnicity. This has been true of critics in the non-western world,[59] of minoritarian critics based in the West and, more specifically, of those from a British-Asian background. Thus, Perminder Dhillon-Kashyap accuses *Laundrette* of creating 'a new victim, the white fascist',[60] who is the prey of unscrupulous immigrant entrepreneurs. bell hooks, by contrast, charges Kureishi with making a 'spectacle' of Otherness rather than really challenging the traditional gaze of western cinema and the assumptions which lie behind it.[61] In both critics' view, Kureishi's vision is, indeed, quasi-racist. Kureishi is to some extent vulnerable to the charge of 'Orientalism' which has been brought against him.[62] If Riaz is a version of the stereotype of the 'Oriental despot', so Ali in 'My Son the Fanatic' (LBT) corresponds to that of the Islamic fanatic of colonial discourse. Equally, one might see Tania's baring of her breasts in *Laundrette* as conforming to stereotypes about 'Oriental' women's forward sexuality. One should note also that, at various moments, Kureishi's British-Asian protagonists explicitly identify with the dominant gaze. At one point in *The Buddha*, Karim is complicit in an attempted assault on an elderly Asian by yobbish football 'supporters' (Tottenham fans, naturally) and on a school trip to Calais helps beat up a 'frog'. Equally, Shahid in *The Black Album* feels like a 'Britisher in India' on the 'sink' estate (BA, 113). To this extent, Kureishi might be deemed vulnerable to the charge of being a 'coconut' – brown outside, white inside.

Such objections need to be taken seriously, though in the end none of them are fully convincing. hooks's interpretation of Tania rests on the presumption that she is, indeed, simply 'Oriental', rather than *also* a feisty *British* teenager rebelling against constraining family proprieties. The perceptions of Karim and Shahid testify in part to the fact that they, too, are *also* British and in part to the politically inconvenient, but psychologically accurate, truth of their adolescent desire to be part of the dominant cultural formation, even if this means disavowing important parts of themselves while they are growing up.[63]

Shahid's response further attests to his realisation of the abyss between himself and the Bengali family in class and cultural terms (his family origins in middle-class Sevenoaks). In *The Black Album*, too, Kureishi is not *just* reinscribing elements of 'Orientalism', but *simultaneously* (and legitimately) critiquing elements of cultural 'fundamentalism' which disregard internationally-agreed standards of human rights.

Equally, if 'hybridity' rarely disturbs class hierarchies in Kureishi's work, conversely this reminds one that class privilege provides no protection against racism. From Amjad in *Borderline* to Salim in *Laundrette* to Anwar in *The Buddha*, comfortable, well-assimilated British-Asian businessmen are prone to all sorts of abuse, including physical assault. Thus, if class politics (and, indeed, cultural nationalism) provide a gratifyingly clear and easy system of binaries around which to mobilise politically, it does not follow that their success will necessarily entail the end of the other forms of oppression on which Kureishi's work focuses, whether in relation to ethnicity, gender or sexuality. If, as Yousaf argues, Kureishi 'critiques the Right but does not fail to interrogate the failings of the Left', this does not undermine Quart's conclusion that, despite his eschewal of a Manichean political vision, Kureishi belongs unquestionably to the Left, broadly conceived.[64] As Hall argues, the emergence of 'new ethnicities' does *not* necessarily imply the disavowal of politics, but rather the reconstitution of politics as traditionally conceived. Thus, 'it is not a politics which invites easy identifications ... [but is] grounded on the complexity of identifications which are at work.'[65] At the very least, such complexity refutes the argument that Kureishi presents ethnicity as a spectacle of stable Otherness to be passively consumed by a majoritarian audience. As Ray argues of *The Buddha*: 'No one position is favoured, and yet the various voices arguing and interfering with each other do question both the structures of the nation-state and the constraints of ethnicity and national particularity.'[66]

Moreover, the charge that Kureishi's vision of identity amounts to no more than an endorsement of postmodernism's allegedly irresponsible and selfish celebration of difference and

pluralism for its own sake is questionable. He clearly distinguishes between the assumption of new identities for the purpose
of pleasure (without puritanically condemning such playful
experimentation) and more politicised forms of role play. When
Karim and Jamila pretend to be French, Roman and Greek, or
African-American, this is precisely because 'to the English we
were always wogs and nigs and Pakis and the rest of it' (BS, 53);
and when Shahid cross-dresses with Deedee, it is in part in order
to self-consciously test dominant conceptions of gender roles.

   In any case, it is too simple to suggest that Kureishi only
endorses 'hybridity' in the context of individual life choices, if
only because one of the strongest themes of his writing is the
inextricable connection between the 'personal' and 'the
political'. This is regularly insisted on, particularly in Kureishi's
refusal to grant autonomy to the most intimate aspects of
individual affective experience. Of *Laundrette*, Cook justifiably
argues that the relationship between Johnny and Omar 'is never
seen outside politics and history'.[67] In *Sammy and Rosie*,
Sammy and Anna make love on the terrace overlooking the city,
with a police helicopter overhead, Danny and Rosie while being
serenaded by the 'straggly kids'. Both moments symbolise the
interconnection between 'public' and 'private'. Moreover, however
paradoxical it may seem, the embrace of individualism can be
seen, not as a form of evasion, but in a politically positive light –
because of the necessarily 'representative' nature of the experience of the ethnically marked individual. (While all individuals
are ethnically marked, one might suggest that in practice some are
more marked than others.) In *Borderline*, Haroon described his
planned trajectory as a long march through the institutions.
While Yasmin accuses him of abandoning politics, it could instead
be argued that at the very least his proposed path adumbrates the
immanent forms of 'hybridisation' about which Bhabha, following Bakhtin, has written. Social institutions cannot remain
exactly as they were once the 'worm' of ethnicity has entered
their body. Black faces in parliament, the judiciary, the army,
sport and the culture industries too,[68] have an important role to
play in changing such institutions both in themselves and in

their representative role in the eyes of society. (This is the principle underlying all programmes of affirmative action.) As Bakhtin puts it, while not ostensibly disordering or oppositional in the manner of 'conscious' or 'intentional' hybrids, 'unconscious hybrids ... are pregnant with potential for new world views.'[69]

Nor can art be seen simply as being in binary opposition to material forms of political activism, even if it is sometimes seen in such terms both by certain contemporary Marxists[70] and in Kureishi's own work. He is modest about the immediate instrumental political effectivity of his work: 'You would flatter yourself if you thought you could change things by a film or a play or whatever, but perhaps you can contribute to a climate of ideas ... Asking these questions [about how we live] seems to me to be the thing artists can do rather than change society in any specific way.'[71] Thus as Ball has argued, Kureishi's work is potentially enabling in that it adumbrates the outlines of a changed and better world. For example, the final scene of *Laundrette* 'hints at a new order to come ... one that could replace the vengeful satisfaction of Omar as boss and Johnny as boy with a more equitable partnership inspired by the mutuality of erotic love'.[72]

In conclusion, many potential objections to Kureishi's work in this context might be answered through reference to Rushdie's essay 'Minority Literatures in a Multi-Cultural Society'. Here Rushdie distinguishes between two different kinds of minoritarian writing. The first is addressed primarily to the writer's own community and seeks to give it cultural confidence and a voice. The second is addressed primarily to a majoritarian audience and seeks to mediate the concerns of the writer's community of origin in an educative way. While each kind of writing involves what Kobena Mercer has called the 'burden of representation', and each is important, Rushdie argues – like Mercer – that the former runs 'a danger of marginalization from within'.[73] A self-consciously self-directed minoritarian literature is also likely to be confined by the majority society to the status of a 'ghetto' literature. Rushdie has explicitly defended

Kureishi against the demands of some minoritarian political activists, arguing that their criticism 'seeks implicitly to control the writer's choice of subject matter' (precisely the theme of *The Black Album*); contesting the claim that 'a black British writer must write about the black British experience', Rushdie proposes that writers like Kureishi and himself 'might merely wish to write about everything writers want to write about: love, death, money, the whole business of being human ... which have nothing to do with my ethnicity'. (This legitimises the directions taken in some of Kureishi's recent work.)[74]

As indicated in Chapter 1, Kureishi has seconded Rushdie's assertion that 'I simply resist the idea of being representative.'[75] In the first place, he argues that it is necessary to get beyond the kind of 'identity politics' which can at times not only advance social disintegration through separatism, but also play into the hands of the dominant culture: 'I hope there will come a time when we are seen beyond the fact that we have some kind of cultural background that the owners of the media wish to use, sometimes for the best of reasons, sometimes for the worst, and sometimes for a mixture.'[76] Secondly, he has vigorously defended his depiction of Asian Britain in relation to, and in the context of, wider British society. A genuinely democratic, cosmopolitan nation and a renewed, plural sense of what it means to be British, he argues, can only be achieved by the creation of 'diverse British communities of which characters of Asian back-grounds are members'.[77] He has also vigorously defended writers like James Baldwin against criticisms that, by entering the mind of white characters, they are *ipso facto* identifying with the dominant gaze and, in so doing, betraying their supposed communities of origin. In this sense, his work corroborates Spivak's argument: 'If part of [the minority writer's] role is to educate the so-called minorities, part of it is to educate the so-called dominant viewership about the minorities as well.'[78] This also partly explains Kureishi's institutional affiliations. The mass media may be majoritarian in orientation, but they are also likely to be the best means to reach a large British-Asian audience, too. It is doubtful whether – marooned in Gloucester –

Sukhdev Sandhu, for example, would have so quickly found his cultural voice as a British-Asian without the aid of TV. Finally, the strong criticisms of Kureishi from minoritarian critics like Dhillon-Kashyap and hooks are hard to sustain given the response to Kureishi from New Right sympathisers like Norman Stone – particularly when it is exactly the same texts which they are all objecting to. Rather, their combined reactions indicate the degree of Kureishi's success in challenging the 'Purities' of both the majority and minority cultures, each of which pressures the writer to produce 'positive' images of the (single) community to which s/he is supposed to be affiliated.

Such debates point to the high degree of contestation over the possible meanings of 'hybridity' and their applicability to Kureishi's work – and by extension, perhaps, to other minority and postcolonial writing. As his best critics have recognised, Kureishi's representation and treatment of 'hybridity' is itself hybrid and ambivalent. In large measure, such instability reflects his sometimes unconsolingly honest perception of the uneven, often contradictory and sometimes highly conflictual nature of inter-cultural relations in the contemporary world. As the cultural/political landscape continues to shift at the turn of a new century, further inflecting minority and postcolonial writing and debate about it – and pushing both in new directions as it does so – it remains to be seen whether Kureishi's work has helped to provide a new, enabling paradigm for discussions of cultural identity and belonging; or whether it will be seen in time as a manifestation of what Terry Eagleton has described as the 'premature utopianism' of wishing to live 'in sheer irreducible difference *now*', while the cultural differences represented by class and nation (and by extension, ethnicity and race) remain such obviously determining factors in the contemporary world.[79]

What can be decided at the present moment, however, is that Kureishi has helped to realise what has always been one of his primary aims. As he puts it in 'Dirty Washing':

> I stress that it is the British who have to make these adjustments. It is they who have to learn that being British

isn't what it was. Now it is a more complex thing, involving new elements. So there must be a fresh way of seeing Britain and the choices that it faces: and a new way of being British after all this time.[80]

Insofar as today's Britain has been transformed since the 1960s, and conceptions of national identity and belonging have – however grudgingly – become more plural since Orwell, Priestley and Eliot defined them, forms of 'contemporary world writing' such as Kureishi's have been a crucial catalyst. Nor can one underestimate the importance of the fact that Kureishi, more than any other single artist, has helped to render Asian Britain visible as a subject of cultural representation.

Notes

Chapter 1

1 That the reader's location is crucial to interpretation of Kureishi's work is suggested by the fact that the author once received a letter from Saudi Arabia praising *The Black Album* for exposing the corruptions of the West. See Adnan Ashraf, '"Into the Unknown": An Interview with Hanif Kureishi' (October, 1995) http://www.walrus.com/-adnan/kureishi.html: 5.

2 On the liabilities of 'local' or 'regional' writing, see Salman Rushdie, 'Minority Literatures in a Multi-Cultural Society', in Kirsten Holst Petersen and Anna Rutherford, eds, *Displaced Persons* (Aarhus, Denmark: Seklos, 1987): 34. For an argument against overvaluing 'world writing' at the expense of such work, see Stefano Manferlotti, 'Writers from Elsewhere', in Iain Chambers and Lidia Curti, eds, *The Postcolonial Question: Common Skies, Divided Horizons* (London: Routledge, 1996): 189. For Kureishi's own comments on his relationship to 'local' and 'world' writing, see Kenneth Kaleta, *Hanif Kureishi: Postcolonial Storyteller* (Austin, Texas; University of Texas Press, 1998): 7 and Ashraf, '"Into the Unknown"': 5.

3 There is a deep-rooted tendency in 'British' cultural historiography to conflate 'English' and 'British', which has been increasingly criticised from within the non-English nations of the United Kingdom. I will endeavour to keep the two terms distinct when practicable. For a subtle discussion of the differences as they relate to postcolonialism, see Simon Gikandi, *Maps of Englishness: Writing Identity in the Culture of Colonialism* (New York: Columbia University Press, 1996).

4 Compare Rushdie, 'The New Empire Within Britain', in *Imaginary Homelands: Essays and Criticism 1981–1991* (1991; Harmondsworth: Penguin, 1992): 129–38.

5   The term 'immigrant' often has negative connotations – mainly because in practice it almost exclusively applied to members of ethnic minorities, which are not intended in this text. It also conflates British-born members of the nation's ethnic minorities with those born elsewhere and often fails to register the fact that many 'immigrants' do not settle permanently in the 'host' culture. For example, Binoo in Kureishi's *Borderline* and Minoo in *My Son the Fanatic* dream of returning to Pakistan (Minoo, indeed, does so). Nonetheless, the term is often indispensable. For further discussion of such terms and associated concepts like 'diaspora', see Avtar Brah, *Cartographies of Diaspora: Contesting Identities* (London: Routledge, 1996); Iain Chambers, *Migrancy, Culture, Identity* (London: Routledge, 1994); James Clifford, *Routes: Travel and Translation in the Late Twentieth Century* (London: Harvard University Press, 1997); and Robin Cohen, *Global Diasporas: An Introduction* (London: UCL Press, 1997). John McCleod points out that 'migrancy has effects which last long after the act of migrating has ceased'. *Beginning Postcolonialism* (Manchester: Manchester University Press, 2000): 210. However, since Kureishi rarely 'looks back' to the subcontinent, describing him as 'immigrant', 'migrant' or 'diasporic' is problematic.

6   'Race' and 'ethnicity' are equally problematic terms, but again indispensable. On the genealogy and meanings of the former term, see Paul Gilroy, *'There Ain't No Black in the Union Jack': The Cultural Politics of Race and Nation* (London: Hutchinson, 1987); Robert Young, *Colonial Desire: Hybridity in Theory, Culture and Race* (London: Routledge, 1995) and Les Back and John Solomos, eds, *Theories of Race and Racism: A Reader* (London: Routledge, 2000); of the latter, Werner Sollers, ed., *Theories of Ethnicity: A Classical Reader* (Basingstoke: Macmillan, 1996); John Hutchinson and Anthony D. Smith, eds, *Ethnicity* (Oxford: Oxford University Press, 1996) and Pnina Werbner and Tariq Modood, eds, *Debating Cultural Hybridity: Multi-Cultural Identities and the Politics of Anti-Racism* (London: Zed, 1997). While taking Stuart Hall's point that every individual is ethnically-marked and that 'the English are just another ethnic group', I will be using the adjective in its habitual sense to describe members of ethnic minorities. See 'The Local and the Global: Globalization and Ethnicity', in Anthony D. King, ed., *Culture, Globalization and the World System* (Basingstoke: Macmillan, 1991): 21. While rejecting the idea that ethnicity is foundational, I would disagree with Berthold Schoene's argument, supposedly paraphrasing Kureishi, that everybody 'is entitled to their own singular ethnicity'. Ethnicity is *social* in character and cannot be so voluntarily chosen or disavowed. See

'Herald of Hybridity: the Emancipation of Difference in Hanif Kureishi's *The Buddha of Suburbia*', *International Journal of Cultural Studies* 1.1 (1998): 123.

7   'Liberal', too, is a problematic term, encompassing a range of meanings from traditional humanist thinking to support for unbridled free market economics.

8   For diametrically opposed Marxist and 'liberal' interpretations of the politics of globalisation, see Aijaz Ahmad, *In Theory: Classes, Nations, Literatures* (London: Verso, 1992) and Francis Fukuyama, *The End of History and the Last Man* (Harmondsworth: Penguin, 1992). On the issue of whether globalisation encourages cultural homogenisation or diversification, see King, *Culture, Globalization and the World-System*. Other important discussions include Arjun Appadurai, *Modernity at Large: Cultural Dimensions of Globalization* (New Delhi: Oxford University Press, 1997); Mike Featherstone, ed., *Global Culture: Nationalism, Globalization and Modernity* (London: Sage, 1990); David Harvey, *The Condition of Postmodernity* (Oxford: Blackwell, 1989); and John Tomlinson, *Globalization and Culture* (Cambridge: Polity, 1999).

9   Compare Hall, 'The Local': 36. Once more, 'fundamentalism' is a contested term, with pejorative connotations which are not intended in this text. For analysis of the discourses around 'fundamentalism', see Bobby Sayyid, *A Fundamental Fear: Eurocentrism and the Emergence of Islamism* (London: Zed, 1997).

10   Donald Weber argues that Kureishi is 'more helpfully situated as a striking variation on American "ethnic" writers, especially Philip Roth, than as an example of "Black British" expression'. '"No Secrets Were Safe From Me": Situating Hanif Kureishi', *Massachusetts Review* 38.1 (1997): 130.

11   Mercer, 'Black Art and The Burden of Representation', *Third Text* 10 (Spring) 1990: 61–78. For an influential argument that all 'minoritarian' art is necessarily politicised and communally representative, see Abdul JanMohamed and David Lloyd, 'Introduction: Towards a Theory of Minority Discourse: What is to be Done?', in JanMohamed and Lloyd, eds, *The Nature and Context of Minority Discourse* (Oxford: Oxford University Press, 1990): 1–16. For Kureishi's opinions on Roth, see 'Dirty Washing', *Time Out*, 795, 14–20 Nov., 1985: 26.

12   Dick Hebdige, *Subculture: The Meaning of Style* (London: Methuen, 1979), traces such fusions through a wide range of post-war musical and subcultural fashions. Compare Hall, 'The Local': 38–9.

13   As Jan Aarte Scholte argues: 'Much global culture is youth culture.'

Globalization: A Critical Introduction (Basingstoke: Macmillan, 2000): 177.

14 Colin MacCabe, 'Interview: Hanif Kureishi on London', *Critical Quarterly* 41.3 (1999): 48.

15 For an account of the relationship between pop and anti-racist politics, see Gilroy, *'There Ain't No Black'*; on pop and British-Asian anti-racism more specifically, see Virinder Kalra *et al.*, 'Re-Sounding (Anti)Racism, or Concordant Politics? Revolutionary Antecedents' in Sanjay Sharma *et al.*, eds, *Dis-Orienting Rhythms: The Politics of the New Asian Dance Music* (London: Zed, 1996): 127–55.

16 Compare Stuart Hall, 'Old and New Identities, Old and New Ethnicities' in King, *Culture, Globalization and the World-System*: 65.

17 Kureishi, *The Mother Country*, unpublished typescript in author's possession: 77.

18 Kureishi has recently commented that most American culture is 'junk' ; see MacCabe, 'Interview': 52.

19 Compare Hall, 'The Local': 24. He adds that while global culture 'remains centred in the West … it is not centred in the same way [as before]'. (28) For an account of South Asian communities and their migration to Britain, see R. Ballard, ed., *Desh Pardesh: the South Asian Presence in Britain* (London: Hurst, 1994). Between 1979 and 1991, the ethnic minority population of Britain grew from 3.4 per cent to 5.5 per cent of the population, with the population of South Asian origin estimated at 840,000 in 1991. See Marc Porée, *Hanif Kureishi: The Buddha of Suburbia* (Paris: CNED-Didier Concours, 1997): 94, and Elaine Dubourdieu, 'The Buddha, Britain and "Black" Immigration', in François Gallix, ed., *The Buddha of Suburbia* (Paris: Ellipses, 1997): 133.

20 Compare *The Buddha*: 141; see also Rushdie's description of the immigrant in *Imaginary Homelands*: 394.

21 On the 'world city', see John Eade, ed., *Living in the Global City: Globalisation as a Local Process* (London: Routledge, 1997) and Richard V. Knight and Gary Gappert, eds, *Cities in a Global Society* (London: Sage, 1989); on the emergence of multicultural London, see Anthony D. King, *Global Cities: Post-Imperialism and the Internationalization of London* (London: Routledge, 1996); Anne Kershen, ed., *London: the Promised Land? The Migrant Experience in a Capital City* (London: Avebury, 1997) and Gerd Baumann, *Contesting Culture: Discourses of Identity in Multi-Ethnic London* (Cambridge: Cambridge University Press, 1996). According to Anna Marie Smith, 3 per cent of London's

population was 'black' in the late eighteenth century. See *New Right Discourse on Race and Sexuality* (Cambridge: Cambridge University Press, 1994): 134.

22 'Translation' has become a key term in postcolonial studies, with a spectrum of applications ranging from the linguistic to the sociological. See Rushdie, *Imaginary Homelands*: 9–21; Homi Bhabha, *The Location of Culture* (London: Routledge, 1994), especially 'Articulating the Archaic', 'DissemiNation' and 'How Newness Enters the World'; and Susan Basnett and Harish Trivedi, eds, *Postcolonial Translation: Theory and Practice* (London: Routledge, 1999).

23 Kureishi remembers his father in 'My Father's Gift', *The Sunday Telegraph Magazine*, 26 April 1998: 15–18.

24 Compare MacCabe, 'Interview': 52.

25 William Leith, 'Sex, Drugs and a Mid-Life Crisis', *The Observer*, 'Life' Section, 23 March, 1997: 8. Compare Suzie MacKenzie, 'All for Love', *The Guardian*, 'Weekend' section, 2 May, 1998: 25–7.

26 In contrast to the present volume, Kaleta's *Hanif Kureishi* is a critical biography and consequently seeks out connections between the work and the man. In discussing *The Buddha*, for example, Kaleta argues that 'the autobiographical connections between Kureishi and Karim, between fact and fiction, become irresistible' (72). Alamgir Hashmi, by contrast, warns against biographical approaches to Kureishi's work, because it leads to 'inevitably negative judgements of both the man and his work'! 'Hanif Kureishi and the Tradition of the Novel', (1992), *Critical Survey* 5.1 (1993): 25–6.

27 Jane Root, 'Scenes from a Marriage', *Monthly Film Bulletin* 52.622 (November, 1985): 333.

28 *The Guardian*, 7 May, 1998: 21.

29 Lucy Johnston, 'Hanif and the Spurned Woman', *The Observer*, 10 May, 1998: 9.

30. *Ibid*: 8.

31 Leith, 'Sex, Drugs': 8.

32 The problem of unreliable memory is highlighted in the 'Introduction' to *Outskirts and Other Plays*. Kureishi misremembers one of the married couples in *Birds of Passage* as Ted and Jean whereas, of course, they are called Ted and Eva. The most serious inaccuracy is the rendering of the title of his first play, *Soaking the Heat*, as *Soaking up the Heart*.

33 Johnston, 'Hanif': 8.

34   Kureishi is not, of course, the first writer to engage with British-Asian experience. Anita Desai's *Bye Bye Blackbird* (1969), V. S. Naipaul's *In a Free State* (1971) and Kamala Markandaya's *The Nowhere Man* (1972) address the issue but, unlike these writers, Kureishi was born in Britain. Stephen Frears' reaction to the script of *Laundrette* is indicative of the radical novelty of Kureishi's subject matter at the time: 'Nobody had ever written from that perspective before. It was astonishing because [Kureishi] got it so right. That someone could be … so confident about it, make the jokes, be on the inside.' Cited in Susan Torrey Barber, 'Insurmountable Difficulties and Moments of Ecstasy: Crossing Class, Ethnic, and Sexual Barriers in the Films of Stephen Frears' in Lester Friedman, ed., *British Cinema and Thatcherism: Fires Were Started* (London: UCL Press, 1993): 224. Frears reflects on his collaborations with Kureishi in Lester Friedman and Scott Stewart, 'Keeping His Own Voice: An Interview with Stephen Frears' in Wheeler Winston Dixon, ed., *Reviewing British Cinema 1900–1992: Essays and Interviews* (New York: State University of New York Press, 1994): 221–40.

35   Kureishi states that he doesn't know how studying philosophy has affected his writing (MacCabe, 'Interview': 46.) But it becomes an important framework in his most recent writing; see Chapter 5.

36   See Marcia Pally, 'Kureishi Like a Fox', *Film Comment* 22.5 (Sept–Oct 1986): 52. For hostile non-western critical accounts of Kureishi, see Hashmi, 'Hanif Kureishi': 32; for hostile accounts by western minority critics, see Nahem Yousaf, 'Hanif Kureishi and "the Brown Man's Burden"', *Critical Survey* 8.1 (1996): 15ff; Kaleta, *Hanif Kureishi*: 45ff and 219; and Sarita Malik, 'Beyond "The Cinema of Duty"?: The Pleasures of Hybridity: Black British Film of the 1980s and 1990s', in Andrew Higson, ed., *Dissolving Views: Key Writings on British Cinema* (London: Cassell, 1996): 209. Some of these will be discussed in Chapter 6.

37   As Ali Rattansi argues, 'generalizations about "British Asians" [are] a foolhardy project except at a highly abstract level.' See 'On Being and Not Being Brown/Black-British: Racism, Class, Sexuality and Ethnicity in Post-Imperial Britain', *Interventions: International Journal of Postcolonial Studies* 2.1 (2000): 128. Compare Malik's assertion that 'British-Asian' is 'a fluid evolving entity, which cannot be reduced to any one thing'. 'Beyond': 213.

38   On intergenerational conflict in Kureishi, see Suresht Renjen Bald, 'Negotiating Identity in the Metropolis: Generational Differences in South Asian British Fiction', in Russell King *et al.*, eds, *Writing Across Worlds: Literature and Migration* (London: Routledge, 1995): 70–88.

39 On families in *The Buddha*, see Sylvia Mergenthal, 'Acculturation and Family Structure: Mo's *Sour Sweet*, Kureishi's *The Buddha of Suburbia*, Ishiguro's *A Pale View of Hills*', in Eckhard Breitinger, ed., *Defining New Idioms and Alternative Forms of Expression* (Amsterdam: Rodopi, 1996): 119–27. For the films' treatment of the family, see note 22 to Chapter 3.

40 However, Kureishi admires Forster the novelist. See 'England, Bloody England', *The Guardian*, 15 Jan., 1988: 19.

41 Chinua Achebe, 'Named for Victoria, Queen of England', *Morning Yet on Creation Day: Essays* (London: Heinemann, 1975): 70. For more on the relationship between Kureishi and postcolonial and minority writing respectively, see Gayatri Spivak, '*Sammy and Rosie Get Laid*', in *Outside in the Teaching Machine* (London: Routledge, 1993): 243–54; Manferlotti, 'Writers from Elsewhere': 189–98; Kate Flint, 'Black Swans and the Black Country: Identity, Nationhood and Black Writing in Contemporary Britain', in Jacqueline Lo *et al.*, eds, *Impossible Selves: Cultural Readings of Identity* (Melbourne: Australian Scholarly Publishing, 1999): 72–84; and Cynthia Carey, 'Hanif Kureishi's *The Buddha of Suburbia* as a Post-Colonial Novel', *Commonwealth: Essays and Studies: Special Issue no. SP 4* (Dijon, France) 1997: 119–25.

42 Kureishi has disavowed 'the politics of blame' on the grounds that: 'It's a kind of trap that white people put black people into.' Root, 'Scenes': 333.

43 For more on this colonial trope, see Gail Ching-Liang Low, 'White Skins/Black Masks: the Pleasures and Politics of Imperialism', *New Formations* 9 (winter) 1989: 83–104.

44 See S. H. Alatas, *The Myth of the Lazy Native: A Study of the Image of the Malays, Filipinos, and Javanese from the Sixteenth to the Twentieth Centuries and its Functions in the Ideology of Colonial Capitalism* (London: Cass, 1977).

45 Kureishi, *Mother Country*: 41.

46 Ashraf, '"Into the Unknown"': 5. In strong contrast to my argument, however, Hashmi suggests that Kureishi draws on non-western cultural material in *The Buddha*. 'Hanif Kureishi' asserts that 'commentators have been consistently oblivious to the dual tradition to which Kureishi belongs' (26) and attempts to link Kureishi to an 'Asian line of [literary] descent' (32). Narayan and Tharoor are invoked as intertexts on the basis that some of their work includes the trope of rascally gurus. The link is also allegedly manifest in Kureishi's sarcastic narrative tone of voice, which Hashmi claims is distinctively Pakistani. Given the Royal Court

connection, a more probable source for Haroon is Matura's play *As Time Goes By*; and a sarcastic narrative voice is common in contemporary British fiction – for instance in the work of Martin Amis. Similarly, I am not persuaded by Fawzia Afzal-Khan's (admittedly tentative) description of Kureishi as a Pakistani writer on the grounds that he (sometimes) writes about Pakistani immigrants to Britain. Given that Kureishi has only visited Pakistan twice, briefly, and usually represents it as a (monoglot) outsider, the label is unconvincing. See 'Pakistani Writing in English: 1847 to the Present: A Survey', *Wasafiri* 21 (Spring, 1995): 58–61. Compare Hashmi, 'Current Pakistani Fiction', *Commonwealth Novel in English* 5.1 (1992): 59–64. I am unconvinced by similar arguments offered in respect of *The Buddha* by a range of French critics. See Dominique Vinet, '*The Buddha of Suburbia*: le Carnaval des Mythes', *Études Britanniques Contemporaines* (Montpellier, France), 13, Janvier, 1998: 57–74; Michèle Hita, 'Identité, Union et Voyeurisme' in Gallix, *The Buddha of Suburbia*: 37–44; Michel Naumann, 'Humour et Entre-Deux; Les Pensées Indiennes et Occidentales dans *The Buddha of Suburbia*', ibid: 118–28. All three accounts seem counter-intuitive.

47   Kureishi has recently described how Rushdie provoked him into writing fiction by challenging him to prove his credentials as a 'serious' writer (screenplays evidently didn't count). See MacCabe, 'Interview': 42.

48   For more on the links between *Midnight's Children* and *The Buddha*, see Vinet, '*The Buddha*'.

49   Homi Bhabha, 'Introduction: Narrating the Nation', in Bhabha, ed., *Nation and Narration* (London: Routledge, 1990): 7. This claim must be treated sceptically. Were it wholly true, much of the work of writers like Achebe, Ngugi and Narayan would be excluded from the postcolonial canon. Moreover, a considerable amount of contemporary western writing, including some of the work of Grass and Calvino, might be described as 'magic realism'.

50   Chinua Achebe, 'The African Writer and the English Language', in *Morning Yet*: 62.

51   Rushdie, *Imaginary Homelands*: 17.

52   For further discussion of postmodern elements in Kureishi's work, see John C. Ball, 'The Semi-Detached Metropolis: Hanif Kureishi's London', *ARIEL: A Review of International English Literature* 27.4 (1996): 22ff; Jörg Helbig, '"Get Back to Where You Once Belonged": Hanif Kureishi's Use of the Beatles-Myth in *The Buddha of Suburbia*', in Wolfgang Klooss, ed., *Across the Lines:*

Intertextuality and Transcultural Communication in the New Literatures in English (Amsterdam: Rodopi, 1998): 81ff, and Hashmi, 'Hanif Kureishi': 26.

53   Kureishi has argued that: 'Once you accept a world-view - be it Marxist or religious - you've given over freedom ... Doubt is the most crucial human faculty of all.' Pally, 'Kureishi': 52.

54   My use of terms like 'third way' and 'third space' owes much to Bhabha's elaboration of such concepts. See Jonathon Rutherford, 'Interview with Homi Bhabha: The Third Space', in Rutherford, ed., *Identity: Community, Culture, Difference* (London: Lawrence and Wishart, 1990): 207–21.

Chapter 2

1   Shortly afterwards, ironically, Kureishi began work on *Sleep With Me*, which opened at the National Theatre in April 1999.

2   Only four of Kureishi's early plays are readily available. *Soaking the Heat* (1976, about student life) and *The Mother Country* (1980, about the relationship between a Pakistani immigrant father and his British-born son) were performed, but never published. This chapter will therefore focus on the plays in *Outskirts and Other Plays* (London: Faber, 1992), with some reference to *Tomorrow-Today!*, in *Outskirts, The King and Me, Tomorrow-Today!* (London: Calder, 1983).

3   Compare MacCabe, 'Interview': 47.

4   William Gaskill, *A Sense of Direction: Life at The Royal Court* (London: Faber, 1988): 34.

5   This opinion was widespread amongst British novelists of the 1970s, especially younger ones. See my 'Apocalypse Now?: The Novel in the 1970s', in Moore-Gilbert, ed., *The Arts in the 1970s: Cultural Closure?* (London: Routledge, 1994): 152–75. This volume also analyses the major cultural debates in progress when Kureishi began his career.

6   Catherine Itzin, *Stages in the Revolution: Political Theatre Since 1968* (London: Methuen, 1980): xiv. This remains the best account of political 'fringe'. Important accounts by some of its luminaries include John McGrath's *A Good Night Out: Popular Theatre: Audience, Class, and Form* (London: Methuen, 1981), David Hare's *Writing Left-Handed* (London: Faber, 1991) and David Edgar's *The Second Time as Farce: Reflections on the Drama of*

Mean Times (London: Lawrence and Wishart, 1988), all of which have influenced my approach to Kureishi's plays.

7   Hare, *Writing*: 15.

8   Cited in Itzin, *Stages*: 25.

9   The 'Introduction' to Moore-Gilbert, *The Arts in the 1970s* contains a survey of debates about the state of the nation in the decade.

10   A similar pattern is evident in British film. See Andrew Higson, *Waving the Flag: Constructing a National Cinema* (Oxford: Clarendon, 1995): 274ff.

11   For a good account of feminist 'fringe', see Micheline Wandor, *Look Back in Gender: Sexuality and the Family in Post-War British Theatre* (London: Methuen, 1987).

12   Itzin's list of 'fringe' plays provides tantalising evidence of earlier British-Asian dramatists. In 1976, Jamal Ali's *The Treatment/ Dark Days, Light Nights* played at the Soho Poly and in 1977 the King's Head staged Ali Salim's *Caramba*. I've not been able to trace these texts. Vincent Ebrahim, who played Haroon/Farouk in *Borderline*, has told me that Kureishi was the only British-Asian dramatist he was aware of at the time. (Telephone interview on 19 July, 1998. Subsequent references to Ebrahim's opinions are taken from this interview.) For a fellow playwright's view of British-Asian drama, see Jatinder Verma, 'Cultural Transformations' in Theodore Shank, ed., *Contemporary British Theatre* (Basingstoke: Macmillan, 1994), 55–61.

13   Rattansi argues that 'it is from these sections of the working class that complaints of second-class status "in their own country" … are particularly popular and are part of a culture of resentment and anger so many of whose victims are the black and brown people who almost inevitably personify for these marginalized English the causes of their social exclusion.' 'On Being': 132.

14   For an analysis of the discourse around mugging in 1970s Britain, see Stuart Hall *et al.*, eds, *Policing the Crisis: Mugging, the State, and Law and Order* (London: Macmillan, 1978).

15   Compare Rushdie's assertion that 'the real gift which we can offer our communities is not the creation of a set of stereotyped positive images to counteract the stereotyped negative ones, but simply the gift of treating black and Asian characters in a way that white writers seem very rarely able to do, that is to say as fully realized human beings, as complex creatures, good, bad, bad, good.' 'Minority Literatures': 41.

16   Bhabha, *Location*: 119.

17   Edward Said, *Orientalism* (1978; Harmondsworth: Penguin, 1991): 208. By contrast to Said, Kureishi's work suggests that West *and* East fantasise about each other.

18   Kureishi, *Mother Country*: 42.

19   See 'Can the Subaltern Speak?', in Patrick Williams and Laura Chrisman, eds, *Colonial Discourse and Post-Colonial Theory: A Reader* (Hemel Hempstead: Harvester Wheatsheaf, 1993): 66–111. My own text might be vulnerable to such charges.

20   Compare Spivak, *The Post-Colonial Critic: Interviews, Strategies, Dialogues*, ed. Sarah Harasym (London: Routledge, 1990): 156.

21   Compare Spivak, *In Other Worlds: Essays in Cultural Politics* (London: Routledge, 1987): 250.

22   Itzin, *Stages*: 89.

23   On Kureishi's attitude to Brecht, see Ria Julian, 'Brecht and Britain: Hanif Kureishi in Interview with Ria Julian', *Drama: Quarterly Theatre Review* 155 (1987): 5–7.

24   Gaskill, *Sense of Direction*: 20.

25   For accounts of the working methods of Joint Stock, see Gaskill, *Sense of Direction*, Hare, *Writing* and Rob Ritchie, ed., *The Joint Stock Book: The Making of a Theatre Collective* (London: Methuen, 1977).

26   Cited in Itzin, *Stages*: 258.

27   HK. In contrast to Kureishi's interpretation, Ebrahim recollects that objections to white actors playing British-Asian characters were the prime reason for the threats.

28   This was for an MA in drama at Essex University which Kureishi did not finally pursue (HK).

29   Vivien Mercier, 'The Mathematical Limit', *The Nation*, CLXXXVIII, 14 Feb., 1959: 144.

30   For more on Orton, see John Lahr's *Prick Up Your Ears: The Biography of Joe Orton* (London: Allen Lane, 1978). Frears directed the film of *Prick up Your Ears* (1987).

31   This also has echoes of *The Caretaker* by Pinter (1960, revived at the Mermaid in 1972), a playwright whom Kureishi greatly admires (HK). *Birds of Passage* has echoes of *The Homecoming* (1965, revived at The Garrick, 1978). Stella's homecoming is as ambivalently received as Teddy and Ruth's and Stella is further linked to Ruth through the theme of prostitution.

32   This is not the only citation of Russian literature in the play. Asif is likened to the protagonist of Goncharov's *Oblomov* (1859).

33 In an interview with me on 27 July, 1998.

34 David Nokes, 'Anthem for Doomed Youth?', *The Times Literary Supplement*, 4 Dec., 1981: 8. For a fuller account of the immediate critical reception of Kureishi's plays, see Kaleta, *Hanif Kureishi*, Chapter 1.

35 Itzin, *Stages*: 311.

36 Cited in *ibid*: 150 and 169.

37 Some measure of Kureishi's success in this respect is provided by Sukhdev Sandhu's touching account of the effect of *Laundrette* on his cultural formation in provincial Gloucester in the 1980s. See 'Paradise Syndrome' (review essay on *Midnight All Day*), *London Review of Books*, 18 May, 2000: 32–5.

38 Cited in Itzin, *Stages*: 188 and 59.

39 Compare *The Buddha*: 207, 258, 267 for Kureishi's jaundiced reflections on 'fringe' politics.

40 Note how Kureishi anticipates the trajectory of Hall and Bhabha in this respect. Their abandonment of traditional Left thinking becomes definitive only after Thatcher's defeat of the miners. See Hall, 'Old and New': 64; Bhabha, *Location*: 27ff.

41 Hare, *Writing*: 63.

Chapter 3

1 *Laundrette* cost $900,000 to make. See Pally, 'Kureishi': 50; on the costs of *Sammy and Rosie*, see Graham Broadstreet, 'Casebook 1: *Sammy and Rosie Get Laid*', *Screen International* 652.3 (14 May, 1988): 50–1.

2 MacCabe, 'Interview': 41.

3 John Hill argues that Kureishi's films pay little attention to working-class experience. See *British Cinema in the 1990s: Issues and Themes* (Oxford: Clarendon, 1999): 205. This is not really true even of the white working class (consider Johnny in *Laundrette* and most of Clint's posse in *London Kills Me*.)

4 *Ibid*: 44.

5 For more on the New Right's view of the 1960s, see Bart Moore-Gilbert and John Seed, eds, *Cultural Revolution? The Challenge of the Arts in the 1960s* (London: Routledge, 1992): 1–14.

6 Rushdie, *Imaginary Homelands*: 87–101.

7   Kureishi nick-named 'Raj Revival' films 'easterns', arguing that they performed a comparable ideological function in Britain to 'westerns' in American culture. See 'Dirty Washing': 25.

8   'Raj Revival' cinema even used white actors to play Asian roles, notably Alec Guinness as Godbole in *A Passage to India*.

9   It's worth pointing out that Peter Cattaneo's *The Full Monty* (1997), one of British cinema's biggest hits in the 1990s, was originally conceived for a predominantly non-white cast. The change in the film itself to a predominantly white cast was made for 'commercial' reasons. See Paul George and Pascoe Sawyers, '"Full Monty" Stripped of Black Origins', *The Observer*, 7 Sept., 1997: 27. For discussion of the representation of ethnicity in the visual media, see Marie Gillespie, *Television, Ethnicity and Cultural Change* (London: Routledge, 1995); Lola Young, *Fear of the Dark: 'Race', Gender and Sexuality in the Cinema* (London: Routledge, 1995); Valerie Smith, *Representing Blackness* (London: Athlone, 1997) and Matthew Bernstein and Gaylyn Studlar, eds, *Visions of the East: Orientalism in Film* (London: Tauris, 1997).

10   Rafi's next words are: 'And cunty fingers'. The two lines echo the line 'Tea and toast with cunty fingers' in Craig Raine's poem 'Bed and Breakfast', in *The Onion, Memory* (Oxford: Oxford University Press, 1978): 17.

11   There is a large critical literature on 'Heritage' discourse. Key texts include Patrick Wright's *On Living in an Old Country: The National Past in Contemporary Britain* (London: Verso, 1985) and Robert Hewison, *The Heritage Industry: Britain in a Climate of Decline* (London: Methuen, 1987).

12   Curiously, there are echoes of such attitudes in the anti-German sentiment of both *London Kills Me* and *My Son the Fanatic*.

13   Compare Hall's argument that 'when the era of nation-states in globalization begins to decline, one can see a regression to a very dangerous form of national identity which is driven by a very aggressive form of racism.' 'The Local': 26.

14   For other 'London' films of the 1980s, see Hill, *British Cinema*: 206.

15   Conversely, Kureishi's films also contest the 'chocolate box' vision of rural England in 'Heritage' cinema through lyrical evocations of urbanscape. Notable examples include the sunset over London which Sammy sees from the motorway and the night crossing of the Thames in *Sammy and Rosie*. Compare *My Son the Fanatic*.

16   Kureishi's films at times differ substantially from the scripts. In the cinema version of *Laundrette*, it is never clear that Omar is

mixed-race (as is Cherry, which has important implications for her critique of cultural 'in-betweens'). Nor is it apparent that his mother has committed suicide. Similarly, in the film of *London Kills Me*, nothing is made of Clint's chronic eczema, nor of Stone's profession as a purveyor of second-hand porn and weapons, which in the script undermines his critique of the posse's lifestyles.

17 Higson argues that pastoralism is the dominant mobilising myth of British national cinema. *Waving the Flag*: 274.

18 Yasmin Alibhai-Brown, 'Nations Under a Groove', *Marxism Today*, Nov./Dec. 1988: 47.

19 For more on Kureishi's vision of London, see Ball, 'Semi-Detached': 7–27. See also Sukhdev Sandhu, 'Pop Goes the Centre: Hanif Kureishi's London', in Laura Chrisman and Benita Parry, eds, *Postcolonial Theory and Criticism* (Cambridge: Brewer, 1999): 133–54; and Bart Moore-Gilbert, 'London in Hanif Kureishi's Films', *Kunapipi*, XXI.2, (1999, this is part of a special issue on 'postcolonial London'): 5–14; and MacCabe, 'Interview'.

20 As noted earlier, Kureishi admires Forster the novelist; but he condemns 'glamourised travesties of novels by the great E. M. Forster, [as] the sort of meaningless soft-core saccherine [*sic*] confection that Tory ladies and gentlemen think is Art'. See 'England, Bloody England': 19. Higson provides a more temperate account of such films, which nonetheless criticises their conservative ideology, in *Waving the Flag*: 273. For a defence of recent film versions of Forster's novels, see Jeffrey Richards, *Films and British National Identity* (Manchester: Manchester University Press, 1997).

21 Radhika Mohanram, 'Postcolonial Spaces and Deterritorialized (Homo)Sexuality: The Films of Hanif Kureishi', in Gita Rajan and Radhika Mohanram, eds, *Postcolonial Discourse and Changing Cultural Contexts: Theory and Criticism* (London: Greenwood Press, 1995): 121.

22 For more on Kureishi's treatment of the family, gender and sexuality and their relation to discourses of national identity, see Gayatri Spivak, 'In Praise of *Sammy and Rosie Get Laid*', *Critical Quarterly* 31.2 (1989): 80–8. A longer version of this essay appears as Spivak, '*Sammy and Rosie Get Laid*'. (Spivak offers further reflections on Kureishi in 'The Burden of English' in Carol Breckenridge and Peter van der Veer, eds, *Orientalism and the Postcolonial Predicament: Perspectives on South Asia* (Philadelphia: University of Pennsylvania Press, 1993): 134–57); and Mohanram, 'Postcolonial Spaces': 117–34.

23 The concept of the 'rainbow coalition' can be dated back to Raymond Williams, ed., *The May Day Manifesto 1968* (Harmondsworth: Penguin, 1968).

24 Gilroy, *'There Ain't No Black'*: 225.

25. *Ibid*: 228.

26 For a more detailed account of the politics of subcultural style, see Hebdige, *Subculture*.

27 Gilroy, *'There Ain't No Black'*: 233.

28 *Ibid*.

29 Colette Lindroth, '*The Waste Land* Revisited: *Sammy and Rosie Get Laid*', *Literature/Film Quarterly* 17.2, (1989): 95–8. Kureishi's interest in Eliot can be traced back to *Outskirts*. See Kaleta, *Hanif Kureishi*: 20.

30 Spivak, 'In Praise': 80; compare Hill, *British Cinema*: 206. One might also describe the difference between Kureishi's first two films in terms of the distinction that Higson makes between the 'observational' and 'participatory' gazes which are constructed for their respective viewers. See *Waving the Flag*: 275.

31 Pally describes *Laundrette* as a 'Romeo-meets-Romeo' film. 'Kureishi': 50.

32 Stone, 'Through a Lens Darkly' and 'Sick Scenes from English Life', *The Sunday Times*, 'Arts and Leisure', 10 Jan., 1988: 1. Kureishi riposted acidly in 'England, Bloody England'. He also took revenge by naming the unpleasant second-hand gun- and porn-dealer in *London Kills Me* after Stone.

33 See Kaleta, *Hanif Kureishi*, for the immediate critical reception of each film.

34 MacCabe, 'Interview': 42.

35 Ranita Chatterjee, 'An Explosion of Difference: The Margins of Perception in *Sammy and Rosie Get Laid*', in Deepika Bahri and Mary Vasudeva, eds, *Between the Lines: South Asians and Postcoloniality* (Philadephia: Temple University Press, 1996: 173); Sandeep Naidoo, Untitled Review of *Sammy and Rosie Get Laid*, *Bazaar* 4–6 (Spring, 1988): 16.

36 Pally, 'Kureishi': 53; Compare Pam Cook, '*My Beautiful Laundrette*' (review), *Monthly Film Bulletin* 52.622 (Nov., 1985): 333.

37 For defences of the style of *Sammy and Rosie*, see Ball, 'Semi-Detached': 18ff; Kaleta, *Hanif Kureishi*: 52–6; Hill, *British Cinema*: 215–18; Higson, *Waving the Flag*: 276ff; Sandhu, 'Pop': 144ff;

Spivak, 'In Praise': *passim*; and Leonard Quart, 'The Politics of Irony: The Frears-Kureishi Films' (1992), reprinted in Dixon, *Reviewing British Cinema*: 241–8.

38 Root, 'Scenes': 333.

39 bell hooks, 'Stylish Nihilism: Race, Sex and Class at the Movies', in *Yearning: Race, Gender, and Cultural Politics* (1990; London: Turnaround, 1991): 161. While hooks's essay is particularly damning, others who see aspects of Kureishi's films as politically conservative include Barber, 'Insurmountable Difficulties': 235; and Porée, *Hanif Kureishi*: 81; see also note 36 to Chapter 1.

40 Una Chaudhuri, 'The Politics of Exile and the Politics of Home' in Patrick Colm Hogan and Lalita Pandit, eds, *Literary India: Comparative Studies in Aesthetics, Colonialism, and Culture* (Albany, NY: State University of New York Press, 1995): 147.

41 Compare Hebdige, *Subculture*: 90–99.

42 Chatterjee, 'Explosion of Difference': 180.

43 Lindroth, '*Waste Land*': 97; compare Spivak, who finds the ideological meanings of Kureishi's treatment of lesbianism in *Sammy and Rosie* 'blurred'. 'In Praise': 83; and hooks, who asserts that 'Rafi and Danny use sexuality as a way to escape their inability to respond politically'. 'Stylish Nihilism': 160.

44 Compare MacCabe, 'Interview': 42.

45 It is ironic that British film-making in the 1980s was often paradigmatically Thatcherite in its entrepreneurialism. Kureishi records how Frears was 'slightly miffed by the realization of how much Thatcher would approve of us: we're a thrifty, enterprising, money-making small business ... she'd just praise our initiative for doing something decent despite the odds' (SR, 72–3).

46 Kureishi's experience in film influences his fiction. Sangeeta Ray argues that there is 'an exaggerated simulation of cinematic techniques', in *The Buddha*, 'The Nation in Performance: Bhabha, Mukherjee and Kureishi', in Monika Fludernik, ed., *Hybridity and Postcolonialism: Twentieth Century Indian Literature* (Tübingen, Germany: Stauffenburg, 1998): 232. Kureishi has stated of *The Black Album* that 'I have always known the novel I'm writing now will be a movie', Kaleta, *Hanif Kureishi*: 116.

Chapter 4

1   See Kaleta, *Hanif Kureishi*: 49.

2   Directing this film involved a change of heart for Kureishi. A few years earlier he had declared: 'I'm not keen to move into directing – it takes up far too much time.' Root, 'Scenes': 333.

3   I will not be analysing the television version of *The Buddha* because it is so faithful to the text. As Kureishi has commented: 'I just wrote what was in the book ... I just did it straight. It's the same as the book.' Cited in Kaleta, *Hanif Kureishi*: 87. There are some differences, however; the New York scenes are cut and, of course, it is not narrated in the first person, though Karim has some voice-overs.

4   Bill Buford, 'The End of the English Novel', *Granta* 3 (1980): 8.

5   *Ibid*: 16.

6   MacCabe, 'Interview': 42.

7   Rushdie, '*Midnight's Children* and *Shame*', *Kunapipi* 7.1 (1985): 1–19.

8   For more on *The Buddha* as picaresque, see Seema Jena, 'From Victims to Survivors: the Anti-Hero in Asian Immigrant Writing With Special Reference to *The Buddha of Suburbia*', *Wasafiri* 17 (Spring, 1993): 3–6; Matthew Graves, 'Subverting Suburbia: the Trickster Figure in Hanif Kureishi's *The Buddha of Suburbia*, in Gallix, *The Buddha*: 70–78 and Jan Borm, '"Thank God I have an Interesting Life": Le Picaresque Dans *The Buddha of Suburbia*', *ibid*: 79–87.

9   It could be argued that the 'condition of England' novel has always sought to expose the illusory homogeneity of national life, while seeking to imagine real unity.

10   For more on Kureishi and Wells, see Hashmi, 'Hanif Kureishi': 27.

11   Compare *ibid*. The film is also one of Jay's favourites in *Intimacy* (I, 20).

12   Kureishi acknowledges the influence of Kingsley Amis (and Evelyn Waugh). See Kaleta, *Hanif Kureishi*: 77. As this suggests, there is some overlap between the sub-genre of the 'university novel' and the explorations of changing class identities by writers like Braine. There is an intriguing echo of the title of one Amis novel in *Intimacy*, when Jay exclaims 'I want it now! I' (I, 51).

13   There is now a large literature on the relationship between English Studies and 'Englishness'. See, for example, Francis Mulhern, *The*

Moment of Scrutiny (London: New Left Books, 1979); Chris Baldick, *The Social Misssion of English Criticism 1848–1932* (Oxford: Clarendon, 1983); and Brian Doyle, *English and Englishness* (London: Routledge, 1987). On the changing nature of 'Englishness' more generally, there is an even larger one. See, for example, Wright, *On Living in an Old Country*; Hall, 'The Local'; Raphael Samuel, *Patriotism* and *Theatres of Memory*, 2 vols (London: Verso, 1994 and 1998); Linda Colley, *Britons: Forging the Nation 1707–1837* (London: Yale University Press, 1992); Gikandi, *Maps of Englishness*; Jeremy Paxman, *The English: Portrait of a People* (London: Michael Joseph, 1998).

14   *Atlantic Monthly*, 263.5 (May, 1989): 56–62.

15   I deal in detail with such issues in relation to Lodge, Bradbury and other post-war 'university novelists' in 'Anglo-Saxon Attitudes: Empire, Race and English Studies in Contemporary University Fiction', *Wasafiri*, 26, Autumn 1997: 3–8.

16   MacInnes made a comeback in the 1980s. Julien Temple's film of *Absolute Beginners* (1959) appeared in 1987. Some of his essays were reprinted in *England, Half English* (London: Chatto, 1986), a title with obvious resonances for Kureishi's work. For an analysis of correspondences between the two writers, see Steven Connor, *The English Novel in History: 1950 to the Present* (London: Routledge, 1996): 90–8.

17   It could be argued that the real innocents in *The Buddha* are Haroon and Changez, rather than Karim.

18   Sandhu argues that 'the urge to be free, mobile, and to escape from the shackles of domesticity have been central motifs of all pop.' 'Pop': 135. Kureishi's concern with mobility may not, then, be specifically postcolonial in orientation.

19   In '"Get Back"', Helbig analyses the privileged role given to the Beatles in *The Buddha*. In Helbig's eyes, this is partly because the group is 'the most British of British pop bands' (77), although he usefully reminds one that in their clothes (the Nehru jackets), music (particularly after exposure to Ravi Shankar) and, one might add, lifestyle (after exposure to the Maharishi), the Beatles were themselves influenced by Indian culture and thus represented an early instance of the kind of cultural syncretism which so interests Kureishi. Helbig further reminds one that in 'Eight Arms to Hold You', John Lennon is described as the central figure of the age and points out that at school Karim learns the lyrics of 'I am the Walrus' off by heart. He concludes that Lennon's song illuminates one of the novel's central concerns, being 'ultimately

all about … the urge to dissolve not only meanings, but any kind of borderlines, categories, and hierarchies'. (80) For another reading of *The Buddha*'s use of pop, see Claude Chastagner, 'Quelques Pistes Rock Pour La Lecture de *The Buddha of Suburbia*', *Études Britanniques Contemporaines* (Montpellier, France), 13, Janvier, 1998: 1–10.

20   It could be argued that 'Prince' tried to transcend identity/identification altogether in insisting latterly on being described as 'The Artist Formerly Known as Prince' and rendering his name as a squiggle.

21.   Karim's surname, Amir, translates as 'Prince'.

22   Gauri Viswanathan points out that the same 'liberal humanist' universalism underpinned colonial thinking about educational programmes for Indian subjects. Officials like T. B. Macaulay and Charles Trevelyan insisted on 'the universality of a single set of [principally English literary] works … in an effort to assimilate individuals [of different races] to a single identity'. See *Masks of Conquest: Literary Study and British Rule in India* (New York: Columbia University Press, 1989): 167.

23   Said argues that seemingly 'positive' stereotypes about the 'spiritual' East still represent an assertion of the colonisers' will-to-power through knowledge. See *Orientalism*: 150.

24.   See *ibid*: 6, 138 and 207ff.

25.   See Sara Suleri, *The Rhetoric of English India* (Chicago: Chicago University Press, 1992): 132–48.

26   See Jenny Sharpe, *Allegories of Empire: The Figure of Woman in the Colonial Text* (Minneapolis: Minnesota University Press, 1993).

27   For more on Kureishi and Kipling, see Émilienne Baneth-Nouailhetas, 'Karim/Kim: Mutations Kiplingiennes dans *The Buddha of Suburbia*', *Q/W/E/R/T/Y: Arts, Littératures & Civilisations du Monde Anglophone* 7 (1997): 183–90; my 'Hanif Kureishi's *The Buddha of Suburbia*: Hybridity in Contemporary Cultural Theory and Artistic Practice', *ibid*: 191-208; and Schoene, 'Herald': 109–28.

28   Kipling, *Kim* (1901; Harmondsworth: Penguin, 1987): 49.

29   However Karim, seventeen when *The Buddha* opens, is roughly Kim's age at the end of his adventures.

30   Stephen Slemon, 'Modernism's Last Post' in Ian Adam and Helen Tiffin, eds, *Past the Last Post: Theorizing Post-Colonialism and Post-Modernism* (Hemel Hempstead: Harvester Wheatsheaf, 1993): 3.

31   Bhabha, *Location*: 188.

32   See Richard Cronin, 'The Indian English Novel: *Kim* and *Midnight's Children*', *Commonwealth Essays and Studies*, 8.1 (1985): 57–73; and Suleri, *Rhetoric*: 174–206.

33   Rushdie, *The Moor's Last Sigh* (1995; London: Vintage, 1996): 39.

34   This is another habit which Karim shares with the protagonist of Braine's *Room at the Top*.

35   Compare Hall, 'The Local': 21.

36   Said, *Orientalism*: 3; compare Hall, 'Old and New': 48–9.

37   As *The Black Album* points out, that most seemingly 'Oriental' of spices, chili, in fact derives from the New World. This suggests that globalisation is the culmination of very long histories of trade between widely-dispersed nations. Compare Hall, 'Old and New': 48–9.

38   Accepting that Kipling is a determining presence in *The Buddha*, Gerard Siary concludes that Karim, like Kim, finally achieves stable selfhood. See 'Identité Optionelle/Identité Bloquée: *The Buddha of Suburbia* de Hanif Kureishi's [*sic*] et *The Remains of the Day* de Kazuo Ishiguro', *Etudes Britanniques Contemporaines* (Montpellier, France), 13, Janvier, 1998: 53. I can't agree.

39   Kureishi's essays strongly criticise this aspect of Enoch Powell's politics. See, for example, 'The Rainbow Sign' and 'Finishing the Job' (MBL).

40   Macaulay's style is recommended as a model to the Pakistani father in 'We're Not Jews' (LBT), by a 'liberal' neighbour.

41   For a theoretical account of mimicry as a form of self-defence, see Bhabha, *Location*: 85–92.

42   Spivak, *In Other Worlds*: 202; Compare Spivak, *Post-Colonial Critic*: 10–11, 45, 109.

43   On the emergence and decline of the term 'Black' as a political category, see Hall, 'Old and New': 53–7; compare Hall, 'New Ethnicities' (1988), in Stuart Hall, *Critical Dialogues in Cultural Studies*, eds. David Morley and Kuan-Hsing Chen (London: Routledge, 1996): 441–9 and Rattansi, 'On Being': 118–34. For defences of its continuing purchase, see Sharma *et al.*, *Dis-Orienting Rhythms*: 3 and John Hutnyk, 'Adorno at Womad: South Asian Crossovers and the Limits of Hybridity-Talk', in Werbner and Modood, eds, *Debating Cultural Hybridity*: 121. In 'Black Art': 73ff, Mercer provides qualified support, as does Hall in 'Old and New': 56.

44   Bhabha, *Location*: 92.

45   Kureishi's vision is often consonant with the Caribbean tradition of cultural criticism which provides a more balanced account of hybridity than Bhabha's often utopian conception of the advantages of 'ambivalence'. See my *Postcolonial Theory: Contexts, Practices, Politics* (London: Verso, 1997): 180ff. Note Kureishi's account of his painful 'identity crisis' during a visit to Pakistan where he was seen neither as British nor Pakistani but, ironically, as a 'Paki' (MBL, 81).

46   Kureishi argues that 'racism is the Trojan Horse within the Labour Movement' (MBL, 96). There is a long history of suspicion of the conflation of issues of class and race, particularly the subordination of the latter to the former. See, for example, Frantz Fanon, *Black Skin, White Masks*, trans. C. L. Markmann (London: Pluto, 1986). Hall, Bhabha and Gilroy extend such arguments to the contemporary period.

47   Kureishi's text corroborates the anxieties expressed by Gayatri Spivak about the 'benevolence' of western feminists towards the 'subaltern'. See 'Can the Subaltern Speak' and 'French Feminism in an International Frame' (1981) in Spivak, *In Other Worlds*: 134–53. Compare Chandra Talpade Mohanty, 'Under Western Eyes: Feminist Scholarship and Colonial Discourse', *Boundary 2* (Spring/Autumn, 1984): 71–92; and Brah, *Cartographies*: 84–127.

48   On the tropes associated with the colonial gaze, see Mary Louise Pratt, *Imperial Eyes: Travel Writing and Transculturation* (London: Routledge, 1992).

49   Spivak, 'Can the Subaltern Speak': 93.

50   Positive accounts of *The Buddha* will be discussed in Chapter 6. Less enthusiastic responses include Porée, who complains of Kureishi's repetitiveness, inability to manage the transitions in the novel and its conservative political vision; see *Hanif Kureishi*: 12, 64, 81; Connor, who complains that the ending 'collapse[s] into a routine kind of emotional piety', *The English Novel*: 96; and Yousaf, who concludes that Kureishi 'tri[es] to do too much' in the text, 'Hanif Kureishi': 18.

51   Anthony K. Appiah, 'Identity Crisis', *New York Times*, Section 8, 17 Sept, 1995: 42.

52   See Pally, 'Kureishi': 50.

53   Amy Gutmann, ed., *Multiculturalism: Examining the Politics of Recognition* (1992; Princeton: Princeton University Press, 1994): 8.

54   *Ibid*: 5. Compare Pnina Werbner's argument that anti-racism is

split between 'universalists who affirm equality, citizenship and individual rights [and] multiculturalists who make claims for collective cultural rights, each accusing the other of being racists'. 'Introduction: The Dialectics of Cultural Hybridity' in Werbner and Modood, *Debating Cultural Hybridity*: 10.

55 See Schoene, 'Herald': 124.

56 Note, however, that the 'divine aubergine' is not an invention, but is based on a true-life event in Leicester; a friend sent Kureishi newspaper clippings about the said vegetable.

57 For an account of the dilemmas posed to 'liberal' Muslims by 'fundamantalism', see Akeel Bilgrami, 'What is a Muslim? Fundamental Commitment and Cultural Identity', *Critical Inquiry* 18 (Summer, 1992): 821–43. Kureishi's position is not altogether clarified in recent interviews. He has recently described himself as a 'liberal', while the pronominal shifting between 'they' and 'we' betrays his ambivalence towards Islam. However, he remains harsh on 'fundamentalism'. See MacCabe, 'Interview': 51, 54. Compare Ashraf, '"Into the Unknown."'

58 Hence, as Koushik Banarjea and Jatinder Barn argue, 'the sonorous voices of dissent [can be] debilitatingly labelled "simplistic" or the multi-purpose "fundamentalist"'. 'Versioning Terror; Jallianwalla Bagh and the Jungle', in Sharma *et al.*, *Dis-Orienting Rhythms*: 207.

Chapter 5

1 Much of Singer's work concerns the conflict between religious tradition and secularism, often posed – as it is in Kureishi's – in terms of conflicts between fathers and sons. See, for example, Singer's *In My Father's Court* (1966). Singer is also fascinated by promiscuous sexuality. Like Cheever's, Kureishi's stories often revolve around the 'erotic bitterness' of adultery and infidelity. See *The Stories of John Cheever* (1979; London: Vintage, 1990). Kureishi's work also echoes Cheever's 'determination to trace some moral chain of being' (*ibid*: vii) through the messy human relations that he anatomises. Like many of Carver's, some of Kureishi's stories are unconsolingly bleak and spare depictions of 'low-rent tragedies' involving middle-aged affective entrapments, relationship breakdown and isolation, often leavened with grotesque or gothic humour. See, for example, the tales in *What We Talk About When We Talk About Love* (1981; London: Harvill, 1996).

2 'The Argentine Ant' can be found in *Adam, One Afternoon and*

Other Stories (1957; London: Minerva, 1997). Like the protagonist of 'Flies', Calvino's narrator is jobless and has a young son and a wife from whom he is alienated. However, in contrast to Kureishi's story, they are eventually reconciled. 'The Duel' can be found in Chekhov, *The Duel and Other Stories* (Harmondsworth: Penguin, 1984). Many of its themes and details are reworked in 'Lately'. While Chekhov's stories often deal with marital disharmony, *Intimacy* has particularly strong echoes of Chekhov's 'Lady with Lapdog'. Like Dmitry, Jay is a middle-aged roué who is alienated from his austere wife and expresses powerfully misogynistic sentiments. Like Dmitry, he comes to realise that he has fallen in love with the young woman whom he has unfeelingly seduced. Much of Jay's musing on the necessity of curiosity as a motive for living is prefigured in Dmitry's philosophy. See Chekhov, *Lady With Lapdog and Other Stories* (Harmondsworth: Penguin, 1964). Carver's 'Intimacy' is a first-person, present-tense account of a visit by a writer (who holds 'to the dark view of things') to his former wife, who accuses him of exploiting her by representing her in his fiction. Not only does this have clear parallels with 'That Was Then', but Kureishi's choice of title for his novella intriguingly implies his anticipation of the controversies that it would generate. See Carver, *Elephant* (1988; London: Harvill, 1998): 48.

3   Kureishi's tale may also be an intervention in the debate provoked by the Anglican vicar Toby Forward's hoax on Virago Press in 1987. Purporting to be a collection of stories by a teenage Asian girl, Rahila Khan, the printed copies of his *Down the Road, Worlds Away* were pulped just before publication.

4   Kureishi's latest work, *Gabriel's Gift* continues this pattern. A deconstructive approach, by contrast, might suggest that ethnicity remains significant precisely because of its (seeming) absence, so that the turn from ethnicity is important *because* of Kureishi's background and previous interests. Thus, Kureishi comments of the use of the English country-house genre in *Sleep With Me*, 'that amuses me very much, as an Indian, writing about that'. MacCabe, 'Interview': 49.

5   *Midnight All Day*, too, was widely assumed to be profoundly autobiographical. See Justine Ettler, 'Free At Last From the Chains of Marriage. So Why the Long Face?', *The Observer*, 'Review', 21 Nov., 1999: 15; and James Hopkins, 'The Horror of Being Hanif', *The Guardian*, 30 Oct., 1999: 10.

6   At the Purcell Room reading of *Intimacy* in 1998, Kureishi professed great admiration for Strindberg, especially *The Father* and *The Dance of Death*. In the former, Laura declares that 'love

between the sexes is a battle'. Intriguingly, in the context of Kureishi's development, the Captain responds: 'It's like racial hatred, this.' Strindberg, *Miss Julie and Other Plays*, trans. Michael Robinson (Oxford: Oxford University Press, 1998): 37–8.

7   One wonders what Ronald Shusterman makes of the recent work, given his complaint that *The Buddha* 'sometimes seems like a *Bildungsroman* without the *Bil*'. See 'Neither/Nor: Non-Binary Logic and the Question of Knowledge in *The Buddha of Suburbia*', *Études Britanniques Contemporaines* (Montpellier, France), 13, Janvier, 1998: 46.

8   The debate corresponds closely with that in Chekhov's 'The Duel' between Layevsky (the out-of-date 'man of the eighties') and von Koren, representing a new, ruthless Social Darwinism.

9   The film of *My Son the Fanatic* is very different at times from the script. Dialogue is added and cut, scenes are cut and reordered and some roles radically simplified. I will try to respect these differences in my account. The cutting of scenes relating to Farid's adoption of Islam caused friction between Kureishi and the director, Udayan Prasad. See Richard Brookes, 'Anger over Cuts to Kureishi Film', *The Observer*, 11 May, 1997: 3; See also Dan Glaister, 'Cannes at 50: British Author Threatens to Kill Journalist', *The Guardian*, 10 May, 1997: 7.

10   Tom Charity, 'Fundamental as Anything', *Time Out*, 29 April–6 May, 1998: 14; cited in Tim Adams, untitled discussion of *Intimacy*, *The Observer*, 10 May, 1998: 26.

11   While *Intimacy* is clearly not a traditional first-person autobiography, the genre has become markedly more experimental in recent years. For example, J. M. Coetzee's *Boyhood: A Memoir* (1997) is written in the third person.

12   See, for example, many of the works in Sage's 'Men and Masculinity' series. In *Unreasonable Men: Masculinity and Social Theory* (London: Routledge, 1994), Victor Seidler suggested that it was at that date 'hard to judge men's accounts of their own experiences because often these personal accounts are not forthcoming'. (109) Several best-selling accounts are now available, including some discussed here. For 'post-feminist' analyses of the 'crisis of masculinity', see Ros Coward, *Sacred Cows: Is Feminism Relevant to the New Millennium?* (London: Harper Collins, 1999) and Susan Faludi, *Stiffed: The Betrayal of the Modern Man* (London: Chatto, 1999). However, many feminists are convinced that patriarchy is as strong as ever. See Germaine Greer, *The Whole Woman* (London: Vintage, 2000) and Imelda Whelehan, *Over-*

loaded: Popular Culture and the Future of Feminism (London: Women's Press, 2000).

13   Like Karim in *The Buddha* (and Rushdie), Kureishi is a Tottenham supporter. Note the regrettable anti-Arsenal sentiment expressed in one of the scenes in *Sammy and Rosie*.

14   Hornby, *Fever Pitch* (1992; London: Indigo, 1996): 130.

15   The motif of 'boulder-pushers' in *The Golden Notebook* draws on Camus's *Myth of Sisyphus* (1942). The emphasis on rebellion in both Lessing's text and *Intimacy* invokes Camus's *The Rebel* (1953). Sartre wrote a short story called 'Intimacy' which has clear parallels with Kureishi's text. It recounts Lulu's coming to a decision to leave her husband for another man (in the end, however, she changes her mind). While framed by a third-person narrative, much of it is recounted in Lulu's interior monologue. See Sartre, *Intimacy* (London: Panther, 1960). Sartre's *Flies* (1947), may be the source of the title of the story in *Love in a Blue Time*.

16   Lessing, *The Golden Notebook* (1962; London: Granada, 1973): 189.

17   Ros Coward, *Sacred Cows*: 131.

18   Caroline Moore, 'The Rat's Tale', *The Sunday Telegraph*, 'Review', 19 April, 1998: 13.

19   Lessing, *The Golden Notebook*: 9.

20   *Ibid.*

21   Susan Faludi, *Backlash: The Undeclared War Against American Women* (New York: Crown, 1991).

22   To adapt Nick Hornby's comments in *Fever Pitch*, 'this kind of confessional from a man, however New he is, is regrettably still not acceptable' (62). By contrast, there are many texts by women which recount the experience of abandonment. In 1999 alone, two autobiographical accounts were serialised in national newspapers – Margaret Cook's narrative of the breakdown of her marriage to Tony Blair's Foreign Secretary, *A Slight and Delicate Creature*, and *The Heart-Shaped Bullet*, by *The Observer* journalist Kathryn Flett. Their fictional counterparts, from Lessing's *The Golden Notebook* (1962) to Shyama Perera's *Bitter Sweet Symphony* (2000), are legion. Of course, there are also innumerable male fictions about adulterous women, including Sartre's *Intimacy* and two of the uxorious Asif's favourite texts, Tolstoy's *Anna Karenina* and Flaubert's *Madame Bovary*.

23   As indicated earlier, as recently as 1997, Kureishi disclaimed any desire to write more plays. He explains his change of mind partly

in terms of a reaction against working in conditions of solitary confinement (HK).

24 Strindberg also wrote first-person narratives which caused great scandal for their supposed resemblances to the playwright's stormy private life, for example *Inferno* (1897).

25 Prior to its opening, Kureishi described *Sleep With Me* to me as 'Chekhov meets Joe Orton' (HK).

26 Chekhov, *Ivanov*, in *Plays*, trans. E. Fen (Penguin: Harmondsworth, 1959): 93. 1997 saw David Hare's revival of *Ivanov* at the Almeida, shortly before Kureishi began work on *Sleep With Me*.

27 The woman in question, Nina, has the same name as the girl for whom Jay falls in *Intimacy*.

28 The play was significantly modified during its run. Some of Stephen's more hysterically misogynistic lines were cut and Julie given more dignity and emphasis. Sophie became more obviously manipulative, making Stephen's behaviour less exceptional. The ending became more affirmative, with greater stress on reconciliation between Barry and Sophie, and Stephen and Julie showed more emotion, particularly towards the end.

29 Chekhov, *Ivanov*: 105.

30 *Ibid*: 48 and 90.

31 Robert Butler, 'Tragedy Without the Tears', *The Independent on Sunday*, 'The Critics', 25 April, 1999: 6.

32 Anthony Holden, 'Not in Front of the Children', *The Observer* 'Review', 25 April, 1999: 8. Michael Billington argued that the characters' 'twin gods are really Mills and Boon … Scratch Hanif Kureishi and you discover Barbara Cartland.' See Billington, 'Glittering Ponces', *The Guardian*, 23 April, 1999: 18. Similarly disobliging were Hal Jensen's 'Something for the Week-End?', *TLS*, 21 May, 1999: 19, and Patrick Marmion's '*Sleep with Me*', *Time Out*, 28 April–5 May, 1999: 134.

33 Chekhov, *Ivanov*: 91.

34 Porée, *Hanif Kureishi*: 12.

35 Ashraf, '"Into the Unknown"': 6.

36 Kureishi, 'One Year On', *The Guardian* G2, 21 Feb., 2000: 15. This is consonant with his comments to Anthony Clare, *In the Psychiatrist's Chair*, BBC Radio Four, 4 Oct., 1998. Compare his praise for the relative liberalism of Britain compared with many European countries. MacCabe, 'Interview': 53.

37 Sandhu, 'Paradise': 35.

38 Holden, 'Not in Front': 8.

39 Hopkins, 'Horror': 10.

40 Jaggi, 'Lost in a City of Vampires', *The Guardian* G2, 10 April, 1997: 13. Flint interprets Kureishi's 'presentism' as a deliberate disavowal of historical Britain, 'Black Swans': 75.

41 Moore, 'Why I applaud the Books of Men who Tell it like it is', *The Independent*, 15 May, 1998: 21; compare Adams, 'Untitled discussion': 25.

42 'RW', 'Sonny Muslim', *The Guardian*, 'Review', 1 May, 1998: 7.

43 Binding, 'Masks and Rituals', *Independent on Sunday*, 31 Oct., 1999: 10.

44 Barnacle, 'Dark Deeds in Medialand', *The Sunday Times*, 'Culture', 7 Nov., 1999: 51.

45 Charity, 'Fundamental': 15.

46 Robson, 'Short but Bittersweet', *The Sunday Telegraph*, 'Review', 7 Nov., 1999: 16.

47 Hopkins, 'Horror': 10.

Chapter 6

1 One project mentioned in the press is a collaboration between Kureishi and Andrew Lloyd Webber on a musical about 'Bollywood'. While Kureishi has disclaimed this, he has a number of future projects in mind. These include a film, provisionally entitled *The Mother*, intended for TV; a novel, provisionally entitled *The Body* in which old people have young brains transplanted into them; this device will be used to explore issues related to ageing and identity. He has also expressed interest in 'another Asian doo-dah', in the form of a novel fictionalising the strike at Grunwick's in 1978, by British-Asian women workers (HK).

2 Spivak, 'In Praise': *passim*; Hall 'Old and New': 60 and 'New Ethnicities': 444–9.

3 Cited in Poree, *Hanif Kureishi*: 11.

4 Rushdie, 'Minority Literatures': 40.

5 Sandhu, 'Paradise': 33. See note 34 to Chapter 1 and note 12 to Chapter 2 for earlier novels and plays about Asian Britain, and Parminder Dhillon-Kashyap, 'Locating the Asian Experience', *Screen*, 29.4 (1988): 120–6, and Malik, 'Beyond': 207ff., for earlier films.

6   As evidence of this might adduce three major events held in London in the summer of 1999 alone. First, in June, Goldsmiths College hosted a conference on 'Subcontinental Britain: Diasporic Culture and Politics', addressing topics as diverse as the commodification of British-Asian popular music and the political responsibilities of British-Asian writing. July saw a three-day event at the Royal Festival Hall, entitled 'Continental Drift: Asian Writing in Transit', discussed below. In the same month, the Whitechapel Art Gallery hosted a three-week-long series of events involving the visual arts, music, film, photography and creative writing, supported by lectures and seminars, entitled 'Zerozerozero: British Asian Cultural Provocation'. One sign of the increasing cultural self-confidence of Asian Britain is the publicity for the 'Coming of Age' South Asian Dance Festival at the Royal Festival Hall in August, 2000 which declares: 'South Asian culture is officially cool. Everywhere we look it has a growing influence. Fashion, music, the club scene, dance, cinema, comedy, theatre. East is West, you could say.'

7   See Sandhu, 'Paradise': 35.

8   Schoene, 'Herald': 111.

9   Telephone interview with Parv Bancil, 10 Aug., 1999.

10 Cited in Yousaf, 'Hanif Kureishi': 17.

11 Ahmad, 'The Politics of Literary Postcoloniality', *Race and Class* 36.3 (1995): 17; Sandhu, 'Pop': 142.

12 Young, *Colonial Desire*: 21. For a different genealogy of hybridity, see Nikos Papastergiadis, 'Tracing Hybridity in Theory' in Werbner and Modood, *Debating Cultural Hybridity*: 257–81. For discussions of earlier theorisations of 'hybridity' in postcolonial criticism, see my *Postcolonial Theory*: 180–84. For other discussions of the concept, see Bill Ashcroft *et al.*, *The Empire Writes Back: Theory and Practice in Post-Colonial Literatures* (London: Methuen, 1989): 33–7; Ania Loomba, *Colonialism/Postcolonialism* (London: Routledge, 1998): 173–83; Monika Fludernik, 'The Constitution of Hybridity: Postcolonial Interventions', in Fludernik, ed., *Hybridity and Postcolonialism: Twentieth-Century Indian Literature* (Tübingen: Stauffenberg Verlag, 1998). For negative accounts of the concept, see below.

13 Fludernik, 'Constitution': 19-55. For another discussion of Bhabha, see my *Postcolonial Theory*: 114–51.

14 Rushdie, *Imaginary Homelands*: 394.

15 For more on this topic, see Smith, *New Right Discourse*.

16   'Multi-culturalism' is, of course, a highly-contested term. For
     fuller discussions of its different meanings and applications, see
     David Theo Goldberg, ed., *Multi-Culturalism: A Critical Reader*
     (Oxford: Blackwell, 1994) and Gutmann, *Multiculturalism*.

17   A specific endorsement of Rushdie's reading of *Satanic Verses*
     comes in *Location*: 225.

18   Bhabha, 'Foreword' to Fanon, *Black Skin, White Masks*: xvii–xviii.

19   *Ibid*: ix.

20   Bhabha, *Nation*: 313-4. Compare Said's conception of international
     cultural negotiations in the contemporary world as being 'contra-
     puntal' rather than 'symphonic' in nature. *Culture and Imperialism*
     (London: Chatto, 1993): 386.

21   Hall, 'Old and New': 59.

22   Cited in Mohanram, 'Postcolonial Spaces': 125

23   See Fludernik, 'Constitution': 21, 29–30, and my *Postcolonial
     Theory*: 119, 137.

24   Ashcroft *et al.*, *Empire*: 34.

25   Rushdie, 'The Empire Writes Back with a Vengeance', *The Times*,
     3 July 1982: 8.

26   Spivak, 'In Praise': 82, 87; Hall, 'Old and New': 59–60. Compare
     Hall, 'New Ethnicities': 449; and Ray, 'Nation': 235.

27   Schoene, 'Herald': 109.

28   *Ibid*: 117.

29   Yu-Cheng Lee, 'Expropriating the Authentic: Cultural Politics in
     Hanif Kureishi's *Buddha of Suburbia*', *EurAmerica: A Journal of
     European and American Studies* 26.3, (1996): 3.

30   But see note 46 to Chapter 1.

31   Yousaf, 'Hanif Kureishi': 16, 22.

32   Kaleta proposes a rather different perspective on Kureishi's
     'hybridity' by arguing that his subject always 'presents the world
     cinematically … whether he is writing screen-plays or prose'.
     Kaleta, *Hanif Kureishi*: 10. See also note 46 to Chapter 3.

33   Manferlotti, 'Writers': 194.

34   Helbig, '"Get Back"': 77.

35   *Ibid*: 78. Chastagner, too, makes the point that Karim listens
     mainly to white British pop. 'Quelques Pistes': *passim*.

36   A. Robert Lee, 'Changing the Script: Sex, Lies and Videotape in
     Kureishi, Dabydeen and Phillips', in A. Robert Lee, ed., *Other*

Britain, Other British: Contemporary Multicultural Fiction (London: Pluto, 1995): 80; Schoene, 'Herald': 117.

37   Werbner, 'Introduction': 8. On the repressive implications of post-colonial theorisations of hybridity see my *Postcolonial Theory*: 193ff and, in the context of Gilroy's work specifically, Hutnyk, 'Adorno': 123–8.

38   Hashmi, 'Hanif Kureishi': 27. Compare Spivak: '[E]ven if one knows how to undo identities, one does not necessarily escape [their] historical determinations', 'French Feminism': 144. As *New Ethnicities, Old Racisms?*, ed. Phil Cohen (London: Zed, 1999) suggests, racism continues to flourish despite all the talk of 'new ethnicities'. Barber argues that Kureishi's first two films attest to 'the seemingly insurmountable difficulties' facing cross-race relationships, 'Insurmountable Difficulties': 222.

39   Ball, 'Semi-Detached': 24.

40   A. Robert Lee, 'Changing': 71

41   Kaleta, *Hanif Kureishi*: 7: In fact, Kureishi expressed almost identical sentiments as early as 1986; See A. Robert Lee: 'Changing': 69.

42   Rushdie, *Imaginary Homelands*: 15. See also note 45 to Chapter 4.

43   However, it is important not to overdo the current reaction against the seemingly inexorable spread of the concept of 'hybridity' and, more particularly, its apparent hegemony in postcolonial criticism. While, as Bhabha and Young point out, hybridity was a colonial strategy of control, it was accompanied by hostility to miscegenation. Such hostility continues unabated in some quarters; as Kureishi points out, 'racists find mixing terrifying', MacCabe, 'Interview': 51. 'Half-caste' was widely used as a pejorative term while he was growing up. Duncan Sandys, a Tory Minister, identified 'half-castes' as social 'misfits' (MBL, 75). This helps explain Kureishi's later disavowals of being 'in-between'. Until the 1980s hybridity was still often seen in very negative terms, even by Left and 'liberal' observers. See V. G. Kiernan's ethnocentric account of the effects of 'New Commonwealth' migration on Britain in *Imperialism and Its Contradictions*, ed. Harvey Kaye (London: Routledge, 1995): 191–214; note Q. D. Leavis's alarm at the prospect of unassimilable minorities in *The Englishness of the English Novel* (Cambridge: Cambridge University Press, 1983): 325; and Martin Green's reprehensible remarks on the advent of multiracial London in *Dreams of Adventure, Deeds of Empire* (London: Routledge, 1980), especially xii–xiii. However, as Kureishi's work reminds us, hostility to hybridity does not come

only from the dominant formation. *The Black Album* and *My Son the Fanatic* explore the 'nativist' rejection of hybridity. Compare Cherry's hostility to 'in-betweens' in *Laundrette*: 19–20.

44   Sharma *et al.*, *Dis-Orienting Rhythms*: 3.

45   Ella Shohat, 'Notes on the "Post-Colonial"', *Social Text* 31–2 (1992): 109; compare Rey Chow: 'What Bhabha's [model of] "hybridity" revives, in the masquerade of deconstruction, anti-imperialism, and difficult "theory", is an old functionalist notion of what a dominant culture permits in the interest of maintaining its own equilibrium', *Writing Diaspora: Tactics of Intervention in Contemporary Cultural Studies* (Bloomington: Indiana University Press, 1993): 35. Perhaps the strongest denunciation comes from John Hutnyk, who sees hybridity as 'a rhetorical cul-de-sac which trivialises Black political activity ... in favour of middle-class conservative success stories in the Thatcher-with-a-bindi-spot mould', 'Adorno': 122.

46   See Young, *Colonial Desire*: 55–89.

47   Schoene, 'Herald': 115. Kureishi himself commented that he wanted to fill 'a hole in the centre of English writing'. See Yousaf, 'Hanif Kureishi': 13.

48   Yousaf, 'Hanif Kureishi': 13.

49   The converse is also true, however, if one accepts that globalisation *both* homogenises *and* increases diversification.

50   Hall argues that contemporary capitalism 'lives culturally through difference and ... is constantly teasing itself with the pleasures of the transgressive Other', 'The Local': 31. Compare the scathing critiques of the marketing of 'World Music' in Hutnyk, 'Adorno' and Ashwani Sharma, 'Sounds Oriental: the (Im)possibility of Theorizing Asian Musical Cultures', in Sharma *et al.*, *Dis-Orienting Rhythms*: 27–9.

51   Ahmad, *In Theory: Classes, Nations, Literatures* (London: Verso, 1992): 123–58.

52   Such ideas have been taken up by a variety of Marxist and *marxisant* critics. See, for example, Benita Parry, 'Signs of Our Times: A Discussion of Homi Bhabha's *The Location of Culture*, *Third Text* 28/29 (1994): 5–24 and Neil Lazarus, *Nationalism and Cultural Practice in the Postcolonial World* (Cambridge: Cambridge University Press, 1999).

53   Flint, 'Black Swans': 74. Hall answers this problem by demanding that difference must be thought through historically rather than seen as a process of endless shiftings. 'Old and New': 50–1.

54 Rushdie, 'Minority Literatures': 36. Compare Hall: 'Hardly anybody is one of us any longer', 'The Local': 26.

55 Ashraf, '"Into the Unknown"': 2.

56 *Ibid*: 3.

57 Ball, 'Semi-Detached':21.

58 Sanjay Sharma, 'Noisy Asians or "Asian Noise"?', in Sharma *et al.*, *Dis-Orienting Rhythms*: 33; compare Sandhu, 'Pop': 136, and Schoene, 'Herald': 122.

59 See Yousaf, 'Hanif Kureishi' and Hashmi, 'Hanif Kureishi': *passim*.

60 Dhillon-Kashyap, 'Locating': 15.

61 hooks, 'Stylish Nihilism': 161.

62 For example by Mahmood Jamal; see Yousaf, 'Hanif Kureishi': 23.

63 Compare Sandhu's account of growing up the provinces and wanting 'anything we thought would make us truly English. Not only would we laugh at malicious jokes … but, eager to ingratiate ourselves, we'd try to trump them', 'Paradise': 33. As Ray argues, Bhabha's theory of hybridity 'erases the other side of migrant experience that is conformist, unexceptional, and ordinary' by over-emphasising diasporic experience as contestatory, 'The Nation': 226.

64 Yousaf, 'Hanif Kureishi': 21; Quart, 'Politics of Irony': 248.

65 Hall, 'Old and New': 60.

66 Ray, 'Nation': 235.

67 Cook, '*My Beautiful Laundrette*': 333.

68 Kureishi has recently commented approvingly on the emergence of 'Asian' directors of films which have nothing to do with ethnicity, for example Shekhar Kapur's *Elizabeth* (1998) and Anand Tucker's *Hilary and Jackie* (1998). See MacCabe, 'Interview': 48.

69 Cited in Werbner, 'Introduction': 5. A recent study indicated that by 2010, whites would be an ethnic minority within London and that by 2100, they would be a minority within Britain. See *The Observer*, 3 Sept., 2000: 1 and 17. The cultural consequences of this 'unconscious' process of hybridisation are likely to be infinitely more far-reaching than any number of 'conscious' acts of hybridisation.

70 This might be inferred from certain Marxist attacks on 'the exorbitation of discourse' as a mode of opposition in postcolonial criticism. See, for example, Benita Parry, 'Problems in Current Theories of Colonial Discourse', *Oxford Literary Review* 9 (1–2): 27–58; Ahmad, *In Theory*; E. San Juan jr., *Beyond Postcolonial*

Theory (New York: St Martin's Press, 1998); compare Ashwani Sharma, 'Sounds Oriental': 28; Werbner, 'Introduction': 7; Hutnyk, 'Adorno': 119ff. While such charges are strictly aimed at postcolonial critics rather than postcolonial artists, it is difficult to see how the latter can logically be exempt from the same charge. By contrast, Spivak insists that one must first 'change the imaginary in order to be able to act on the real', 'French Feminism': 145. Compare Rushdie: 'some of us will wish … to leap in and join the fight, some of us may wish to wait cautiously for the fires to die down and then in the calm of the aftermath to try and say what they had meant to say or simply to weave them into our stories, and I don't think that they are mutually exclusive responses', 'Minority Literatures': 42.

71 Yousaf, 'Hanif Kureishi': 20; compare Rushdie, 'Minority Literatures': 42.

72 Ball, 'Semi-Detached': 17; compare Rushdie, 'Minority Literatures': 40–1 and Schoene, who argues that such utopian visions are necessary in formulating the strategic goals of political action, 'Herald': 118.

73 Rushdie, 'Minority Literatures': 38. Discomfort with such labels as 'minoritarian', 'ethnic', etc. has been expressed by comparable figures to Kureishi, like the sculptor Anish Kapoor. Kapoor declined to exhibit his work at the major show of post-war 'ethnic' art at the Hayward Gallery in 1991, on the grounds that he did not want to be pigeon-holed as an 'Asian artist'. See Marianne MacDonald, 'The Colour Issue', *The Observer*, 'Life', 12 April, 1998: 8. The choreographer Shobana Jeyasingh has expressed similar sentiments.

74 *Ibid*: 40. Again, one could argue that Kureishi's ethnicity is an inescapable issue insofar as what is significant about his recent trajectory is where it began.

75 *Ibid*.

76 Ashraf, '"Into the Unknown"': 3.

77 Yousaf, 'Hanif Kureishi': 19; compare Hall, 'Old and New': 61.

78 Spivak, '*Sammy and Rosie*': 244.

79 Eagleton, 'Nationalism, Irony and Commitment' in Terry Eagleton *et al.*, *Nationalism, Colonialism and Literature* (Minneapolis: University of Minnesota Press, 1990): 23-4; compare Schoene 'Herald': 61.

80 Kureishi, 'Dirty Washing': 26. This might be taken to corroborate Bhabha's argument that diasporic writing has the power to explode 'the [dominant] metaphor of a *heimlich* national culture', *Nation*: 316.

Selected texts by Kureishi

Birds Of Passage (Oxford: Amber Lane Press, 1983).

The Black Album (London: Faber, 1995).

Borderline (London: Methuen, in association with the Royal Court Theatre, 1981).

'The Buddha of Suburbia', *Harper's* 274.16 (June, 1987): 45–51.

The Buddha of Suburbia (London: Faber, 1990).

'Dirty Washing', *Time Out*, 795, 14–20 Nov., 1985: 25–6.

'England, Bloody England', *The Guardian* 15 Jan., 1988: 19.

'Esther', *Atlantic Monthly*, 263.5 (May, 1989): 56–62.

'Erotic Politicians and Mullahs', *Granta* 17 (Autumn 1985): 139–51.

'The Flesh Made Word', BBC Radio 3, 18 Aug., 1997.

The Faber Book of Pop, co-edited with Jon Savage (London: Faber, 1995).

Gabriel's Gift (London: Faber, 2001).

Intimacy (London: Faber, 1998).

'London and Karachi', in Raphael Samuel, ed., *Patriotism: The Making and Unmaking of British National Identity*, vol. 2, *Minorities and Outsiders* (London: Routledge, 1989): 270–88.

London Kills Me (London: Faber, 1991).

Love in a Blue Time (London: Faber, 1997).

Midnight All Day (London: Faber, 1999).

The Mother Country. Unpublished typescript in Kureishi's possession.

My Beautiful Laundrette and Other Writings (London: Faber, 1996).

'My Father's Gift', *The Sunday Telegraph* 'Magazine', 26 April, 1998: 15–18.

My Son the Fanatic (London: Faber, 1997).

'One Year On', *The Guardian* G2, 21 Feb., 2000: 15.

Outskirts, The King and Me, Tomorrow-Today! (London: John Calder and New York: Riverrun Press, 1983).

Outskirts and Other Plays (London: Faber, 1992).

Sammy and Rosie Get Laid: The Script and the Diary (London: Faber, 1988).

Sleep With Me (London: Faber, 1999).

Selected Kureishi criticism, reviews and interviews

Adams, Tim, Untitled discussion of *Intimacy, The Observer* 10 May, 1998: 25.

Afzal-Khan, Fawzia, 'Pakistani Writing in English: 1947 to the Present: A Survey', *Wasafiri* 21 (Spring, 1995): 58–61.

Allison, Terry and Renée Curry, '"All Anger and Understanding": Kureishi, Culture, and Contemporary Constructions of Rage', in Curry and Allison, eds, *States of Rage: Emotional Eruption, Violence, and Social Change* (New York: New York University Press, 1996): 146–66.

Appiah, Anthony K., 'Identity Crisis' (review of *The Black Album*), *New York Times*, Section 8, 17 Sept., 1995: 42.

Ashraf, Adnan, '"Into the Unknown": An Interview with Hanif Kureishi' (October, 1995) http://www.walrus.com/-adnan/kureishi.html

Bald, Suresht Renjen, 'Negotiating Identity in the Metropolis: Generational Differences in South Asian British Fiction', in Russell King *et al.*, eds, *Writing Across Worlds: Literature and Migration* (London: Routledge, 1995): 70–88.

Ball, John C., 'The Semi-Detached Metropolis: Hanif Kureishi's London', *ARIEL: A Review of International English Literature* 27.4 (Oct., 1996): 7–27.

Baneth-Nouailhetas, Émilienne, 'Karim/Kim: Mutations Kiplingiennes dans *The Buddha of Suburbia*', *Q/W/E/R/T/Y: Arts, Littératures & Civilisations du Monde Anglophone* 7 (1997): 183–90.

Barber, Susan Torrey, 'Insurmountable Difficulties and Moments of Ecstasy: Crossing Class, Ethnic, and Sexual Barriers in the Films of Stephen Frears' in Lester Friedman, ed., *British Cinema and Thatcherism: Fires Were Started* (London: UCL Press, 1993).

Barnacle, Hugo, 'Dark Deeds in Medialand' (review of *Midnight All Day*), *The Sunday Times* 'Culture', 7 Nov., 1999: 51.

Billington, Michael, 'Glittering Ponces' (review of *Sleep with Me*), *The Guardian*, 23 April 1999: 18.

Binding, Paul, 'Masks and Rituals' (review of *Midnight All Day*), *The Independent on Sunday*, 31 Oct., 1999: 10.

Böhner, Ines Karin, *My Beautiful Laundrette und Sammy and Rosie Get Laid: Filmische Reflexion von Identitatsprozessen* (Frankfurt: Peter Lang, 1996).

Broadstreet, Graham, 'Casebook 1: *Sammy and Rosie Get Laid*', *Screen International* 652.3, (14 May, 1988): 50–1.

Brookes, Richard, 'Anger over Cuts to Kureishi Film', *The Observer*, 11 May, 1997: 3.

Butler, Robert, 'Tragedy without the Tears' (review of *Sleep With Me*), *The Independent on Sunday*, 'The Critics', 25 April, 1999: 6.

Carey, Cynthia, 'Hanif Kureishi's *The Buddha of Suburbia* as a Post-Colonial Novel', *Commonwealth: Essays and Studies: Special Issue no. SP 4* (Dijon, France, 1997): 119–25.

Charity, Tom, 'Fundamental as Anything' (interview/review of *Intimacy* and *My Son the Fanatic*), *Time Out*, 29 April–6 May, 1998: 14–15.

Chastagner, Claude, 'Quelques Pistes Rock Pour La Lecture de *The Buddha of Suburbia*', *Études Britanniques Contemporaines* (Montpellier, France), 13, Janvier, 1998: 1–10.

Chatterjee, Ranita, 'An Explosion of Difference: the Margins of Perception in *Sammy and Rosie Get Laid*', in Deepika Bahri and Mary Vasudeva, eds, *Between the Lines: South Asians and Postcoloniality* (Philadephia: Temple University Press, 1996: 167–84.

Chaudhuri, Una, 'The Politics of Exile and the Politics of Home', in Patrick Colm Hogan and Lalita Pandit, eds, *Literary India: Comparative Studies in Aesthetics, Colonialism, and Culture* (Albany, NY: State University of New York Press, 1995): 141–9.

Clare, Anthony, *In the Psychiatrist's Chair* (Interview with Kureishi), BBC Radio 4, 4 Oct., 1998.

Commonwealth: Essays and Studies: Katherine Mansfield, Hanif Kureishi. Special Issue no. SP 4 (Dijon, France, 1997).

Connor, Steven, *The English Novel in History: 1950 to the Present* (London: Routledge, 1996).

Cook, Pam, '*My Beautiful Laundrette*' (review). *Monthly Film Bulletin* 52.622 (November, 1985): 333.

Dhillon-Kashyap, Perminder, 'Locating the Asian Experience', *Screen*, 29.4 (1988): 120–6.

Dubourdieu, Elaine, 'The Buddha, Britain and "Black" Immigration', in Gallix, ed., *The Buddha of Suburbia*: 131–47.

Ettler, Justine, 'Free At Last From the Chains of Marriage. So Why the Long Face?' (review of *Midnight All Day*), *The Observer*, 'Review', 21 Nov., 1999: 15.

Flint, Kate, 'Black Swans and the Black Country: Identity, Nationhood and Black Writing in Contemporary Britain', in Jacqueline Lo *et al.*, eds, *Impossible Selves: Cultural Readings of Identity* (Melbourne: Australian Scholarly Publishing, 1999): 72–84.

Gallix, François, ed., *The Buddha of Suburbia* (Paris: Ellipses, 1997).

Glaister, Dan, 'British Author Threatens to Kill Journalist', *The Guardian*, May 10, 1997: 7.

Gross, John, 'Deliciously, Desperately Awful People.' (review of *Sleep With Me*), *The Sunday Telegraph* 'Review', 25 April, 1999: 7.

Hall, Stuart, 'New Ethnicities' (1992) in Stuart Hall, *Critical Dialogues in Cultural Studies*, eds, David Morley and Kuan-Hsing Chen (London: Routledge, 1996): 441–9.

Hall, Stuart, 'Old and New Identities, Old and New Ethnicities', in Anthony D. King, ed., *Culture, Globalization and the World System* (Basingstoke: Macmillan, 1991): 41–68.

Hashmi, Alamgir, 'Current Pakistani Fiction', *Commonwealth Novel in English* 5.1 (1992): 59–64.

Hashmi, Alamgir, 'Hanif Kureishi and the Tradition of the Novel' (1992; reprinted in *Critical Survey* 5.1 (1993): 25–33.

Helbig, Jörg, '"Get Back to Where You Once Belonged": Hanif Kureishi's Use of the Beatles-Myth in *The Buddha of Suburbia*', in Wolfgang Klooss, ed., *Across the Lines: Intertextuality and Transcultural Communication in the New Literatures in English* (Amsterdam: Rodopi, 1998): 77–82.

Higson, Andrew, *Waving the Flag: Constructing a National Cinema in Britain* (Oxford: Clarendon Press, 1995).

Hill, John, *British Cinema in the 1990s: Issues and Themes* (Oxford: Clarendon, 1999).

Hita, Michèle, 'Identité, Union et Voyeurisme' in Gallix, *The Buddha of Suburbia*: 37–44.

Holden, Anthony, 'Not in Front of the Children.' (review of *Sleep With Me*), *The Observer* 'Review', 25 April, 1999: 8.

hooks, bell, 'Stylish Nihilism: Race, Sex and Class at the Movies', in *Yearning: Race, Gender, and Cultural Politics* (1990; London: Turnaround, 1991): 155–63

Hopkins, James, 'The Horror of Being Hanif' (review of *Midnight All Day*), *The Guardian*, 30 Oct, 1999: 10.

Jaggi, Maya, 'Lost in a City of Vampires' (review of *Love in a Blue Time*), *The Guardian* G2, 10 April, 1997: 13.

Jena, Seema, 'From Victims to Survivors: The Anti-Hero in Asian Immigrant Writing With Special Reference to *The Buddha of Suburbia*', *Wasafiri* 17 (Spring, 1993): 3–6.

Jensen, Hal, 'Something for the Week-End?' (review of *Sleep With Me*), *Times Literary Supplement*, 21 May, 1999: 19.

Johnston, Lucy, 'Hanif and the Spurned Woman' (review of *Intimacy*), *The Observer*, 10 May, 1998: 8–9.

Julian, Ria, 'Brecht and Britain: Hanif Kureishi in Interview with Ria Julian', *Drama: Quarterly Theatre Review* 155 (1987): 5–7.

Kaleta, Kenneth C., *Hanif Kureishi: Postcolonial Storyteller* (Austin, Texas: University of Texas Press, 1998).

Kureishi, Yasmin, 'Intimacies: A Sister's Tale', *The Guardian*, 7 May, 1997: 7.

Lawley, Sue, *Desert Island Discs* (interview with Kureishi), BBC Radio 4, 21 April, 1996.

Lee, A. Robert, 'Changing the Script: Sex, Lies and Videotape in Kureishi, Dabydeen and Phillips', in A. Robert Lee, ed., *Other Britain, Other British: Contemporary Multicultural Fiction* (London: Pluto, 1995): 69–89.

Lee, Yu-Cheng, 'Expropriating the Authentic: Cultural Politics in Hanif Kureishi's *Buddha of Suburbia*', *EurAmerica: A Journal of European and American Studies* 26.3 (1996): 1–19.

Leith, William, 'Sex, Drugs and a Mid-Life Crisis' (interview), *The Observer*, 'Life' 23 March, 1997: 6–8.

Lindroth, Colette, '*The Waste Land* Revisited: *Sammy and Rosie Get Laid*', *Literature/Film Quarterly* 17.2 (1989): 95–8.

MacCabe, Colin, 'Interview: Hanif Kureishi on London', *Critical Quarterly* 41.3 (1999): 37–56.

MacKenzie, Suzie, 'All for Love' (interview/review of *Intimacy*), *The Guardian* 'Weekend', 2 May, 1998: 25–8.

Malik, Sarita, 'Beyond "The Cinema of Duty"? The Pleasures of Hybridity: Black British Film of the 1980s and 1990s', in Andrew

Higson, ed., *Dissolving Views: Key Writings on British Cinema* (London: Cassell, 1996): 202–15.

Manferlotti, Stefano, 'Writers from Elsewhere', in Iain Chambers and Lidia Curti, eds, *The Postcolonial Question: Common Skies, Divided Horizons* (London: Routledge, 1996): 189–98.

Marmion, Patrick, '*Sleep With Me*' (review) *Time Out*, 28 April–5 May, 1999: 134.

Mergenthal, Sylvia, 'Acculturation and Family Structure: Mo's *Sour Sweet*, Kureishi's *The Buddha of Suburbia*, Ishiguro's *A Pale View of Hills*', in Eckhard Breitinger, ed., *Defining New Idioms and Alternative Forms of Expression* (Amsterdam: Rodopi, 1996): 119–27.

Mohanram, Radhika, 'Postcolonial Spaces and Deterritorialized (Homo)Sexuality: The Films of Hanif Kureishi', in Gita Rajan and Radhika Mohanram, eds, *Postcolonial Discourse and Changing Cultural Contexts: Theory and Criticism* (London: Greenwood Press, 1995): 117–34.

Moore, Caroline, 'The Rat's Tale' (review of *Intimacy*), *The Sunday Telegraph*, 'Review', 19 April, 1998: 13.

Moore, Suzanne, 'Why I applaud the Books of Men who Tell it like it is' (review of *Intimacy*), *The Independent*, 15 May, 1998: 21.

Moore-Gilbert, Bart, 'Hanif Kureishi's *The Buddha of Suburbia*: Hybridity in Contemporary Cultural Theory and Artistic Practice', *Q/W/E/R/T/Y: Arts, Litteratures & Civilisations du Monde Anglophone* 7 (Octobre, 1997): 191–208.

Moore-Gilbert, Bart, 'London in Hanif Kureishi's Films', *Kunapipi*, XXI.2 (1999): 5–14.

Naidoo, Sandeep. Untitled Review of *Sammy and Rosie Get Laid*, *Bazaar* 4–6 (Spring, 1988): 16.

Naumann, Michel, 'Humour et Entre-Deux; Les Pensées Indiennes et Occidentales dans *The Buddha of Suburbia*', in Gallix, *The Buddha of Suburbia*: 118–28.

Nokes, David, 'Anthem for Doomed Youth?' (review of *Borderline*), *The Times Literary Supplement*, 4 Dec., 1981: 8.

Pally, Marcia, 'Kureishi Like a Fox', *Film Comment* 22.5 (1986): 50–5.

Porée, Marc. *Hanif Kureishi: The Buddha of Suburbia* (Paris: CNED-Didier Concours, 1997).

Quart, Leonard, 'The Politics of Irony: The Frears-Kureishi Films' (1992), in Wheeler Winston Dixon, ed., *Reviewing British Cinema*

1900–1992: Essays and Interviews (New York: State University of New York Press, 1994): 241–8.

Ray, Sangeeta, 'The Nation in Performance: Bhabha, Mukherjee and Kureishi', in Monika Fludernik, ed., *Hybridity and Postcolonialism: Twentieth Century Indian Literature* (Tübingen, Germany: Stauffenburg, 1998): 219–38.

Robson, David, 'Short but Bittersweet' (review of *Midnight All Day*), *The Sunday Telegraph* 'Review', 7 Nov., 1999: 16.

Root, Jane, 'Scenes from a Marriage', *Monthly Film Bulletin* 52.622 (November, 1985): 333.

Rushdie, Salman, 'Minority Literatures in a Multi-Cultural Society', in Kirsten Holst Petersen and Anna Rutherford, eds, *Displaced Persons* (Aarhus, Denmark: Seklos, 1987): 33–42.

'RW', 'Sonny Muslim' (review of *My Son the Fanatic*), *The Guardian*, 'Review' 1 May, 1998: 7.

Sandhu, Sukhdev, 'Paradise Syndrome' (review essay on *Midnight All Day*), *London Review of Books*, 18 May, 2000: 32–5.

Sandhu, Sukhdev, 'Pop Goes the Centre: Hanif Kureishi's London', in Laura Chrisman and Benita Parry, eds, *Postcolonial Theory and Criticism* (Cambridge: Brewer, 1999): 133–54.

Schoene, Berthold, 'Herald of Hybridity: The Emancipation of Difference in Hanif Kureishi's *The Buddha of Suburbia*', *International Journal of Cultural Studies* 1.1 (1998): 109–27.

Shusterman, Ronald, 'Neither/Nor: Non-Binary Logic and the Question of Knowledge in *The Buddha of Suburbia*', *Études Britanniques Contemporaines* (Montpellier, France), 13, Janvier, 1998: 41–50.

Siary, Gérard, 'Identité Optionelle/Identité Bloquée: *The Buddha of Suburbia* de Hanif Kureishi's [*sic*] et *The Remains of the Day* de Kazuo Ishiguro', *Études Britanniques Contemporaines* (Montpellier, France), 13, Janvier, 1998: 51–6.

Spivak, Gayatri C., 'The Burden of English', in Carol Breckenridge and Peter van der Veer, eds, *Orientalism and the Postcolonial Predicament: Perspectives on South Asia* (Philadelphia: University of Pennsylvania Press, 1993): 134–57.

Spivak, Gayatri C., 'In Praise of *Sammy and Rosie Get Laid*', *Critical Quarterly* 31.2 (1989): 80–8.

Spivak, Gayatri C., '*Sammy and Rosie Get Laid*', in *Outside in the Teaching Machine* (London: Routledge, 1993): 243–54.

Stone, Norman, 'Through a Lens Darkly' and 'Sick Scenes from English Life', *The Sunday Times*, 'Arts and Leisure', 10 Jan., 1988: 1–2.

Vinet, Dominique, '*The Buddha of Suburbia*: le Carnaval des Mythes', *Études Britanniques Contemporaines* (Montpellier, France), 13, Janvier, 1998: 57–74.

Weber, Donald, '"No Secrets Were Safe From Me": Situating Hanif Kureishi', *Massachusetts Review* 38.1 (1997): 119–35.

Yousaf, Nahem, 'Hanif Kureishi and "the Brown Man's Burden"', *Critical Survey* 8.1 (1996): 14–25.

Selected further reading

Achebe, Chinua, *Morning Yet on Creation Day* (London: Heinemann, 1975).

Ahmad, Aijaz, *In Theory: Classes, Nations, Literatures* (London: Verso, 1992).

Ahmad, Aijaz, 'The Politics of Literary Postcoloniality', *Race and Class* 36.3 (1995): 2–20.

Alibhai-Brown, Yasmin, 'Nations Under a Groove', *Marxism Today* (Special Issue) Nov/Dec., 1998: 47.

Ashcroft, Bill, Helen Tiffin and Gareth Griffiths, *The Empire Writes Back: Theory and Practice in Post-Colonial Literatures* (London: Methuen, 1989).

Bhabha, Homi, 'Foreword' to Frantz Fanon, *Black Skin, White Masks*, trans. C. L. Markmann (London: Pluto, 1986): xvii–xviii.

Bhabha, Homi, ed., *Nation and Narration* (London: Routledge, 1990).

Bhabha, Homi, *The Location of Culture* (London: Routledge, 1994).

Brah, Avtar, *Cartographies of Diaspora: Contesting Identities* (London: Routledge, 1996).

Buford, Bill, 'The End of the English Novel', *Granta* 3 (1980), 7–16.

Chekhov, Anton, *Plays*, trans. E. Fen (Harmondsworth: Penguin, 1959).

Chow, Rey, *Writing Diaspora: Tactics of Intervention in Contemporary Cultural Studies* (Bloomington: Indiana University Press, 1993).

Eagleton, Terry, 'Nationalism, Irony and Commitment', in Terry Eagleton *et al.*, *Nationalism, Colonialism and Literature* (Minneapolis: University of Minnesota Press, 1990): 23–42.

Fanon, Frantz. *Black Skin, White Masks*, trans. C. L. Markmann (London: Pluto, 1986).

Fludernik, Monika, ed., *Hybridity and Postcolonialism: Twentieth-Century Indian Literature* (Tübingen: Stauffenberg, 1998).

Gaskill, William, *A Sense of Direction: Life at the Royal Court* (London: Faber, 1988).

Gilroy, Paul, *'There Ain't No Black in the Union Jack': The Cultural Politics of Race and Nation* (London: Hutchinson, 1987).

Gutmann, Amy, ed., *Multiculturalism: Examining the Politics of Recognition* (1992; Princeton: Princeton University Press, 1994).

Hall, Stuart, 'The Local and the Global: Globalization and Ethnicity', in Anthony D. King, ed., *Culture, Globalization and the World System* (Basingstoke: Macmillan, 1991): 19–39.

Hare, David, *Writing Left-Handed* (London: Faber, 1991).

Hebdige, Dick, *Subculture: The Meaning of Style* (London: Methuen, 1979).

Hornby, Nick, *Fever Pitch* (1992; London: Indigo, 1996).

Hutnyk, John, 'Adorno at Womad: South Asian Crossovers and the Limits of Hybridity-Talk', in Werbner and Modood, *Debating Cultural Hybridity*: 106–36.

Itzin, Catherine, *Stages in the Revolution: Political Theatre since 1968* (London: Methuen, 1980).

Kipling, Rudyard, *Kim* (1901; Harmondsworth: Penguin, 1987).

Lessing, Doris, *The Golden Notebook* (1962; London: Granada, 1973).

McLeod, John, *Beginning Postcolonialism* (Manchester: Manchester University Press, 2000).

Mercer, Kobena, 'Black Art and the Burden of Representation', *Third Text* 10 (Spring, 1990): 61–78.

Moore-Gilbert, Bart, *Postcolonial Theory: Contexts, Practices, Politics* (London: Verso, 1997).

Rattansi, Ali, 'On Being and Not Being Brown/Black-British: Racism, Class, Sexuality and Ethnicity in Post-Imperial Britain', *Interventions: International Journal of Postcolonial Studies* 2.1 (2000): 118–34.

Rushdie, Salman, 'The Empire Writes Back with a Vengeance', *The Times*, 3 July, 1982: 8.

Rushdie, Salman, *Imaginary Homelands: Essays and Criticism, 1981–991* (Harmondsworth: Penguin, 1991).

Rushdie, Salman, '*Midnight's Children* and *Shame*', *Kunapipi* 7.1 (1985): 1–19.

Rushdie, Salman, *The Moor's Last Sigh* (1995; London: Vintage, 1996).

Said, Edward, *Culture and Imperialism* (London: Chatto and Windus, 1993).

Said, Edward, *Orientalism* (1978; Harmondsworth: Penguin, 1991).

Sharma, Sanjay *et al.*, eds, *Dis-Orienting Rhythms: The Politics of the New Asian Dance Music* (London: Zed, 1996).

Slemon, Stephen, 'Modernism's Last Post' in Ian Adam and Helen Tiffin, eds, *Past the Last Post: Theorizing Post-Colonialism and Post-Modernism* (Hemel Hempstead: Harvester Wheatsheaf, 1993): 1–12.

Smith, Anna Marie, *New Right Discourse on Race and Sexuality* (Cambridge: Cambridge University Press, 1994).

Spivak, Gayatri C., 'Can the Subaltern Speak?', in Patrick Williams and L. Chrisman, eds, *Colonial Discourse and Post-Colonial Theory: A Reader* (Hemel Hempstead: Harvester Wheatsheaf, 1993): 66–111.

Spivak, Gayatri C., 'French Feminism in an International Frame' (1981), in Spivak, *In Other Worlds: Essays in Cultural Politics* (London: Routledge, 1987): 134–53.

Spivak, Gayatri C., *The Post-Colonial Critic: Interviews, Strategies, Dialogues*, ed. Sarah Harasym (London: Routledge, 1990).

Werbner, Pnina and Tariq Modood, eds, *Debating Cultural Hybridity: Multi-Cultural Identities and the Politics of Anti-Racism* (London: Zed, 1997).

Young, Robert J. C., *Colonial Desire: Hybridity in Theory, Culture and Race* (London: Routledge, 1995).

Index

(Note: 'n.' after a page reference indicates the number of a note on that page).